COLOURED

HOW CLASSIFICATION BECAME CULTURE

TESSA DOOMS
LYNSEY EBONY CHUTEL

JONATHAN BALL PUBLISHERS

JOHANNESBURG • CAPE TOWN

Originally published in South Africa in 2023 by
JONATHAN BALL PUBLISHERS
A division of Media24 (Pty) Ltd
PO Box 33977
Jeppestown
2043

ISBN 978-1-77619-149-9
ebook ISBN 978-1-77619-150-5

www.jonathanball.co.za
www.twitter.com/JonathanBallPub
www.facebook.com/JonathanBallPublishers

Cover by Sean Roberts
Set in Minion Pro 11/15

For my father, Lesole Elliot Dooms, who found his name, once lost.

Tessa Dooms

For Meryl Nicole Moses, and all the girls with skin like earth and hair like clouds, too good for this world, but who lit it nonetheless.

Lynsey Ebony Chutel

CONTENTS

Foreword   vii

Introduction: #ColouredLivesMatter
Tessa Dooms and Lynsey Ebony Chutel   xi

1. Social orphans: Not Black enough, not White enough
   Tessa Dooms   1

2. Lucky Coloureds and forgotten ancestors
   Lynsey Ebony Chutel   17

3. No, Trevor Noah isn't Coloured
   Tessa Dooms   40

4. Musical roots
   Tessa Dooms   52

5. *Huiskos*: Identity on a plate
   Lynsey Ebony Chutel   67

6. *Awê! Ma se kind*: Finding our mother tongues
   Lynsey Ebony Chutel   84

7. *Kerksuster* or *straatmeit*?
   Tessa Dooms   104

8. Of men, manne and 'moffies'
   Lynsey Ebony Chutel   117

9.   On the margins: Coloured political identity in South Africa
         Lynsey Ebony Chutel   137

10. Reclaiming Krotoa
         Tessa Dooms   157

11. Reclaiming the past, reinventing the future
         Tessa Dooms   170

     Notes   179
     Acknowledgements   187
     About the authors   189

FOREWORD

One of the foremost sentiments that colours my childhood memories can be encapsulated by the word 'wrong'. My first education as a racialised person taught me that I was wrong in a world that balanced itself on the tightrope of absolute differences. For better or worse, being a full-something was always better than being a half-nothing. Inadequacy became a way to define my existence: for being Coloured, for being a *waterslams*, for being queer – never quite right and never quite enough.

'What are you?' is a question that has assaulted me many times throughout my life, and the search for the answer set me off on my own journey of academic inquiry. Though I have somewhat relented in trying to answer the question, not least because of its dehumanising phrasing, I can say I have found one answer to a different question: 'Who are you?' Tessa Dooms and Lynsey Ebony Chutel offer me an answer with *Coloured*.

Despite our histories of collective trauma and colonial wounding, South Africans genuinely do not know much about each other. Our social literacies are overwhelmingly informed by party politics that dominate our social imagery. Alienated from each other by colonialism and apartheid, and now distracted by politricks, we have not taken the time to get to know each other beyond the essentialist caricatures we have been mesmerised by. However, this book loudly disrupts this damning trajectory.

Coloured does not miss a single opportunity to remind us of an important truth: White supremacy lied to us all and none of us has escaped its conditioning, but we can reclaim our histories. When we say we are Coloured, we are not bound to a reductive definition of the positionality as a colonial invention created for the purpose of lubricating the apartheid state's terror machine. We are Coloured because of a specific wounding and historical trajectory that birthed circumstances necessitating survival. Out of that need to survive, we created cultures that don't enjoy uniformity, but most certainly overlap with the histories of other racialised people in South Africa.

Though we reclaim and celebrate our pride in being who we are, we can never shy away from our complicity with the harm and oppression meted out to other Black people who share our histories. Despite also being acted upon by an oppressive system, we can never understate the agency Coloured people have always had to make different choices when called upon to show solidarity towards other Black people. With utmost compassion, Coloured calls us all to account for our complicity and anti-Blackness while offering us facts that confront the epistemologies of ignorance in which we have been incentivised to participate.

Colouredness produces a highly politicised existence, the mechanics of which can be attributed to South Africa's particular form of racecraft in which a buffer race was created to attenuate the reaction of a numerically preponderant Black population to violent oppression. However, in spite of this, Coloured people also live in a beautiful banality that is unaffected by the bigger politics that hope to define us. There are things that are just frivolously Coloured, that we understand and internalise as 'us'. We are by no measure monolithic and, in fact, engage in healthy contestation about how we express our ethnic identities, but it is in the crevices of the overlaps that we meet each other. In the everyday of being Coloured, away from the discourse and debate, we have food, music, dance and storytelling that stitches a quilt of magic under which we all can find the comfort of belonging. It is where we matter, unconditionally.

When we talk about Coloured identity, there is often an anxiety to produce evidence of what makes this identity and how long ago it was established – as if artefacts and timelines legitimise human existence. We have made and unmade Coloured identities and cultures repeatedly throughout our histories, and if one thing binds us all it is our ability to adapt and respond to our circumstances. Despite many of those circumstances being characterised by pain and dispossession, we have employed creativity and humour in lifesaving ways, forming perhaps the most significant inheritance we have gifted each other throughout generations.

With all that we have to consider, *Coloured* also asks us to interrogate the harmful practices we have adopted as culture. We are confronted with the gender and sexual politics that shape the experiences of Coloured women and queer people in even more specific ways. As we grapple with effects of racial capitalism and patriarchy, we become aware of how we have mistaken pathology for praxis. The complicated relationships we have with prejudice and power and the dishonesty that sustains them require interrogation, starting on these pages.

Coloured offers yet another entry into the archive in which I also live. It is an archive of lives and experiences that has been buried alive, and is now exhumed on these pages. It matters that ordinary lives are given voice in this book. The experiences documented here are simultaneously ordinary and spectacular, simply for their ability to make the point that something terrible happened in this place called South Africa and we are all trying our best to make sense of it.

Tessa and Lynsey advance such important work with Coloured, amid a dearth of honest and accurate reflections of Coloured experiences that do not shy away from discomfort but also do not reduce lives to classifications. Here, we are called in and instructed to love ourselves enough to destroy the conditioning of our early induction into White supremacist patriarchy, while also developing a vision for a future of Colouredness. A future that builds bridges across the divides we have taken to maintaining, to our detriment.

This book is first and foremost for *Coloured* people, but is certainly not exclusively so. There are many conversations we must have as racialised people in this country with many wounds to heal. When we have those conversations, I hope we show up with facts, accountability and empathy. *Coloured* offers us a wonderful guide for how we start and sustain such conversations.

Jamil F. Khan, critical diversity scholar and author of
Khamr: The Makings of a Waterslams

INTRODUCTION:
#COLOUREDLIVESMATTER

In 2020, the death of yet another Black man in the United States sparked global outrage and solidarity with the #BlackLivesMatter movement. George Floyd's death, in full public view and recorded as a White police officer would literally not take his knee off the cuffed man's neck, brought home the enduring racial inequality not only in the US but also in Europe, South America and Asia. It was a reminder that, in many of these countries' Black neighbourhoods, the police are an extension of a system designed to oppress people of colour.

Across the Atlantic, 16-year-old Nathaniel Julies, a Coloured boy, was shot at point-blank range by a police officer while returning home from the local shop in Eldorado Park, a township southwest of Johannesburg. Just as the racist tropes of African Americans created the environment for Floyd's killing, Julies was a young Coloured man, in a Coloured neighbourhood, trapped by tropes of violence and gangsterism. Except Julies had Down syndrome and was well known in the community as a harmless, helpful and generally pleasant child. Yet somehow, his very presence posed a threat so great that it required lethal force. The officers accused of killing Julies were Coloured and Black, an awful reminder of how the South African policing system is inherently hostile to people of colour, irrespective of the race of the officers. And while we still don't know the motive behind the killing, it's hard not to see this as a form of internalised racism, an example of how little a Coloured boy's life mattered even to the people who look like him.

The wave of anger about police brutality quickly spread from Eldorado Park to the rest of the country. Soon, other townships joined, and the protests took on a greater significance to become a demonstration against the hopelessness and nihilism of young Coloured people who felt left behind by a system that was meant to take them into a non-racial future. Soon, #ColouredLivesMatter began to pop up on social media and on the placards people carried as they marched to the police station. As the issue gained national attention, Tessa Dooms, a sociologist and political analyst, was called in to news broadcast studios to help South Africans understand the anger they saw unfolding on television in the dramatic clashes between community members and police. Lynsey Ebony Chutel, a journalist, was assigned to the story to talk to the grieving family, the community and the police in an attempt to understand what had happened and what the moment meant.

Both of us also happen to be Coloured women who grew up in Eldorado Park. In our professional roles, we found ourselves trying to translate our childhood communities, but also their present-day frustrations, while positioning it all in a global movement to explain how the hashtag #BlackLivesMatter had been subverted into a very specific ethnic – but still Black – identity.

Explaining the nuances between these positions is difficult on an ordinary day, but doing so in a context of high emotions, in the glare of the media as the country – and the world – watched and listened, was a much harder task than we imagined. The terms 'Black' and 'Coloured' mean so many things to so many people that a crude one-liner in a news report or radio interview cannot do them justice – and made contributing to public discourse a daunting experience. It was in the midst of this struggle to do justice to a complex story of one Coloured family's pain and one Coloured community's anger that the idea of this book was conceived.

To begin to explain the alienation of young Coloured people today, we had to look back to the creation of this community, in whose fractured history is the story of South Africa itself. We hoped to begin by responding to the base question: what, if anything, distinguishes Coloured identity from that of other groupings of Black people? This led to many more questions that too few people ask about what it means to be Coloured in South Africa.

Not nearly enough has been written about Coloured identity in South Africa historically, and certainly not about the contemporary experiences of Coloured people in the context of a post-apartheid society seeking to redress the injustices of our brutal past and build a more equitable society into the future. Mixed-heritage and creolised people's stories, the world over, are generally found on the margins of history. The stories of these communities are often deemed too opaque, complex, revealing of malevolence that others would prefer to remain hidden, and even inconvenient among other oppressed groups fighting for their own right to be heard and seen in the struggle for justice and power.

Yet there are many books about race: about what race and racism are, about how systems of racism define and confine people and strip them of their voices and places in the world. Each of those books has some relationship to normative ideas about how Coloured identity can best be understood. Books that are more specifically about slavery, colonialism and apartheid shed further light on the making of Coloured identities. While all useful, not many of these offerings of reflection and analysis can – or should – replace the understanding of Coloured identity as experiences rather than historical facts.

Coloured identity cannot be reduced to a racial classification, one that codifies people to legitimise or delegitimise them. Coloured identity *is* us. Coloured people, so identified by choice and by force, are not only the experts on Colouredness – we are the essence of what it means to be Coloured. Understanding Coloured identity requires people who are not Coloured to be willing to look beyond the stereotypes, listen past the generalisations, and look into the eyes, souls, hearts and minds of Coloured communities with a desire to learn. A deep need exists within Coloured communities not to be spoken about, or even spoken to, but to be seen and to be heard.

We offer this book, then, as a mirror to reflect Coloured life – and a projection to show this life to people who too often think they know us. It is a book for Coloured people, by Coloured people, a book of Coloured and colourful stories from varied corners of the South African vista, past, present and future. We have written this book not only to capture stories of Colouredness, but also to evoke those stories in efforts to welcome all who care to know that Coloured lives truly do matter.

The very word 'Coloured' is loaded. To some, it is a slur, which made the hashtag even more controversial as it spread. To others, it is a burden. To others still, it is a unifier in a country where ethnic identity politics are beginning to replace the ideals of non-racialism and Black Consciousness that toppled apartheid. Who are Coloured people? Are they San or Khoe, Malay or mixed, and where in South Africa do they fit in? And then the enduring, but also insulting, question: do Coloured people even *have* a culture?

These are questions that we, the authors, have grappled with in our own lives, too. Our histories are so different, yet we are of the same ethnic group. Was being from Eldorado Park enough to make you Coloured? Not in the slightest. How about having mixed heritage? Most South Africans have a mixed cultural and ethnic heritage. To look at the markers of race – skin tone, hair texture, physical features – is to participate in the racism of White supremacy and the colourism that has already divided Coloured families and communities.

A harder question, still, to answer was whether we needed to be called Coloured at all. Many thought the classification would fall away along with the Colour Bar; not only has it held on, but a generation of so-called born-frees also clings to this identity. With so many wounds still gaping, so much healing still to be done, perhaps three decades after the end of apartheid was too soon to let go of four centuries of pain. But if we do hold on to this apartheid-era categorisation, what meaning will it take on?

We all know well enough that history is not neutral and that, at various epochs in the greater South African story, Coloured history and the question of identity have been used for the state's political purposes. We hope that you will take the history in this book as an inspiration to explore your own, but also to deconstruct the mistruths that have peppered Coloured identity and kept us on the margins instead of recognising that our stories are the stories of this country. We need not ask who we are, because we have always belonged.

Our first conversation about writing this book was one of the shortest and clearest conversations we have had as friends and co-authors. A book about Coloured identity had been an ambition for us both for a long time. The prospect of writing it together gave us each great comfort as we could tackle this sensitive and intimidating mission within the confines of a trusted friendship. That friendship was a gift to this book. What we knew intuitively is that it could not be a book about ourselves. But as we dug through archives, interviewed Coloured South Africans and made sense of contemporary events, it became impossible to ignore our own stories. It became intensely personal and challenged our own long-held assumptions.

As we wrote, we also knew that this book needed to be about people, rather than about history or theory. But we use history in this book as a tool for understanding the present. There is certainly room for more theorisation of Colouredness as an identity and, although we reference some of the great theoretical debates in South Africa's landscape about identity politics, this book is more about better understanding Coloured people's realities than it is about abstracting their experiences in conceptual musings. We ask you to read this book with your head *and* your heart. Take in the stories of Coloured communities from Limpopo to the Cape Peninsula with all the ebbs and flows of facts and feelings that make them accessible, even if you are not familiar with Coloured life. The people we interviewed have told many of these stories for the very first time. Even some of our own stories were spoken for the first time as we wrote this book. We are grateful that people trusted us with their deepest – and, in many cases, darkest – recollections. We realise, too, that history can be murky at times; while we have endeavoured to give an accurate account, we still look forward to learning new or different information about the history of Coloured communities that will help advance the debates about the place of Coloured communities in our society.

If you are not a Coloured South African, this book is for you too. Consider it a guide through and into Colouredness from the most intimate view we could provide. You may know all the stereotypes, but we invite you to learn about the experiences of Coloured people – the food, music and languages that bring Coloured cultures to life. To experience the debates about hair and skin from inside our communities and understand how they are about so much more than aesthetics. To pay homage with us to the political heroes of Coloured communities, the internal contestations about power and the ongoing and ever-changing struggle for legitimacy and relevance in the broader national question. To peep through the keyhole of history and get a glimpse of the twists and turns that are the making and remaking of Colouredness, and of how these fit into South Africa today. We hope that, in the parallels we draw with the Black South African experience but also with African American and other international experiences of racial subjugation, you will find that we have more in common than segregationists would have us believe.

This is a story that begins in slavery and colonialism, and the forced labour and exploitation these necessitated. We examine apartheid and its laws, particularly its two most socially and economically destructive tools: the Population Registration Act and the Group Areas Act of 1950, which created a classification – Coloured – and applied it carelessly and at whim. The stroke of an apartheid bureaucrat's pen wiped out the histories of entire communities, and forced removals invented new communities of convenience with no consideration of the people it forced together. We start, then, by attempting to animate the experience and consequences of apartheid classification, and move to explain the cultures that this classification lost and found through hair, music, language and food, and which constitute legitimate, albeit disparate, cultural experiences of Colouredness.

We cannot shy away from the social tensions that Colouredness represents in relation to other oppressed groups in South Africa, and we attempt to amplify as many voices and causes in Coloured communities' intracultural political battles. Colouredness in South Africa has always been characterised by resistance, but at times these political formations existed to ensure proximity to Whiteness and a separation from Blackness. What does it mean when that form of political identity makes a resurgence? But most importantly, this book is a call to reclamation. It signals that the questions of the marginality of Coloured people are as valid as they are misleading.

While various iterations of Coloured identity have thrived on the idea of isolation, Coloured people, in all their guises, have never been marginal in an honest version of the South African story. Yet the response to Julies's killing was once again wrapped in a narrative of isolation and marginalisation, of a forgotten people left to fend for themselves. The hashtag that set us off on this journey could be seen as yet another example of that marginality. But we have come to understand that it is the heartbreaking response of a people who feel erased from the South African story. Erasure is not a sign of marginality – it is an active attempt to keep salient stories out of the main narrative because they expose fissures in our society that are not easy to face or to fix.

It is our hope that this book will bring the subjugated but seminal stories of Coloured South Africans in the country's past and present to the surface. That reading and discussing it will enable difficult conversations, within Coloured communities, between Black communities and, broadly, among people of the world who care about the direction in which the arc of history bends. South Africa, like many societies across the world, is grappling with what it will take to build a more just, more equitable society that delivers quality of life to all. If this book moves those endeavours forward, in even a small way, it will have been worth the effort.

1. SOCIAL ORPHANS:
NOT BLACK ENOUGH, NOT WHITE ENOUGH

Tessa Dooms

Atlanta, Georgia, is 13 558 kilometres from Johannesburg. In 2007, as a 22-year-old postgraduate student of sociology, I travelled to the US for the first time. There, I was set to present the findings of my research to public health scholars at Emory University's Rollins School of Public Health. As a girl born and raised in Eldorado Park, a historically Coloured township, the idea of travelling to the US was barely a thought, no less a dream, I had growing up. American popular culture had, however, been an important part of my socialisation. From following daily soapies like *Days of Our Lives* and *The Bold and the Beautiful*, to being immersed in African American music cultures from R&B to gospel, I grew up feeling that I knew American cultures well – and that these cultures knew me.

I was bursting with excitement when presented with my first opportunity to travel to the US. Strangely, my excitement was less about the opportunity to present my work on sexual health at one of the leading public health institutions of learning in the world than it was about being a Coloured girl from Eldorado Park in America. Atlanta was the perfect place to have my debut experience of America. As a city with a large African American population, it was an ideal place to realise that my affinity with American culture was, in fact, mostly about real and imagined ties to Blackness as an experience of historical and cultural links to my identity as a Coloured person. So much about Atlanta and its African American communities reminded me of life in Eldorado Park: a shared love for R&B, gospel, soul and jazz; churches being central to organising the social life and fabric of communities; a focus on style and swag.

There was also the distinct lingering presence of segregation, as the city still had neighbourhoods that were considered Black. A sense that, regardless of the passing of civil rights laws and of time, even a large African American community could still feel the implied othering that only historical marginalisation can bring.

Like African Americans, Coloured communities in South Africa carry in their cultural DNA marks of being products of imposition, miscegenation, misrecognition, dispossession and slavery. When Malay people were shipped to Africa and African people were shipped to America, they became part of communities that are products of slavery which forcefully dislocated them from their homes and birthrights – people who, in a brutal process of being displaced, were dispossessed of their heritage only to be told that they were unrecognisable in new lands. Needing to form new communities, born out of structural violence, rape and other dehumanising practices, their realities were often a mishmash of communities bound by the convenience and inconvenience of others, while attempting to forge new ways of living together and becoming cohesive and functional communities. To my mind, Colouredness was so closely related to African Americanness that I may as well have been African American as I walked the streets of Atlanta. Through Atlanta's vibrant culture, language and music, Black people lived the streets of the city, but not without tensions. Much like Johannesburg, Atlanta is a sprawling metropole with huge highways connecting neighbourhoods that are very different. Atlanta's Buckhead is like Johannesburg's Sandton – fancy, rich – and for a child like me from Eldorado Park it has living conditions made for TV. Eldorado Park is more like Atlanta's Oakland or Lakewood, communities with low-income families, underresourced schools and children who play in the streets while their parents hustle to make a living. These communities, rich and poor, coexist in an awkward dance to build a society. Importantly, not all the rich are White people in a city like Atlanta. Black wealth and Black inequality exist. What comes with this Black inequality is the familiar tension of growing up Coloured in post-apartheid South Africa: what made some people, who were once marginalised and oppressed, worthy of better lives while other lives do not improve or get worse?

I could feel the similarities. Our histories of oppression. Our racial tensions. Our obvious inequalities. Atlanta felt like home because it mirrored the feeling of technically being free, living in a city where many people look like you but are still an economic and cultural minority. As one of the US's Blackest cities, in a way Atlanta felt like home. So, imagine my surprise when a clash of sensibilities became the most memorable culture shock of my trip.

Within my first few days in Atlanta, I was standing in a medium-sized lecture hall to deliver my presentation in front of approximately a hundred staff and students of the Rollins School. The white walls and neatly packed chairs made for a sterile setting, given life only by the professors and students who packed the room, which went from empty to standing room only within minutes. I was exhilarated. I looked out at a crowd of diverse faces, people of various ages and racial backgrounds. My research was on religion and sexual health among South African youth. For my sociology honours research paper, I had conducted interviews with teenage South Africans from lower- and middle-income communities, asking them about the role that religious messages had played in their own sexuality and decisions about sex.

Nervous about the sensitive subject matter, I was far from calm and collected. I began my presentation with an explanation of the demographics of the teens who had participated in the research – which, of course, included their racial profiles. I listed them as Black, White, Indian, Coloured – all common racial signifiers that any person in South Africa would encounter when completing a standard government form. As I uttered the word 'Coloured', something changed in the room. The word moved through it like a choking gas. Some gasped; others looked on in shock. What had been a room of warm, welcoming faces eager to hear the findings of a young South African student had become an atmosphere of shock and deep discomfort. I searched the faces, trying desperately to understand this shift. Finally, I realised: the word 'Coloured', a term that affirmed my identity, was an insult deeply rooted in a painful past for African Americans.

Historically, the word 'colored' was used in the American lexicon to identify people of African descent, a way of designating them as inferior, unworthy and defective. Being referred to as 'colored' was not a way of telling what you were but a reminder of what you were not – White. Being referred to as Coloured for me, at least as a young and fairly politically naive 22-year-old, had – and continues in many ways to have –

different meanings. To me, the term 'Coloured' reflects my history and represents my culture. It is an expression of my cultural sensibilities and the community that raised me. It is the languages I speak. It is the games I played as a child. It is the food I call home. And yet, similar to the African American experience, Coloured is not a name I gave myself, or my community gave itself. The history of Colouredness as a legal identity marker is of a name given to many communities through a process that often stripped away way more than it offered.

In South Africa, a country principally shaped by race, otherness has defined how Coloured people are perceived from as far back as slavery and colonialism to as recently as apartheid, which ended within my lifetime. It is near impossible to live in South Africa without contending with the baggage of racial classification and profiling. Unlike other African countries, where markers like nationality and ethnicity trump race as identities that bear political and practical meaning, in contexts where colonisers settled and never left, even post-independence, race is politically loaded with ideas about belonging, dignity, humanity and questions of ownership that are as real and consequential today as they were for centuries before 1994.

South Africa was formed through racial antagonisms, with Black pitted against White in a binary from which every other facet of our people's political, economic and social lives, our very destinies, emanates. To be caught in the middle of this binary is just as binding, suspending Coloured people in a sort of in-betweenness that has come to shape our very selves, as community and as individuals. In everything from the family portraits on the wall unit to the Black Economic Empowerment codes of practice, Coloured people embody a racial identity that is neither here nor there. It's a space Coloured people have negotiated in the past and that continues to shape how we navigate the post-apartheid South African reality. The forced formation of Coloured communities, during apartheid and even before it, has created communities that are scarred, both socially and politically.

Colouredness bears many wounds. The birth of Colouredness is pained by slavery, ripped from home to a life of trauma. It is in powerlessness, and the violence of the rape of Black women by colonial masters. It is in the wilful erasure of indigenous language and culture. Even as the idea of Colouredness as a racial identity began to take shape, it was steeped in the rejection of being living proof of the miscegenation that diluted

White claims to superiority. It was also burdened by the shame of needing to hide our Blackness out of a skewed sense of self-preservation. Slavery, then apartheid, separated families, erased heritage and created impossible choices between individual rights and the right to community.

Not Black enough, not White enough: this is the phrase that has become synonymous with Coloured frustration in post-apartheid South Africa. It's heard chanted as a political slogan, or muttered at braais to describe the fruitless job search, yet in many ways these six words hide a deep pain, a sense of orphanhood in post-apartheid South Africa. It is a cry by Coloured people to be seen as fully human and legitimate participants in the South African, African and, indeed, larger human story.

In her article 'What's in a Name?', sociologist Deborah Posel writes compellingly about how the system of racial categorisation in apartheid South Africa was enacted[1]. Referring to the implementation and enforcement of the Population Registration Act of 1950, Posel describes the categorisation process. She details how, in registration offices called Offices for Race Classification, people would physically present themselves to one or two registration officers, who essentially had full discretion and power to give anyone any racial categorisation they deemed appropriate. Empowered by an authoritarian state that regarded most of its citizens as less than human, officials behind a desk decided the destinies of millions of people. They examined hair, eyes, skin and any other phenotypical marker that would inform this racial categorisation. They asked questions as menacingly simple as, 'Who are your parents?' or gave commands as random as, 'Show us the gesture you make to say thank you,' to make a decision about a person's race, and therefore their future.

This interrogation was particularly important when biological characteristics were not definitive enough in the minds of an officer tasked with making this all-important decision. A resulting identity code issued by the officer would dictate the terms of the bearer's life. With an army of bureaucrats to support its brutality, the apartheid system tied itself in legal and procedural knots in efforts to undo centuries of mixing between colonial settlers and indigenous people. The main goal of the Population Registration Act was to create a clear system of White supremacy by being clear about who 'the other' was.

The power that these bureaucrats and the state they served had to categorise people, and the effects of their enactment of it, must never be downplayed. The process of assigning someone a racial identity in apartheid South Africa determined their legal status, quality of life, education opportunities, where they could live and even who they could marry. The moments spent in an Office for Race Categorisation determined – and, in many instances, altered – the fate of many individuals and families for generations. One has to wonder whether these bureaucrats, working from 8 am to 4 pm, with benefits and pensions, ever gave a thought to the lives they altered with a stamp.

VERDUIDELIKING VAN IDENTITEITSNOMMER

Die identiteitsnommer van 13 syfers wat op bladsy 1 van die identiteitsdokument verskyn, is soos volg saamgestel: (a) Die eerste ses syfers verteenwoordig die geboortedatum van die houer, naamlik die eerste twee syfers die jaar, die volgende twee syfers die maand en die vyfde en sesde syfers die dag van geboorte. (b) Die volgende groep (vier syfers) is 'n volgnommer en dui die geslag van die persoon aan. As die 7de tot 10de syfers 0001 tot 4999 is, is die persoon vroulik en as hulle bo 5000 is, dui dit 'n manlike persoon aan. (c) Die derde groep syfers (die 11de en 12de) dui die persoon se burgerskap en bevolkingsgroep soos volg aan:

Bevolkingsgroep	S.A. Burger	Nie-S.A. Burger
(i) Blanke	00	10
(ii) Kaapse Kleurling	01	11
(iii) Maleier	02	12
(iv) Griekwa	03	13
(v) Sjinees	04	14
(vi) Indiër	05	15
(vii) Ander Asiër	06	16
(viii) Ander Gekleurde	07	17

(d) Die laaste syfer (die 13de) is 'n kontrolesyfer wat deel van die nommer uitmaak.

See page 10 for English text.

EXPLANATION OF IDENTITY NUMBER

The identity number consisting of 13 digits and appearing on page 1 of the identity document is made up as follows: (a) The first six digits represent the date of birth of the holder, the first two indicating the year, the next two the month, and the fifth and sixth the day of birth. (b) The following group (four digits) is a serial number and indicates the sex of the person concerned. If the 7th to 10th digits are 0001 to 4999 the holder is a female person, and if they are above 5000 a male person is indicated. (c) The third group of digits (the 11th and 12th) indicates the person's citizenship and population group as follows:

Population group	S.A. Citizen	Non-S.A. Citizen
(i) White	00	10
(ii) Cape Coloured	01	11
(iii) Malay	02	12
(iv) Griqua	03	13
(v) Chinese	04	14
(vi) Indian	05	15
(vii) Other Asian	06	16
(viii) Other Coloured	07	17

(d) The last digit (the 13th) is a control digit forming part of the number.

Kyk bladsy 9 vir Afrikaanse teks.

Pages of an apartheid-era identity document, listing South African racial classifications, including the subcategories created for Coloured identity.

My father's life was forever changed in a registration office like this; as a young boy he went into one of these offices named Lesole but, to be reclassified from Native to Coloured so that he had the same classification as his mother, he changed his name and left the office named Elliot.

Race and racism have always been about affirming and diminishing people's humanity. Racial classifications place people into groups that are accorded a social, political and economic hierarchy. During apartheid, being White or European was the pinnacle. It meant a higher social standing and better life chances in South African society, and being seen as more human than people of African descent. Being 'Native' meant barely being recognised as human – having the lowest status and the worst life chances.

What lay in between became a breeding ground for the otherness and uncertainty that lives within the fabric of South African society to this day.

This is the birthplace of modern Coloured identities. Why modern? Because the Population Registration Act of 1950 did not invent Coloured-ness. During the colonial era, people of so-called mixed racial descent were called 'Kleurling', an Afrikaans word which, directly translated, means 'one with colour' or 'coloured'. 'Coloured' in both South Africa and America was not an affirmation of what a person was, but rather a reminder of what the person was not.

When apartheid became a legal system and race was codified, many different realities awaited the people who walked out of the Office for Race Categorisation registered as Coloured. My father, Elliot Dooms, was 16 years old in 1958 when he was first ushered into such an office. He and his classmates were taken from school without any explanation of where they were going, without parental permission or support.

Before then, my father's life had been uncomplicated – at least, it seemed that way. Raised in the then Northern Cape village of Dithakwaneng, and later Vryburg, a rural town in what is now the North West province, my father grew up speaking a combination of Setswana, Afrikaans and English. From a family of livestock farmers, my father often recounts a blissful childhood spent playing along the river and catching snakes. His primary caregivers were his grandparents, Johannes and Elizabeth Dooms. Johannes was the eldest son of a German soldier and his Motswana wife, Mammila. The name Dooms was evidence of the family's Germanic roots, although the family's cultural heritage was firmly Batswana.

On the day my father and his high school peers unwittingly arrived at the registration office to be racially classified for the first time, he had never thought of himself as anything other than a Motswana boy. He had never heard the word 'Coloured', let alone contemplated the implications of be-ing called this. Wearing his school uniform, and with no parent or adult present to help him understand the weight of his responses, when it was his turn to answer the Registration Officer's questions his answers were candid and innocent. To the question, 'What is your name?', he proudly told the officers that he was Lesole Dooms. Lesole, his Motswana name, was given to him because he was born in 1942, a year associated with war and soldiers. In that office, on that day, the name Lesole became the main marker of my father's identity to those tasked with classifying him. They determined that it was cause enough to classify him as 'Native'.

He left that room clutching his first registration document, his 'dompas', unaware of the implications until he arrived home from school. 'Dompas' is the name given to registration documents, or passes, that Black people had to carry during apartheid. They allowed Black people to be in a place, to pass into and through the place legally. Police could ask for a person's pass at any time, often in insulting ways. It became common for police to refer to the document as a 'dompas', Afrikaans for 'stupid pass' – because while that pass document defined the very existence of Black people, it was just a stupid piece of paper to them, a piece of paper that gave the status of people for whom they had no regard. The police looked forward to using it to intimidate, catch out and harm Black people.

Recounting the events of the day to the elders in the family, my father presented this 'dompas'. It was only at this point that he learnt that the rest of his family had been registered as 'Coloured'. What did it mean to be Coloured? What did it mean to be Native? Lesole had no clue. More importantly, however, what did it mean for him to have been classified differently from his family? A great deal; the most important implication had to do with the enactment of the Group Areas Act of 1950.

By 1958, my family had been moved from Dithakwaneng to the newly formed Coloured township in Vryburg called Colinda. This move was not by choice. The Group Areas Act of 1950 had kicked in and launched a new wave of forced removals in South Africa. It not only entrenched apartheid racial classifications, but also realised segregation in practical terms through spatial inequality. My father, still a child, knew only that the change in location was preceded by his White friends in the village telling him that their parents would no longer allow them to play at the riverside with him. This was followed by my father's grandparents announcing that the family would need to leave the land in Dithakwaneng and move to either Taung or Vryburg, to settle in newly formed settlements. They would no longer be livestock farmers. They would need to establish a new life as shopkeepers.

In the Houses of Parliament and sprawling Union Buildings, the apartheid government was very proud of their segregation policies. They skilfully justified removing people from their ancestral homes and the land that

A woman tending to sheep in Dithakwaneng in 2022.

anchored their livelihoods by claiming that this was nothing more than a mechanism for bringing 'order' to society, as this excerpt from a speech by Senator PZ van Vuuren, speaking in Parliament in 1977, explains:

> We make no apologies for the Group Areas Act, and for its application. And if 600 000 Indians and Coloureds are affected by the implementation of that Act, we do not apologise for that either. I think the world must simply accept it. The Nationalist Party came to power in 1948 and it said it would implement residential segregation in South Africa … We put that Act on the Statute Book and as a result we have in South Africa, out of the chaos which prevailed when we came to power, created order and established decent, separate residential areas for our people.[2]

Although this, of course, was positioned as benign if not benevolent governance, it was, as many acts of violence and oppression in South Africa's history are, essentially a land grab that sought to disenfranchise Black people for the economic and political benefit of White people. Your registration document was a pass that allowed you to fraternise only with people with the same classification as you, unless you were given special permission to be in an area another group lived or worked in.[3]

When my father went home with his registration document for the first time, then, he was essentially breaking the law. Imagine breaking the law by simply going home from school. This is a small yet powerful example of apartheid's power to separate parents from children, brothers from sisters, and to keep lovers from becoming spouses. My father's family had not told him about the collective narrative they had agreed upon to be identified as Coloured. Like many families, mine had predetermined strategies for ensuring that everyone ended up with the same classification and securing the highest possible classification status to improve the family's life chances. Families would alter their surnames – Ndlovu became Oliphant, Nkosi became King. They would deliberately forget their mother tongue and whole parts of their history. What my father's elders had not told him was that he was not to use the name Lesole. So, to answer Posel's 'What's in a name?' question, my father's using his name given at birth – the name that held so much of his identity – in one moment cost him the right to be with his family. And, as he would learn upon his second trip to the Office for Race Categorisation, getting that right back would require him to relinquish his name officially.

Children of the Dooms, Moeketsi and Setzin
families in the 1960s in Mafikeng.

Ironically, it is that very sacrifice which resulted in my father being arrested by the apartheid police a few years later. His aunt, Margaret, a shrewd businesswoman, had managed to organise two pass documents: one that classified her as 'Native' and another that classified her as 'Coloured'. Aunt Margaret was the elder sister of my father's mother, Onica. Although she was not the eldest of the four daughters born to Johannes and Mammila Dooms, Aunt Margaret was certainly the most ambitious and feisty. She had trained as a teacher but became well known in the community as the first person to start multiple shops, mini superettes, in the townships designated for both Natives and Coloureds. No one ever knew how Aunt Margaret managed to get two passes but having them enabled her to run a business in the township area where the majority of Mostwana people lived. Depending on who was asking, she would produce the pass that was most expedient to the situation. My father worked in her shops in Coloured and Native areas, although his pass document only allowed him to work in Coloured areas.

One afternoon, as my father stood behind the counter, uniformed police officers arrived – routine harassment sanctioned by law. They demanded to see my father's documents, which he did not have with him that day. It was recommended that, when he was in an area in which he was not legally allowed, he did not carry his pass. He spoke meekly, not wanting to stir up any trouble. He promised to run home to get it, if they would just give him a few hours. The police allowed him to stay at the shop that day but told him they would return the next day to inspect his documents. When they did, and they realised that he was in fact registered as Coloured after initially having been registered as 'Native', they arrested him for being in the area unlawfully.

The police bundled my father up and took him to a holding cell at the police station where they detained him for hours. He sat in police custody, alone and uncertain, all because of a classification that he had not chosen. A classification for which he had sacrificed his name. Aunt Margaret Dooms, however, was as fierce as she was shrewd and would not let them jail my father. Her reputation in Vryburg was one of a leader who would not cower, not even before the police. She arrived at the police station to negotiate my father's release, determined to ensure that her nephew would not spend a single night in jail.

Young Elliot – no longer Lesole – was released with a warning that day. A warning that meant that working in his family's business, as the shopkeeper in Aunt Margaret's store, could get him arrested again, with more dire consequences next time. He could not risk a next time. Being arrested for being Coloured in the wrong area forced my father to reconsider his life and where he would live it. It ripped him from everything he knew.

He never returned to working for his aunt. That same day, he began making plans to leave Vryburg for Kimberley. Outside of the family home and Aunt Margaret's shop, the church was where he spent most of his time. He knew a pastor in Kimberley who would take him in, help him rebuild. But he soon realised that plan would be complicated in the same ways. The pastor and his church were also in an area demarcated for 'Natives'. He was scheduled to leave for Kimberley within days of his arrest and release. Shortly before he was meant to board the bus, his sister, Ous Koeba, who lived in Johannesburg, arrived to take him to live with her in Eldorado Park, a newly formed Coloured township. She had made a life for herself there, and he could too. The city's demarcations were clearer, with new townships springing up in Johannesburg specifically to keep races apart.

Elliot would be safe in Eldorado Park, as long as he forgot about Lesole. That name does not appear in his contemporary South African identity document but is invoked as a term of endearment by family members who to this day call him Solly – a contraction of Lesole. Having never heard the name Lesole until I was an adult myself, I was always curious about why my father was called Solly. As I've mentioned, many in the family explained that it was short for 'Soldier': my father was born at a time when soldiers walked the streets of Soweto, where his mother lived when he was conceived.

My father still lives in Eldorado Park. Eldo's, as it is affectionately called, is a by-product of the invention of Colouredness. First built in 1965, it was specifically created as a low-income township for Coloured people. South of Johannesburg, Eldo's is adjacent to Soweto, separated by a street and a field. Between the two is Kliptown, the birthplace of the Freedom Charter, where the borders between race are much more porous. Eldo's was created as a shared but bare canvas, where many people with this new identity would come together to piece together their own lives in an ever-expanding, composite community of varied stories, values, norms, traditions, ancestries and ways of life. They were all forced to make this new community work. Like the devastation, emptiness and confusion of a child left orphaned in an instant, the psychology of Colouredness is borne from past ruptures, displacement and a void of information about the past and the future. It should not surprise us, then, that the foundation on which the present was built was shaky. Maya Angelou unknowingly channelled the making of Colouredness when she wrote '[p]rejudice is a burden that confuses the past, threatens the future, and renders the present inaccessible'.[4]

Eldorado Park is where Elliot Dooms made a life for himself. Here, he met Irene Marwa, the woman who would become his wife. It is where he raised his children and truly learnt as an adult what it meant to be Coloured. In Eldo's, his identity as a Coloured man would no longer be a matter of law or circumstance. It would require a deliberate set of life choices about religion, career, culture and language. It took my father many years to make sense of what being classified as Coloured meant for his life. More than twenty years after a faceless bureaucrat decided my father's classification and his future, my father would make that decision for his own children. The dread of that brokenness he had experienced being visited on his children guided him when he decided which language we, his children, should learn. He would not teach us Setswana. My mother, having been raised in Witbank, spoke isiZulu – but she would not pass her mother tongue on to us either. My parents opted to have us speak Afrikaans, the other language they had spoken at home. But they eventually settled on English – yet another choice about our identities that would improve our prospects.

Given the trauma of my father's registration experience, my parents' decision, while strange, was noble. We were born when apartheid was still in full swing. Our births were registered and we were codified as Coloured, living in not a clearly Coloured neighbourhoods. To preserve his family, my father needed to deny his children the opportunity to learn his language. In the 1970s and 1980s, he had little hope that the apartheid regime would be defeated in his lifetime; he planned for a future in which his children may very well have to stand in front of a registration officer, needing to account for their right to be a part of his family.

Apartheid's laws made many Coloured people social orphans. Some were physically separated from their families; others separated from their heritage; and others separated even from themselves, unable to claim their own names. The Coloured communities that apartheid created were like communal orphanages, places with narrow streets and matchbox houses where children with diverse histories met for the first time and realised that they needed to make families of one another instead of longing for the families that had been lost to them forever. Coloured communities are fragile because they hold, in plain sight, unattended and unacknowledged brokenness. Broken families and wounded people. Untold stories and untold pain. In a sense, racism achieves its ultimate goal through Colouredness: stripping people of their humanity. As Steve Biko reminds us, to restore a people and a person's humanity is to affirm their humanity rather than their race.

Not Black enough, not White enough: a lamentation often spoken in Coloured communities in South Africa. The idea of not being enough haunts the psyche of Colouredness and can be traced back to experiences of falling short of Whiteness in the corridors of registration offices. It also includes the shame associated with being a child of a Black mother who was not regarded as human enough to be spared the violence of rape, or good enough to be claimed as a wife, even if she were loved by a White man. Further, it recalls the indignity of slavery. Measuring worth according to race, or being suspended between two racial constructs, strips Coloured people of their humanity and traps them all within race. Not being enough and not having enough are some of the longstanding tropes of Coloured identities. Needing to prove your worth, validate your existence, is a central part of the making of contemporary Colouredness. At the heart of it all is a crisis of belonging.

In post-apartheid South Africa, four centuries after the first colonial and slave masters landed and seven decades after the making of Coloured communities through the Group Areas Act, Coloured people are still in search of belonging and humanity. Our place in South Africa still feels uncertain. While it is true that Coloured people in South Africa do not hold the monopoly on marginalisation and suffering, our plight is no less important than that of other marginal groups. Unemployment, poverty, inequality, crime and poor service delivery are all real problems in Coloured communities. Structural racism, compounded by a dearth of opportunities and class barriers, maintains the legacies of historical oppression.

Born and raised in a Coloured community, I have experienced not only the social ills that result from this brokenness, but also the religion, song, dance, food and family traditions we have used, in unspoken ways, to heal the parts of ourselves and our community that were broken generations before us. The making of culture and shared values in Coloured communities is sacred because it does the heavy lifting of weaving communities together. For better or for worse, the solidarity in Coloured communities is not accidental. From gang culture to church culture, Coloured communities – like orphaned children – have decided to make family of one another and craft new forms of belonging while fighting against the disruption, disrespect and dislocation of racism.

As a Coloured person today, I am a product of a series of social and political events. Some of these events are accidents of history. Others are intentional acts of historical violence and oppression. Some are decisions taken by office clerks in a registration office, and others are deliberate choices made by my family and community between limited and often undesirable outcomes. What is undeniable is that being Coloured is not a simple identity. It is as deeply political as it is cultural. As a social orphan, I decide how to take power back from those who have made decisions for me, and I choose how to define myself. Ultimately, I have settled on identifying as Black and Coloured. In accepting Blackness as a political identity that links me to a history of Black struggle, and Colouredness as a cultural identity that expresses my socialisation, the way I was raised, the languages I speak, the food I eat, the music I listen to and the way I comb my hair, I have chosen to transcend the classification and embrace the culture that is Coloured identity.

It is my cultural experience of Colouredness that makes it an identity I use easily and with pride. Coloured is not my race. I do not identify as Coloured because of the tone of my skin. I identify as Coloured because of shared practices, values and experiences I have with a community that raised me and gave me a sense of belonging in this country. It is an identity that, despite its roots in violence, oppression and pain, has come to mean more to me, and many in the Coloured communities who raised me, than a signifier that I do not 'qualify' for being called White. When I spoke of Coloured identity in that research presentation in Atlanta, then, I was not reinforcing racism's oppressive naming convention. Rather, I was reclaiming not only the word 'Coloured', but also every idea it carries in the hearts and minds of the generations who have made a collective life out of the ruins of apartheid and colonial dispossession.

2. LUCKY COLOUREDS AND FORGOTTEN ANCESTORS

Lynsey Ebony Chutel

It was my cousin Kelsley who figured out that pantihose make better hair than jerseys. She was about nine, I about six, standing in front of the mirror, pretending to have straight hair, knowing then already that we had been unlucky with the thick bushes of kinky, *kroes* hair that puffed in our school plaits or stood as a stubborn thatch of coils when water touched them. We were cute little girls, cousins who dressed alike and had matching rag dolls. We were smart and precocious. Just a pity, was the unsaid message, about our hair. At least it grew beyond our necklines, but it was thick, so very thick, and so very *kroes*. Of course we covered it; of course we wanted someone else's hair.

Pantihose were better than the jerseys we used to play with, pretending that we had beautiful hair, if only in the mirror. Pantihose were long and thin and fitted snuggly on our heads, completely covering our own hair, we discovered. The empty nylon legs swayed like lucky hair was supposed to, and the way our thick, stiff plaits wouldn't, even with ribbons lovingly tied to their ends. Pantihose also came in colours that were closer to what we thought, even as young as six and nine, hair was supposed to look like. My mother's preferred colour, called Blackmail, looked like a shiny, blackish-brown mane, with the seam working nicely as middle parting.

The jerseys would fall over our eyes when we would flip our fabric hair, standing in front of the mirror practising for the day when we would have pretty hair. Jerseys were multicoloured, thick and woolly, too close to the hair we were trying to get away from. The hair that tangled and knotted, that was thick and *gekoek*, that we resented as we sat at our mothers and aunts feet. The comb was a symbol of terror; rollers were torture. All a necessary step to make our hair acceptable. Each Sunday, I would sit at my aunt Joan's feet, and we would begin a ritual that started when I was in nappies – wash, detangle, comb, roll, blow and plait. None of it was gentle, not to my memory. When I was a baby, my aunt would wait until I was asleep, weaving my hair into pantihose cut into little strips. When I was a toddler, she would chase me around with the hairdryer. The story goes that once I made it all the way to the front gate of our backroom in Bosmont. Joan, with her beautiful waves, had learnt how to tame her own hair as a child, and is still the family's de facto hair-weaving magician.

Lynsey Ebony Chutel, the author (right), with her older cousin
Marice Phillips in 1988.

When we were children, our family never really sent Kelsley and I the overt message that our hair was ugly. They didn't have to. The need to tame it, the threats that necessitated it – 'people will laugh at you', 'birds will nest in you' – and the ritual that reinforced it all sent a message that the way our hair grew from our heads was not good enough. It also taught us to associate our hair, our very appearance, with pain. No one who was rich or famous on TV had hair like ours. Our mothers and aunts, who were neither rich nor famous, didn't have hair like ours either. Instead, every few weeks they would tame their hair with relaxer or straightener; their ability to withstand the choking smell of the white cream seemed a strength. Our mothers also covered their acceptable, straightened hair with pantihose. Displaying the versatility of nylon and the innovation of Coloured women, a *swirlkous* was cut from the girdle of an old pair of pantihose. The holes where the legs had been cut off were knotted to form a tight cap that would wrap around the straightened hair, keeping it acceptable in a cone or a hive of hair overnight. When you washed, it would keep dreaded moisture away until your hair was ready to be revealed, swaying in the wind. Unless it rained and your hair shrivelled back to its naturally kroes state. Then you and your hair went home, as Coloured people say.

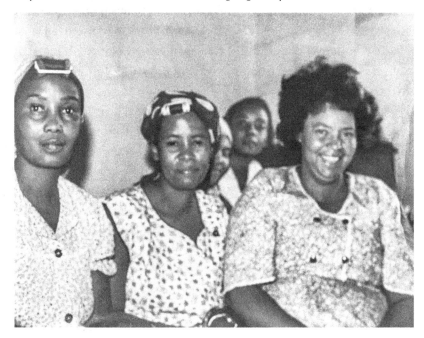

(Left – Right) Van Vooren sisters Sannie, Emma, Martha and Maureen with their cousin Christine Slava, preserve their curls after a wedding in Utrecht, KwaZulu-Natal, 1979.

When would we have our turn? Not until we were old enough to handle the burn on our scalps, and to master the swirl that would preserve its results. Worse, we would need to prove that we could manage our own hair so that it would not break off in chunks like that of the other unlucky girls with *kroes* hair, whose bad luck was compounded by the bald patches of chemical burn. Our mothers wouldn't let us relax or straighten our hair until we were 13. The family rule felt like a burden through our childhoods. It was as if straight hair also signalled a sexual maturity we would need to be ready for, an attention our mothers were trying to put off for as long as possible, even if it was never really said out loud. The rite of passage was marked with the smear of Dark and Lovely's Beautiful Beginnings on zigzagging roots to make them straight and pliable. Until then, it was pantihose – pretend locks in play that turned into an easy *swirlkous* for bed.

Kelsley and I were unlucky in another way: we were brown. Brown like coffee with milk, or muddy water. Thankfully not black *moerkoffie* brown, or black earth brown, but brown nonetheless. We were not lucky Coloureds, with fair skin or light eyes – better if it was both. Bonus points for straight hair, extra bonus if it was naturally pin-straight, but who wants to talk about the hidden bottles of relaxer in the homes of lucky Coloureds? Somehow, though, we were shielded from the worst of our misfortune. Born to unlucky brown mothers and aunts, who made up for their perceived loss in the phenotype by being smart professional women. At boarding school and college, my mother and her sisters were old hands at taming their own hair with the *struikkam* warmed on the open flame of a Primus stove or tin of burning cotton wool dipped in spirits. Later, they risked their hairlines with sulphurous straighteners and Wella became a verb. When it worked, their hair was the talk of the town, hanging like good curtains. But the chemicals could just as easily turn on you, and women became experts at covering bald patches where hair was eaten away by relaxer. Wigs were a handy tool when a comb-over didn't work. Cutting your hair, though, was not an option. The Afro had not yet been embraced by Coloured women in the 1970s, and anyone trying to find a partner or a job dared not risk being *kroes*.

As a student nurse at Somerset Hospital in Cape Town, my mother Lorraine first encountered the material effects of colourism. Pretty as she was, a hazelnut-coloured girl with long, thick hair from small-town KwaZulu-Natal would never snag a Coloured doctor or any fair-skinned Coloured man in Cape Town. The students with the right skin tone and long hair didn't seem to need to apply themselves at all. Never mind, though; my mother was bookish and her best friend Mary McMinn knew her way around rollers. In Cape Town, my mother saw Coloured doctors, physiotherapists and radiographers for the first time. It was also the first time she was exposed to the politics of the anti-apartheid struggle, Robben Island a distant speck from the hospital ward's window. But the rhetoric of political emancipation did not measure up to the colourism that still coloured her experience in the city, to the underlying message being that she was not quite good enough, not quite light enough, to be valued within the Coloured community.

It helped that the matriarch of our family knew exactly who she was and what she stood for, despite a regime that told her otherwise. My grandmother, Martha de Klerk, is a smart, determined, dark-skinned woman, who was in turn the daughter of a proud Zulu woman. Her self-assurance insulated us, for the most part, from the attacks of colourism. Yet even in our little town of Utrecht, a town founded by a handful of families, there was a separate section of the Coloured graveyard for lighter-skinned families. My grandparents, both Coloured but of entirely different hues and experiences, created a family across the colour spectrum. But my family is not immune from colourism; you hear it in the jokes, still, about who is darkest among us, who has the best hair, what strange luck it was that the darkest also had the best hair. Old wounds, wrapped into new jokes.

It helped, also, that Kelsley and I were born later, in the 1980s, when our prospects were not tied to our luck. This experience of colourism, even without formal expression as every little Black girl who has wished for blonde hair, is universal. It is most poetically articulated in Toni Morrison's *The Bluest Eye,* when a young African American girl's prayer for blue eyes hides a pain much older than her years.[1] Pecola's wish is the wish of so many little girls, whispered in languages around the world, in backyards and bedrooms from the US to our little corner in Africa, anywhere where White supremacy, the venom of colonialism, apartheid and Jim Crow, had sunk its fangs into a society. Colourism, an internalised racism that created a racial hierarchy within Black communities, was not just the burden of little girls – it defined the destinies of so many men and women of every age. Pecola's heartbreak, and Kelsley's and my silly games, are perhaps the most naive results of colourism. Our yearning for straight hair was about much more than beauty standards – rather, it was a deeply internalised self-hatred borne from the very creation of Colouredness as a separate racial category. We were children playing out a legacy of othering that had very real consequences for our forebears.

In societies governed by White supremacy, proximity to Whiteness created privilege. For centuries, racism has ascribed moral and economic value to people based on their phenotype. Being light-skinned meant better working conditions, even in the inhumanity of slave plantations in the American south or the British colonies of the Caribbean, with lighter enslaved people working in the home while darker ones worked in the hot sun, picking cotton or hacking sugar cane. Later, wavy hair could mean a job as a clerk rather than a streetsweeper. A straight nose could land a young lady a good husband, with similar features, and the often unspoken hope that they would birth lucky children. The right combination – skin, hair, eyes and nose – could grant an entirely new life: a lucky Black person passing as White. Passing would mean a lifetime of alienation from family and living as an impostor, with the constant fear of being caught out. But it was a choice that many Black people, the world over, have made.

This is neither new nor revelatory, but it is enduring. Racism does not rely on logic, but on efficiency and brutality. The apartheid government was perhaps one of the most successful examples of racism and its ability to create a false hierarchy. Under the apartheid government, the very structure of South Africa's state, politically, economically and socially, was governed by race, a concept we now understand to have no intrinsic value yet is one that has shaped our world. It justified the exploitation of Black people, their inhumane treatment, with theories of race arguing that Black people were not quite whole people.

For people of mixed racial descent, then, the more closely you resembled someone of European descent, the higher up in social strata – the closer to human – you were, but you were still never quite whole. You were something like Shakespeare's Caliban, allowed to live nearby, to serve, to learn what could be useful to your master and to take what little he offered. The only comfort was: at least you were not Black. In real terms, this meant rejecting any features, cultural or physical, that could bring you as a Coloured person closer to being Black and take you further away from being White. The colonial and then the apartheid system encouraged Coloured people wilfully to separate themselves from Black Africans, pitting groups against each other by creating a false hierarchy, with White people at the top. Never mind that the few rungs on the social ladder that were available to people who were not White were so narrow and offered so little – when fighting for the crumbs of White capitalist exploitation, they still mattered.

The insidious power and cruelty of White supremacy is hard to escape, deeply internalised by the Black and Brown people victimised by systemic racism. How much harder it is, then, to disentangle yourself from these racist ideals when your very identity seems to be shaped by racism and a response to it. Coloured identity is wrapped in colonial history, created, some would argue,[2] by White supremacy itself. Coloured people in South Africa, in particular, are the descendants of indigenous Khoe and San, as well as the former enslaved people of the Cape Colony who came from as far afield as the islands of Indonesia and Africa's west coast. Some were also the unclaimed children whom White settlers had with Black and Asian women. Through slavery and subjugation, they lost their languages; to survive on the vineyards and colonial farms, they spoke a creolised Dutch that would become Afrikaans and remain one of the key indicators of perceived differentiation. The descendants of these disenfranchised groups became the Black labour class of emancipated Khoe, San and other enslaved people in the first half of the 19th century, who continued to build the colony.[3] Even then this labour class was diverse, culturally and phenotypically, but already the rulers of the colony had created a division between them and South Africa's indigenous tribes for the purposes of political control and capital gain. This was a group of Black people created by colonialism itself. Their White overseers referred to them as 'half-caste', 'bastards', 'off-whites', 'Cape Boys', and the term that would stick: 'Coloureds'.

The discovery of diamonds in South Africa in 1867, and then gold in 1886, entrenched the material gains to be made from maintaining these differences. To survive, this Black labour class internalised the names they had been called as an identity that would ensure their material survival in colonial capitalism. It was also one of the first instances of the people who would call themselves Coloured deliberately separating themselves from indigenous Africans, already aware that to be closer to Whiteness would bring some advantage, no matter how small.

'The rapid incorporation of significant numbers of Bantu-speaking Africans into the burgeoning capitalist economy serves as the catalyst for assimilated colonial blacks to assert a separate identity and organise politically under the banner of Colouredness,' identity scholar Mohamed Adhikari writes in the book *Burdened by Race: Coloured identities in southern Africa.*[4] Rejected by White society and firmly placed within the class of exploited labour, colonial Black people used this claim of a separate identity to assert a privilege over Africans as they competed for resources doled out by White colonialists.

The early creation of this Coloured identity may have been forged by the influences of Dutch colonialism at the Cape, but it was formalised and disseminated by British colonial attitudes and Cecil John Rhodes's scramble for African resources. It was in this period that the term 'Coloured' itself took hold and came to mean a people of mixed racial origin with a sprinkling of European civility who were regarded more highly, if only slightly, than the African workers. The so-called Civilised Labour Policy, espoused by Prime Minister JBM Hertzog after he took power in 1924 and formalised in the 1926 amendment to the Mines and Works Act (referred to as the Colour Bar Act), not only affirmed this competition among colonial Black people and Africans, but also systematised the segregation between the two groups.

This segregation was enacted over a series of laws that laid the groundwork for the apartheid system, which, at its most legislatively crude, was a series of Acts and amendments that separated South Africans more and more from each other, from the workplace to the park bench. Even as the very classification of Coloured served to corral different peoples and histories, there was an acknowledgement, albeit scurrilous, of some diversity. Even then, though, this was as a matter of control. The 1911 census of the Cape of Good Hope is when we begin to see the word used formally alongside other ethnicities. Before then, in 1865, ethnicities are given as 'European', 'Kafir', 'Hottentot' and 'Other'. 'Malay' is added in 1875, alongside 'Mixed' and 'Other'. Indigenous Black groups are classified as 'Fingo' and 'Bechuana' from about 1891, but by 1911 these classifications had also dissolved into 'Bantu' and then 'Native'.

It was the Population Registration Act of 1950 that gave clear definition to racial differences, but even these definitions demonstrated the speciousness of racial certitude. In 1951, the census lists as population groups 'White', 'Bantu', 'Coloured' and 'Asian'.[5] But even then, Coloured people are further divided, into 'Malay' and 'Other Coloured', and later into 'Cape Coloured' and 'Griqua' – all the way until the 1980s, as the franchise shifted and the Group Areas Act remade communities. Each group had a numbered code, indicated by the final number of the 13-digit ID number; this endured until the end of apartheid. Parliamentary debates from the time of the Bill showed the flimsy foundation that informed one of the apartheid government's most enduring injustices.

While Afrikaner nationalism was informed by the ideology of White supremacy dipped in the pseudo-science of eugenics as proof of racial purity, there was simply no time, resources or commitment to apply this rigour to establishing the Coloured identity, even if it was in the interest of the White nationalist project. According to Posel, the classification protected notions of White purity by ensuring that Coloured blood would not be mixed with White blood through the accidental acceptance of Coloured people into the White race.[6] As Posel quotes one Union of South Africa lawmaker as saying in the debate on the Coloured question:

> It is no use saying that we know these people are Coloured. We know these people are Coloured but, because by repute and common content they are white, we are going to make them white. By so doing, we are going to allow Coloured blood into this race which we, some of us, wish to maintain so wonderfully pure.[7]

But there was no appetite to diversify a system that would unequivocally prove the biological differences between Europeans and Coloured people, and even less so to investigate the differences between Coloured and Black people. For White South Africans building nationhood, uniting a disparate group of settlers into a group that, without irony, called themselves Africans, or Afrikaners, the differentiating factor was a sense of purity, creating distance between themselves and the indigenous people whom God had sent them to civilise – or, at the very least, subjugate. Not unlike colonial pilgrims elsewhere, Whiteness became a driving force as they trekked into this uncharted, supposedly empty land, guided by a divine hand. In the formalisation of a government and a country, this purity would justify their status as the rightful stewards of a land that was not theirs at all. It would justify the plunder of natural resources and the mistreatment of Black people as the other.

It is no wonder, then, that Coloured people, as they began to embrace the classification and internalise its racism, sought to establish and protect a place for themselves at the doorsteps of White people, rather than along-side Black people – even accepting that they were not African, as illogical as this claim is for people of colour born in Africa. It served White people too. As the government of the day created the framework for segregation, they sought public consultations from around the country in what was a rather democratic process, were it not only limited to White men. To discussions about the bureaucracy that would be required in this new classification pro-ject, White nationalist ideologues from across the country contributed their views. Drawing on their experience of animal husbandry and of playing *baas* at the farm attendees of the Murraysburg Boere en Wolwerks Vereeniging meeting in 1951, in records quoted by Posel, posited that '... it is almost impossible to determine with any certainty which people are natives and which people are Coloureds ... It would be an uneconomical waste of time and money to try, throughout the country, to determine a person's race with precision ...'.[8]

The task of deciding the fate of millions of men and women was doled out to junior bureaucrats who would use 'common sense'. 'It is obvious to all: we know that if we see a white man, we know that he is a white man', according to the minutes of a House of Assembly debate on the Population Registration Act in 1950.[9] When the Bill was published, its arbitrary defini-tions of race would become the bedrock of South Africa's segregated society, cruelly enforcing these haphazard classifications as fact and, ultimately, law.

According to the Act, a White person was one who appeared White and who was generally accepted as White but not a person who appeared White but was socially accepted as Coloured. A Native person was a member of 'any aboriginal race or tribe of Africa', while a Coloured person was one who was neither White nor Native.[10] The new Act codified Coloured people's proximity to Whiteness, and gave their random physical traits legal and economic heft. It was no longer just luck – it was law. The Act itself was amended several times over the decades to tighten any loopholes, but as late as 1984[11] the reclassifications continued, with dire consequences for people's lives.

The actual act of classification was even more slapdash and would al-most be laughable were it not for the cruelty that permeated the process. Bureaucrats would fire off a series of questions about height, weight, ancestry, religion, food and, of course, your name. When skin tone was not a clear response, the person's lived experience became a litmus test for race. Levels of education, where you lived, the language you spoke and the accent with which you spoke it were all important. Whether men drank spirits or home-brewed beer, if their wives cooked rice or pap with their meat, and even a sense of how you behaved were all markers of racial classification.

The answers to these questions reveal the colourist hierarchy that would become entwined in the fabric of Colouredness. Hair, on one's head and one's body, were key indicators, as testimonies collated by Posel show: '*Sy hare staan los, sy hare rol nie*';[12] '*Hulle staan reguit; my hare is kroeserig*';[13] '*Daar is baie naturelle what hare op hulle arme het*'.[14] So, too, with skin and facial features: '*fyner as 'n naturel*',[15] or '*my kleur is tussen donkey and ligbruin*'.[16] The recurring theme, '*hulle*' and '*ons*' – us and them – did the real work here, dividing Coloured people from Black as Coloured had been divided from White.

These features would decide what kind of employment you would be eligible for – a clerk or a tea girl, an artisan or a hired hand – what schools your children would attend, where your family could live and ultimately who you could marry. In rural areas like the Transkei, where groups lived in closer proximity and everyone spoke isiXhosa, it was easier to hold on to family and friends and the colour line was much more blurred. In the cities and towns, however where race so clearly defined economic prospects, the colour line could be a canyon, even in places like Noordgesig and Orlando, where Coloured and Black lived but a street away from one another.

In the cities, Coloured people with light eyes and light skin came to be known as the 'lucky Coloureds' and had their pick of the crumbs apartheid doled out to them, earning work in the factories or homes in the form of council flats in Newclare. Darker-skinned Coloured people lived in constant fear that they would be reclassified as Black, ripped from their lives and the little bit of privilege they had accrued. Courtship and marriage too were influenced by this hierarchy. To that end, couples made deliberate choices. Two light-skinned parents could hope for light children, who would intrinsically have value within their community. For a light-skinned man to marry a woman of a slightly darker hue was to do her a favour. She could make up for it with her hair, though, but this could mean a lifetime of sleeping with rollers, rising early and secrets at the hairdresser so that her husband could go his whole life without seeing his wife with wet, shrunken, *kroes* hair.

These choices within the Coloured community defined our identity, our moving away from Black and closer to White, our clamouring for proximity and privilege from the very people who rejected us.

Falling through the cracks of that system could leave one isolated and excluded. My paternal grandmother, Aisha, had three sets of children, each from a man of a different race. Born of a Black mother and German father, she was regularly complimented as a beautiful woman for her pale skin and hazel eyes. But her racial ambiguity, coupled with her class as an uneducated rural woman, proved to be a disadvantage. Her first daughter was from a White man, who abandoned her. Her second group of children was from a Coloured man, who also disappeared. She later married a Malawian migrant, who had come to work in the coalfields of the Natal Midlands. She converted, from Alzina Mbatha to Aisha Chutel, and had six more children.

When her husband died young, she struggled to find support in her community, my Uncle Dean recalled in his own unpublished memoirs. They were Muslim, but not Indian. They were Black, but not Zulu. Their official classification was 'Other Coloured', and my father and his brothers attended an Indian primary school because Weenen's apartheid enforcers didn't know what else to do with them. High school was out of reach, so the brothers moved to Johannesburg, to start a shop, a path not unlike immigrants today. My father, who died when I was young, continued to live between these two worlds. Few knew him by his Arabic name, Rajab; instead, he went by Marshall. Kliptown, that storied corner of Soweto that was neither Black nor Coloured, was where we drove to when he bought stock for his chip shop in Eldo's. As a child, driving around with him after school, we traversed the townships, Pimville, Lenasia and Noordgesig. The Chutels fell through the cracks of classification, and in many ways it forced them to create a culture of their own that was a combination of Zulu, Islam and survival.

This arbitrary legislation also forced Coloured people to reject their history and culture, making them cultural orphans. To be or resemble Black people was a liability, and to admit to any Blackness meant the loss of social and economic status. It meant the denial of close family, exile from communities. The emotional toll is impossible to quantify, but the scale of it can be estimated when, even today, some Coloured South Africans are mistaken for being Black. Being spoken to in isiZulu or Setswana is an offence to some, who are desperate to remain separate. It is particularly true for some of the most economically frustrated among us, whose self-hatred allows the K-word to fall easily from their lips, even as they live cheek by jowl with Black South Africans who experience equal disappointment with post-apartheid South Africa.

Even before apartheid was legislated, the willingness to embrace the darker side of the family tree was swiftly punished. In the early years of the Cape Colony, the Van der Stel family's political dominance was challenged in part because of their mixed heritage. Simon van der Stel was the son of a Dutch East India Company commander and a freed slave, Maria Levens. Van der Stel became governor of the Cape and was succeeded by his son Willem Adriaan. Both tried to change the Van Riebeeck-era policy of hostile engagement with indigenous tribes, particularly the Khoena. Under the two governors, freed enslaved people and free Black colonial labourers grew in social and economic stature and came to be seen as a direct threat to the White settler population. As Adam Tas, described as the chief architect of the Van der Stel family's downfall, wrote of Willem Adriaan van der Stel:

> But as is frequently the case with persons of mixed blood, the throw-back badness occurred in the third generation. The impression that Willem Adrian leaves upon us is that of the half Oriental. His character was not without its more admirable features, but he lacked balance and self-control, and the moral sense seems to have been entirely wanting.[17]

No wonder, then, that in the living rooms of Coloured families centuries later the lighter-skinned ancestors are celebrated in framed photographs while their darker partners or children are left forgotten. Coloured children could tell you their White racial heritage down to a fraction – 'one-eighth Irish on my father's side' – but had no clue that their grandmothers spoke Setswana before their names changed. Family lore often overlooks the deliberate choices people made to align themselves with a certain group to enjoy the economic and social capital afforded to them by legislated segregation. These are stories that play out over and over in Coloured histories and, while this proximity no longer holds the economic advantages it did before 1994, it maintains value within the family and the community.

In Coloured communities, this correlation between social hierarchy and acceptable hair was intertwined with our identity. It served to set us apart from other ethnic groups within South Africa, but also imposed a social and economic hierarchy on the group. Across homes, communities and the country, there is a miscegenation myth that permeates, privileging White and Asian ancestry. It overlooks the Ghanaians, Mozambicans, Angolans and Black South Africans who make up what Stephen Langtry refers to as 'A Coloured Tapestry' on a simple Facebook page of that name which collects the stories of Coloured heritage – all the stories.[18]

Stories like that of Dina van Rio de la Goa, born in Mozambique and enslaved in the Cape in the 1730s. She escaped and joined a community of runaways in what is today Pringle Bay. She and seven others were put on trial and sentenced to a horrendous death: being tied to a pole and strangled. She was 25 and pregnant, and the only reason we know her story is because of her testimony during her trial.[19] This courage was not only deliberately erased by a White supremacist culture – it was perverted to a point of shame. That's why the film *The Making of a Runaway*,[20] an exploration by University of Cape Town students in 2014, is a humble but incredibly important piece of work.

By focusing on the story of this young Mozambican woman, *The Making of a Runaway* not only challenges how slavery in South Africa exists in public memory, but also subverts the colourist hierarchy that existed centuries ago and stubbornly persists in Coloured collective memory. In the Slave Lodge at the Cape, Black women like Dina would have been kept in the basement, along with the other enslaved people from Africa. The enslaved people from Asia had slightly better quarters and the mixed-race enslaved people enjoyed the best of what this humiliating life could offer. It's a hierarchy that is seen throughout the world where Black people have been subjugated, and it is a hierarchy that Coloured people have reproduced, wittingly and unwittingly preserving these categories of oppression.

The apartheid government may have formalised this centuries-old hierarchy through the classification system, but even now, as categories like 'Cape Coloured' and 'Other Coloured' have fallen away, class and privilege in Coloured communities continue to organise around it. They will continue to do so too, because there is a dearth of projects like *The Making of a Runaway* in which Coloured people interrogate the social systems we have not only preserved, but also turned into a sort of culture. We do not have an absence of culture; instead, we have created a culture from preserving good hair and genetic luck. Without interrogating our history, and the way we have created that history, any culture we create will erase women like Dina van Rio de la Goa. The formal codes of racial classification may have long since been done away with, but they remain deeply entrenched in a post-apartheid expression of Coloured identity. Who would we be if we celebrated the story of women like her? Internalising a culture that is based on rejecting heroines like Dina van Rio de la Goa erases so much of our history.

But how do Coloured people begin to embrace a culture based on exploitation? How do we build the codified division established haphazardly by colonial and then apartheid rulers, which reduced rich histories to a number? It was not just Coloured people whose memories were erased. The legends and languages of the amaMpondo, amaHlubi and baLobedu that did not fit neatly into the homeland structure of the amaZulu, ama-Xhosa and so-called Northern Sotho were simply erased by the system, but thankfully preserved by the people who took pride in these histories. While the colonial governments recognised the amaMpondo as a separate people – albeit for purposes of exploitative trade treaties[21] – administratively this group that migrated from the Great Lakes region was filed under amaXhosa.

The amaHlubi, in their fight for recognition, have the *izibongo*, the oral history, that draws a line from *inkosi* Chibi, who ruled a people who migrated from east Africa in the 14th century.[22] Their stones recall Langalibalele's desperate flight to save his tribe from the invading Voortrekker settlers and trace their living descendants[23] in northern KwaZulu-Natal today through their *isithakazelos* (praise poems). Today, the amaHlubi are using these oral histories to challenge the apartheid-era governance system that lumped their history together with a schematic understanding of Zulu culture and tradition. The Rain Queen is the embodiment of baLobedu culture and history, even as apartheid-era language classifications grouped a language with its origins[24] in the ruins of Great Zimbabwe under the umbrella of Northern Sotho. This traditional descendance, too, was tested[25] in court in 2021 as a teenage queen prepared to take the throne in a post-apartheid administration that aims to restore royal power.

Both this court battle and a similar amaMpondo matter from 2019[26] pit cultural power, situated in a shared history and identity, against the post-apartheid government's constitutional promise of freedom and an ideological identity wrapped in the banner of our ahistorical and ethnically agnostic flag. While the legal challenges are largely driven by gaining access to state-issued salaries and a seat in the House of Traditional Leaders, not to mention having a say over a traditional land, they present the opportunity to enter centuries of oral history into legal records, which will in turn inform the future of each group in this new South Africa. As a Coloured person I am envious – and desperate to record my own oral histories. Because if centuries-old, precolonial nations could be plastered over by the bureaucracy that still reverberates in post-apartheid South Africa, what about the intimate erasure within Coloured families whose histories have already been redacted as a means of survival?

Even now, when identity politics and critical race theory have given us the intellectual tools and language to identify the injustices of the colonial and apartheid systems, the messaging has not been dismantled, and still sits in the follicles and cells of the hair texture and skin tone in which so many Coloured people still place social and personal value. In creating our culture, we have relied for too long on our phenotype rather than on our shared history and complex diversity. Even without the enforcement of the apartheid government, we continue to police ourselves based on these arbitrary features.

Nowhere is this more obvious, perhaps, than in a township hairdresser on a Saturday morning. One of my earliest memories is of being a confetti girl with Kelsley at an aunt's wedding. The plan, according to the wedding stylist, was to create little crowns of curls out of our own hair, which would require our hair to be manageable – read 'straight'. And so, as soon as the hairdresser in Eldorado Park Extension Five opened at 8 a.m. that Saturday morning, we were there. Aunt Joan, the guardian of my hair, never left our side; she ensured that, while the hairdresser would make our hair sleek, she would not apply any form of relaxer to our hair, as sometimes happened when hairdressers just did not have the energy or willingness to deal with *kroes* hair. Our hair was only meant to be blown out at temperatures that our old standing hairdryer at home couldn't muster. This rare trip to the hairdresser would mean that we would style our hair no longer in the puffy plaits and school-coloured ribbons, but in ponytails and buns, and even loose – signalling a maturity and a readiness to be sent out into the world. The adults often told us that our hair was fine as it was – thick, rich and beautiful with a *goeie draad* that would relax well one day. But the blowing and the rolling and eventually the ironing (thankfully, not the *struikkam* of my mother's era), followed by the compliments and cooing that followed when our hair was straight, almost nullified the pride they tried to instil in us for our natural hair. Their indirect message was that straight hair was meant for special occasions, like Christmas, funerals and weddings, and so, while they protected our natural hair, it was rarely celebrated.

Preparing for my role as a confetti girl in my aunt's wedding procession, I winced but dared not whine as the hairdresser partitioned my fluffy hair and pulled it around a roller until the flesh of my scalp rose up to meet her determination. When the roller had successfully gathered up all the hair around its hollow plastic shape, a pin would keep it in place, digging into my scalp until the skin at its tip went numb. Despite the pain, it was a point of pride that I used green rollers and a few orange ones on the crown. Kelsley, older and more poised for pain, used orange and yellow ones.

Christmas Eve rollers on Joan de Klerk, who became her family's de facto hairstylist.

I was boosted on a cushion and locked into a standing hairdryer for half an hour. After the timer's ping, a test revealed that my *dik hare* was still wet, so in went my rollered head, like bread into an oven, for 30 minutes more. When at last my hair was dry and the rollers released, the hairdresser gave my scalp a quick massage before handing me over to the more senior hairdresser – the one who could work with my 'type of hair' – for more torture. This next step is one that women around the world know: the high heat and pull of a blow-dry. Except, when you blow Coloured hair, you cannot allow our roots to reveal our secret – that our straight hair is an illusion – and so my already tender scalp was seared by close heat, taming my wiry roots. I remember nearly crying, or actually crying, and my aunt being there to comfort me, not to take me away but just to remind me that this was part of the process, that soon it would be over and I would be pretty. And I was – at least, I finally felt I was – when on the walk back home the wind whipped through my straightened hair and Kelsley and I giggled at the fantasy come true: no pantihose needed, at least not until the *swirlkous* later that night. Once our hair had been moussed and gelled into loops that resembled little tiaras, we made fine confetti girls and the trauma was forgotten.

I would willingly subject myself to this process again and again for years to come – as a bridesmaid for Kelsley's wedding more than two decades later, and again for two more weddings, when I was to take my place in the social strata of family life or send the message that I was well, cared for, valued. And even now, a proud wearer of a natural Afro for more than a decade, I embark on an annual pilgrimage to a hairdresser where I have my hair washed, set and blown, blasted straight with heat in the same way as when I was a confetti girl. I tell myself it makes my Afro more manageable, my ends easier to trim, but the truth is that sitting in the hairdresser feels like home. In many ways, it has come to feel like a ritual of my roots, it has given me a sense of connection to a time when who we were seemed simpler. Whether it is part of a lazy Sunday afternoon with aunts and cousins, or in a trusted hairdresser, the pulling, poking and singeing of hair all feel wonderfully, painfully familiar, even away from home. Being seated between a trusted elder's knees, my hair pulled this way and that, feels profoundly comforting, despite the pain. In a strange way, to have my hair taken care of so meticulously is an act of love.

I have no obvious ties to the Western Cape, no people there, but when I walked into Heloise May's salon in Mount Pleasant in 2021, the feeling was familiar all over again. Between the Kleinrivier Mountains and the rocky Atlantic coastline, Mount Pleasant should be idyllic. Just outside Hermanus, its fishing cottages and row houses would be quaint were it not for the ugly history that built them. It was founded in 1929 as a fishing community for the Coloured people of Hermanus.[27] At that time many chose to live close to their livelihoods in Hermanus, but by 1966 the Group Areas Act had stripped all races of this choice and relocated the Coloured community to the township on the outskirts of the town. Its geographic location served as a buffer to the Black township of Zwelihle, and today, even as only a narrow street separates the townships, they remain worlds apart.

On a temporary stay in the area, I did not live in either township, but locals still required a classification. Throughout my two-month stay in the Western Cape, my dark skin and voluntarily *kroes* hair led to confusion and a demand that I clarify which side of the street I fell on, even in 2021. Everyone from mall security to supermarket tellers looked me up and down, classifying me. The contemporary test was administered in Afrikaans or isiXhosa for efficiency. My English answer made it clear that I was from neither side of the street.

Despite my foreignness as a Joburg Coloured, Mount Pleasant was familiar and easy enough to navigate. Before the mall was built, Mount Pleasant's activity centred on a shopping-cum-community centre, which houses a clinic, a general dealer and three hairdressers. I walked in one Tuesday afternoon (skipping the queues from Friday to Sunday, when the regulars prepared for church and work) with my hair in an Afro tightened by humidity, submitting myself to a combination of research and nostalgia. As had become my habit in Hermanus, I walked in explaining myself, pre-empting the test.

'I'm writing about the Coloured experience in South Africa,' I declared to three quizzical women, pen and notebook in hand, my professional boundary. I tried again in Afrikaans, but that wasn't the problem. The issue was that, although Coloured people – women in particular – spend so much of our time talking about hair, it is treated as an inherent burden or blessing from a European or Asian ancestor, wilfully ignoring the Black ancestry we all carry. Our notions of what makes good hair, or even so-called Coloured hair, are rarely subjected to the critique of why we value it so – even as we try to move away from the merits attributed to straight hair, citing ease and convenience rather than acknowledging the overtly political statement it is to wear your hair naturally in an environment where the past's White supremacy still casts such a long shadow.

'*Nee, nee, ons ken van sulke hare. Ons weet hoe om alle soorte hare te manage,*' said May, the owner. As I settled into the chair, we began to talk about how issues around Coloured hair had changed – or had, at least, begun to. May recalled a former employee who would have balked at my Afro, blamed my parents and accused me of neglect as he twisted my head from left to right, trying to find a strategy for tackling the nest. As more and more young women came into the hairdresser refusing to relax their hair, the former employee had become increasingly obstreperous until she'd had to take him aside for a talk that eventually led to his early retirement. Philecia Figaji, the nail technician who had been forced to drop out of a BSc degree, proudly fingers the wavy bush of her ponytail. She chose to go natural a few years ago, ending years of trips to Cape Town where her grandmother would organise the more than hour-long drive to get her hair straightened. It was like washing away the traces of her mother's poor choice of partner: her father, whose heritage had given her that enviable bush of hair.

May's salon was as much a testament to the resilience of Coloured women as it was a meeting place. A mother of three, she'd struggled to find her way until she began doing hair. It led to her own business and dreams of producing her own natural hair line, which is now being sold in the salon. Her cousin, Anelle May, had a natural flair for taming hair, and so she is able to feed her family as she washes, sets and blows the community's hair. As in so many neighbourhoods in South Africa, the hairdresser, the locus of maintaining our collective colour complex, is also a safe space for women and a key to the financial independence of anyone who could serve this hallmark of Coloured culture. Just like the barbershops and hairdressers of Black America, the hairdressers of Coloured townships are safe spaces where we can let our hair down, or up, as it shrivels under the water. It is also likely why unravelling our culture and identity from our hair types and skin shades will be hard.

As the women rolled my hair – it took several hands, holding mainly orange and yellow rollers because, yes, that still mattered – the conversation turned to life in Mount Pleasant, the frustration, the lack of opportunities, the proliferation of the lolly lounges, or drug dens, the power of the gangs and the injustice of the police that hid behind the suburb's quaint façade. Here, in Hermanus, a haven for European tourists, southern right whales and White tycoons still fat off apartheid money, Coloured people were still living with the maladies of poverty and alienation. Still left out, unable to access the country's wealth. The stories were the same, sometimes worse, along the R43, as in Hawston – the diseases of gangsterism and addiction that had inflamed Cape Town's townships for decades had spread to this historically Coloured seaside town. We commiserated, again, about the similarity of our experiences on opposite ends of the country. Inevitably, sadly, the commiseration turned to anger, and then the familiar divide. My hair finally straight, after four hours of pulling, tugging and talking, the ladies were now comfortable enough with me, this English speaker from Joburg, and the thing emerged that had been lurking beneath their frustration: us and them. Mount Pleasant and Zwelihle, Mannenberg and Gugulethu, Eldorado Park and Soweto, Eersterus and Atteridgeville, Wentworth and Umlazi, Coloured and Black, us and them. Even then, their anger did not turn to the wealthy White South Africans just a little further down the road.

The racialised scramble for crumbs still plays out over a quarter of a century after the end of apartheid. Little open animosity was shown towards the whitewashed beachfront mansions of Hermanus, because that's simply the way it's always been – a testament to the efficacy of the colonial and apartheid systems. Here were working-class South Africans of colour still eking out a living side by side in the shafts and kitchens of White supremacy, still elbowing each other out in the midst of exploitation, albeit of a different kind. Instead of valuing the resilience of that little hairdresser, and the opportunities that women like May have created by serving their community, we other ourselves again and again.

The legacy of colourism is not unique to Coloured communities, and perhaps that is how we will begin to tell a different story, a story that will eventually free us from these categorisations. More than two decades later, as a journalist writing about how film and music were recording a new history of Africa, I happened across the short film *Hair That Moves* by Yolanda Keabetswe Mogatusi.[28] It was heartbreakingly familiar. Buhle is a little girl, precocious and smart, nine or ten, who wants to be a singer –

like every other girl, including Kelsley and I when we were that age. In the poignant story, Buhle yearns for hair that sways in the wind, that will whip when she dances and brush across her face when she cocks her head. Like us, she hangs her school jersey over her head and pretends to have straight hair. Mogatusi's treatment of Buhle's fantasies in the mirror were so tender, without mocking her dreams, that it taught me for the first time that the games Kelsley and I had played, our yearning, was universal. This is how Buhle rehearses for a coveted role in a school play and the adulthood she envisions for herself. It was not unlike Kelsley's and my performances in the mirror, with jerseys and pantihose on our hair. Buhle, though, has a rebellious but unfortunate encounter with relaxer, but it teachers her that neither her talent nor her value lies in her hair. When I wrote about it, I got messages from as far afield as the UK, where Black women had all played the game, heard the same message.

The message to Black girls was universal and vehement: our hair, as it grew from our heads – curly, zigzagged, spiralled, or coiled – was an unruly burden we should restrain as soon as possible. In my family, that meant waiting until we were 13; in other households it would happen as young as two, as if to hide the child's true roots as soon as possible under the guise of manageability.

Natural hair is unruly, difficult and unattractive – all the things you do not want a well-behaved girl and respectable woman to be. That message was communicated loudly through teasing and disapproval, or more subtly in popular culture that reinforced colourism through the absence of women who looked like us in our morning cartoons or late-afternoon soap operas. In the 1990s – when I was a child, and so was South Africa's democracy – the radical joy of the Afro had begun to recede and was being replaced by the straightened hair or weaves that symbolised the era's celebration of capitalism and corporate power, produced in the US and beamed across the world, albeit a few years behind, to our mothers' television sets.

Images of mocha-coloured women with straight, black hair and toffee-coloured men with wavy cuts appeared over and over in the images of pop culture. Unaware that Hollywood was the victim of the same kind of colourism that afflicted us, in Coloured communities these images reinforced the messages of White supremacy beyond political policy to the labour sector, cultural production and even the intimacy of family. By the time it went mainstream, this messaging had crept beneath the skins of people of colour around the world. In communities with a claim to miscegenation – and in the Coloured community in particular – these celebrated images became an internalised identity.

It was a message that was so easy for Coloured people, and Black South Africans too, to accept because it latched on to our already internalised notions of White supremacy. We may have resisted and fought against systemic racism, but the consciousness created by that system has been harder to shake off. Post-apartheid South Africa, consumed with building homes and providing electricity, did not have the resources or the capacity to rebuild our souls. That is slowly changing, at least on our screens, but the conversations in hairdressers and households tell me we still have some way to go.

Kelsley has a daughter now, Erin, who carries the same hair, and burden, as her mother and I. She has beautiful hair, long and thick and wonderfully *kroes*. It also hurts when she has to plait it for school, and every week is a *snot en trane* affair, but it ends with her parents and three brothers standing around her, all cooing about how pretty she looks with her hair straightened and tamed, and how worth it the weekly pain has been. It is all painfully familiar.

Still, Erin is growing up in what should be an entirely different hair culture. At five, she attended a natural hair convention where there were several stalls catering purely to children like her, reinforcing that her hair was beautiful. As she grabbed samples and compliments from each stall, she beamed, proud of the two stiff plaits poking from her head. We were proud, too, and continued to reinforce the message of the beauty of her natural hair. Kelsley has not made the same promise that Erin can relax her hair at 13, and instead they experiment with coconut oil and shea butter and the dozens of products now available to embrace natural hair.

And yet, Erin still yearns to have straight hair. Her confidence is noticeably higher when her hair is blown out. Without anyone telling her, she has figured out that her hair is not a '*goeie draad*'; society's whispers, carried over the centuries, have made another little girl believe its lies. But as we all prepared for another family wedding, ten-year-old Erin decided on her own look: she shirked a blowout for pink-and-purple box braids that celebrated her hair and brought her joy, whipping and waving as she danced.

3. NO, TREVOR NOAH ISN'T COLOURED

Tessa Dooms

Trevor Noah was first introduced to national and international audiences when he released his first one-man show, *The Daywalker*. In this and subsequent stand-up shows, he explains that he is the child of a mixed-raced relationship between his Xhosa mother and Swiss father. Noah explains that the children in his Soweto neighbourhood used the name 'Daywalker' to refer to him. In a time when interracial sexual relations were illegal, being of mixed-race descent with light skin in a Black community raised eyebrows.

Growing up in 1980s apartheid, instead of explaining his mixed heritage, Noah allowed his friends to believe that he had a skin condition called albinism, a melanin deficiency that affects mostly Black and Brown people. While the apartheid government would likely have classified Noah as Coloured, he did not look into a mirror and see a Coloured boy. He did not correct children who saw his lighter skin and assumed albinism by stating that he was Coloured. He knew he was different, but he was not Coloured. Although he was the child of an interracial relationship, being Coloured was not a natural assumption for Noah to make about himself, nor was it the default assumption of his childhood friends. This is because being Coloured has never simply been a matter of racial mixing. In the terms of the age-old nature versus nurture debate, Colouredness is very definitely a matter of nurture over nature, characterised by relationships, geographies, language, fashion sensibilities and music. Noah could not claim Coloured identity because, regardless of the inclinations of a system that would be eager to classify him as such, he lacked the experience of Coloured identity.

Colouredness as an identity marker in South Africa must always be understood in the context of both the country's race-based political structure and its unintended cultural consequences. We have seen how the invention of Coloured as a racial category under apartheid was a clumsy and random process based on a conception of race as a mash-up of biology, culture and geography – and that, when people presented themselves for racial classification, as was the mandate, it was not DNA or even self-identification that determined their classification but the subjective views of a few White men using limited information and their own prejudices. Reducing Coloured identity simply to being 'mixed' represents not only an erasure of many people's histories and experiences, but also a failure to recognise the violence of the classification and the work that followed. Colouredness was created by communities forced together to make their lives work, which has had consequences for self-perception, world views and opportunities. Coloured identity is more than hair and complexion. It is more than an accident of biology. Colouredness is a culture. This cannot be overstated.

So, when internationally renowned comedian Trevor Noah is casually referred to as Coloured, it is a debate I want to have but almost always avoid. A discussion about someone else's identity is deeply personal. However, when it comes to race, the personal is also profoundly political, and the intersections between personal and public identities matter. The explanation of why Trevor Noah, while being a person of mixed racial heritage, is not Coloured says a lot about many misunderstandings of what it means to be Coloured and about oversimplifications of Colouredness that stem mostly from the political and legal history of the category.

In his book *Born a Crime: Stories from a South African Childhood*, Noah tells the story of how his mother, a Black Xhosa woman, met and fell in love with his father, a White Swiss-German man.[1] Owing to the legal and social prohibitions that apartheid placed on love relationships between people of different racial groups, Trevor grew up in Soweto with his mother as his primary parent. In the book, Trevor explains in detail how complicated his appearance and mixed heritage made his mother's life. The central claim to, and of, White exceptionalism in South Africa was threatened not only by Black love and the idea that Black people were capable and worthy of love, but also by the ways in which children born of 'mixed' relationships diminished and exposed the false claim that light skin, light eyes or straight hair were markers of moral superiority – a claim on which White supremacy in South Africa depended.

Trevor Noah's parentage certainly presented the same threat to White-ness that, historically, many Coloured people have. The mythology of White supremacy,[2] which needs to position itself as pure and unblemished by 'lesser' people, relies on four elements to even almost hold together. First, it relies on the identification of other people, Black and Brown people, who present as different to what White people accept as Whiteness. An important step for Whiteness to succeed is for it to make sure that power is distributed to select people. Second, it relies on interpreting physical differences in skin tone, hair, facial features and body types not as mere diversity of human biology, but as defects that can somehow show that some people are 'naturally' superior to others. This, of course, neglects the reality that, as is the case with the lens through which history is told, what is deemed the standard of 'good biology' is about who has the power to interpret the science and who is empowered to translate the science into social policy. White supremacy relies on having the monopoly on what is considered valid science and knowledge to ensure that what is regarded as truth favours Whiteness over all other people.

Third, White supremacy relies on these so-called physical defects be-ing associated with moral inferiority. It is important to remember that race is neither natural nor accidental. For colonial conquest to work, it needed a justification. Race and racism became this justification, with those who undertook those conquests making wild leaps in logic that connected differences in physical appearance with judgements about dif-ferent moralities. The audacity of saying, without fear of contradiction, that the inhumane treatment of Black people was simply a function of a natural order of White superiority is the foundation of a system of op-pression that is irrational and unconscionable. It is a world view that has been normalised and is reflected in the internalised racism experienced by Black people in Africa and the diaspora.

Finally, and most importantly, it relies on a separation from and loath-ing of those physical traits to maintain the lie that the traits justify the inhumane treatment of other people. This is where the threat that children of mixed descent pose to White supremacy comes to the fore. If White men can find Black women attractive enough to have sex with, it contra-dicts ideas that Black people's biology is inferior and undesirable. It creates a category of people who have traces of the biology that Whiteness praises as superior – and a social lineage that, in the bodies of people of mixed descent, literally equalises Blackness and Whiteness.

The underlying driver of racism is fear: that the inadequacy of others will be exposed as a lie, and that the privileges derived from that lie will fall away. The stories of 'mixed' people like Trevor Noah and many Coloured people expose the lies that uphold White supremacy. During colonialism and apartheid, the birth of a mixed-heritage child signalled that a White person, usually a man, had physically desired a woman who was not White – usually a Black woman. This desire offered a different interpretation of Black bodies. It showed that those bodies were beautiful, acceptable and more similar to than different from White bodies.[3]

There are, however, many more told and even more untold stories of this desire leading to sexual violence. In a system that gave White men immense power and exploited Black people, women in particular, sex was no longer about desire. It was about power, as rape always is. Powerful White men preyed on the disempowered Black women who were their slaves and later servants and employees. There are also untold stories of love, secrecy and abandonment, as White people met locals whose beauty, charm, intelligence and passion connected with their hearts. But there are also the babies abandoned in fields, dropped at orphanages, when their appearance betrayed their parents' crimes. While Trevor Noah's story had a happier ending, with his sweet and courageous grandmother as the heroine of his tale, many were not as fortunate.

By the time colonialism and apartheid had been firmly entrenched, these relationships and the children they bore would be flagged as a danger to White supremacy. When mining towns boomed in late-19th century Johannesburg, migrant labour created transient communities where people from different backgrounds met, socialised and had sexual encounters. The 1889 outbreaks of syphilis on the Witwatersrand during the gold rush, narratives soon emerged about the role of 'dangerous Black women' whose feminine charms caused White men to stray into sexual immorality that led to disease. Those White men could not be held accountable for their own decisions and, moreover, their decision to be with Black women required a narrative that justified such an error in judgement.

This was neither the first nor the last time that Black women would be forced to carry the shame of White men's desire for them. History is littered with stories of the oversexualisation of Black women's bodies. From Krotoa, the first indigenous servant of Jan van Riebeeck, who married a Danish settler and was ostracised as a woman with loose morals, to Sara Baartman, the KhoeKhoe woman who became an international colonial exhibit fetishising the curves of the African woman's body, Black women's sexuality has been shamed as a way to justify the gaze of White men.[4] However, children born of mixed-race sexual relations were much harder to explain away, hence the need to create legal distance between Whiteness and people of mixed heritage. As early as 1682, 30 years after the first settlers arrived, the government of Simon van der Stel was commanded to stand against the mixing of races in the colony. The threat posed to White exceptionalism by racial mixing was quickly felt in colonial South Africa. As the number of mixed-race children grew, the claim to White exceptionalism diminished. The slow creep towards creating laws that made sure people of mixed descent were socially and physically distanced from White people resulted in the creation of Coloured identities to protect and entrench White privilege.

I use the word 'mixed' cautiously when talking about Coloured identity. While miscegenation is an important part of how Colouredness is formed, racial mixing is not the only way that Colouredness is socially or legally constructed. It is more accurate to think of Colouredness as a mixture of people from different backgrounds than to think that being of mixed heritage makes someone Coloured. The Population Registration Act of 1950 recognised this reality. While the determination of who would be White (European) or Black (Native) was crudely based on general appearance and parentage, Coloured was the only racial classification that had four distinct types – which, over time, increasingly included cultural markers in the criteria for classification.

As mentioned earlier, a person determined to be Coloured could be Malay, Cape Coloured, Griqua or Other Coloured. Malay Coloureds were those considered to be direct descendants of enslaved Malay with no apparent mixed heritage. 'Cape Coloured' referred to people who were thought to be descendants of a mixed heritage that included Cape colonists, enslaved Malay and indigenous African people like the KhoeKhoe, San or amaXhosa. In reality, even people with no mixed heritage who came from this region and matched the physical or cultural traits of any of the groups not easily classified as White would be classified as Cape Coloured. Similarly, Griquas were classified on the basis of heritage and geography. Mainly found in what is now the Northern Cape of South Africa, Griqua people were people whose heritage was mixed between European colonists and the Nama people, a subset of the KhoeKhoe who in the 1800s lived nomadically between Namibia and the western parts of South Africa.[5]

These first three categories show signs of an apartheid government still confident in its ability to use biology as its tidy benchmark for racial classification. But the inclusion of the fourth category – Other Coloured – demonstrated the inability of the regime to fit Colouredness into neat biological categories. Other Coloureds were not easily identifiable as White, Black, Chinese, or Asian, and were not from the Cape regions. Other Coloureds necessitated the need for greater scrutiny of physical features like hair and complexion, with the added complexity of using cultural markers such as language (particularly the use of Afrikaans), friendships, economic status and even food preferences as ways of excluding as many Black people as possible from the status accorded to Coloured people. More importantly, however, it was to exclude as many people of mixed descent as possible from Whiteness, the ultimate status. When the Group Areas Act of 1950 then created Coloured communities, Colouredness could never again simply be about mixed biology. Culture as opposed to lineage increasingly prevailed, but the system was far from perfect, letting some fall through the cracks while ensnaring others in a world of racial otherness.

The story of Sandra Laing illustrates why classifying people as Coloured on the basis of biology alone was woefully inadequate. Sandra was born in 1955 on the outskirts of a small, predominately White conservative town in the Transvaal to biological parents who were White, but she and her younger brother had features typical of mixed-race people. Her parents, Sannie and Abraham Laing, had light skin and straight hair, but their youngest children were darker with textured, curly hair. In their little town, rumours soon spread that Sannie Laing must have had an affair. And if that wasn't immoral enough in a Calvinist culture, it appeared that her lover had been a Black man.[6] Sannie and Abraham dismissed the rumours as false, united in their account that Abraham was indeed the only possible father to all their children.

While it is unclear whether Sannie and Abraham ever provided a counter-narrative to explain Sandra and her younger brother's distinct appearances, the history of racial mixing in colonial South Africa sheds light on these genetic anomalies.[7] Genealogists tell us that, given that interracial sexual relations – between White Dutch men and Black women in particular – were as old as the colonial settlement project itself, many Afrikaners who appear White have Black ancestors. Apartheid segregation laws and processes were cumbersome in many respects, but when it came down to the fundamental task of practically assessing and registering every person, the bureaucracy lazily confined itself to general appearance to ascertain Whiteness.

The Population Registration Act of 1950 illustrates just how far from genetics and biology the racial classification system was in practice: '"white person" means a person who in appearance obviously is, or who is generally accepted as a white person, but does not include a person who, although in appearance obviously a white person, is generally accepted as a coloured person.'[8] This seldom meant that people who were classified as White were 'pure', however.

Until Sandra went to school, the family was able to raise their children without concern beyond town gossip. At birth, children were ordinarily classified in the same way as their parents had been. But as adults, they would need to present themselves to the Population Registration Office to have their birth classification confirmed or be reclassified. Inevitably, Coloureds were most affected by reclassification. The most common reclassifications involved people being reclassified out of or into Colouredness, often based on life choices such as where they lived or who they married. For example, if a woman who had been classified Coloured as a child married a man classified as Native, the system would consider that woman as having opted out of Colouredness.

Children rarely had dramatic life changes that would require reclassification, and this was for the best as reclassification of a dependant could lead to a separation of that child from their parents. But this would be Sandra Laing's unfortunate fate. When Sandra began attending school at the age of six, her parents sent her to a boarding school in the nearby town of Piet Retief – the same school her older brother had attended. Except that he presented as White. Sandra's relatively darker skin and curly hair meant that not only did she not look like her older brother, but she also did not look like her peers. Until then, Sandra's parents had protected her, keeping her in the bubble of Whiteness that nurtured White children and spared them the realities of apartheid. Unaware of the social meaning attributed to the differences between her appearance and that of others classified as White, Sandra found herself confused and hurt by the ridicule and rejection she had to endure from her schoolmates and teachers. Children scoffed at Sandra, telling her that her skin was dirty and her hair unkempt.

The treatment Laing endured went far beyond schoolyard bullying. Having decided that she did not belong, teachers began lobbying the Department of Education for her removal from the school. Until that point, there had been no social consequences of looking different. Sandra's parents did not treat her like her differences mattered in giving her love and acceptance. It was the judgement of strangers unwilling to see beyond her appearance that would change her life forever. Sandra's school in Piet Retief succeeded in their quest to have her reclassified as Coloured, justifying her expulsion from the school. This change in her legal status criminalised several aspects of her life, none more consequential than her ability to continue to live in her family home. That she lived with her parents made them criminals and pariahs in the eyes of their community.[9]

What did it mean for Sandra Laing to have been classified as Coloured? In the 1960s, it meant being expected to live in an areas exclusively designated for Coloured people, attend schools with other people classified as Coloured, marry Coloured men; and adopt the practices of Coloured people. Culturally, Sandra was a rural *boeremeisie*, fluent in Afrikaans, her mother tongue, and conversant in isiZulu, a language commonly spoken by the children of Black farmworkers in the surrounding Transvaal farming communities. Her parents defied the authorities and refused to let her move to a Coloured community. While the authorities largely turned a blind eye to what was patently an illegal situation, staying with her parents came at a cost to Sandra. She could not attend school consistently and was shunned by her community.

Still, her father fought for his daughter's right to be White. Abraham Laing made an application to the Supreme Court to challenge his daughter's classification, arguing that it was her birthright as a child born of White parents. Although the case itself was unsuccessful, Parliament soon

changed the law to stipulate that children born to White parents be classified as White regardless of their general appearance. With the stroke of a
pen, Sandra was White again.

Sandra's classification as Coloured may have complicated her life, but it
did not result in her living life as a Coloured person. Living as a Coloured
person would require more than classification or DNA. It would require a
lived experience of communities, from the Cape Flats and Wenties Durban
communities to the Nama people in the Karoo and the displaced people of
Westbury – the communities forced together by slavery, colonialism and
eventually apartheid as the 'other' of their times, which went on to build
new common interests and create shared identities. This is the cultural experience that is undeniably the sociocultural DNA of Colouredness – much
more than the experience of having parents who are not of the same race.

This is particularly notable for young, first- or second-generation Coloured people like Genevieve, a 21-year-old woman born and raised in the
suburbs of Bloemfontein to a mother of Nama descent and a Mostwana
father. The eldest of three children, Genevieve describes her identity as
always having been a point of contention for many people in her family
and for her own sense of becoming in the world. Genevieve recalls how her
father's family would often point out the differences in her hair and complexion, othering her in ways that had her questioning her claims to being
a Black person. Unlike Sandra, Genevieve was born in a country no longer
formally segregated by apartheid, but much like Sandra she has always had
to answer the question, 'What are you?' Born to a middle-class family with
parents who could afford to send her to a private, racially diverse but still
predominantly White school, Genevieve found that being a light-skinned
person with loose curls was confusing when her home language was
Setswana and her accent carried the lilts inherited from her Nama mother
who hails from Kenhardt, a small, remote town on the outskirts of Upington. Kenhardt is a quintessential Coloured *dorpie*. Genevieve recalled very
few White people in the town; Black people have only recently moved to
the area as migrant labourers in construction and banking. Mostly, it is a
town filled with people of Nama and other indigenous groups, historically
grouped together as people with so-called Bushman heritage: groups that
today are referred to as part of the 'first nations' communities who are
fighting for the right to be acknowledged beyond, and even outside of,

the blanket Coloured classification into which apartheid bundled them.

Genevieve's mother's family, who identify as Nama, trace their roots to Namibia – which, history tells us, was not always as distinct from South Africa as it is today. Her mother was born in South Africa, but as a child she lived in Namibia with her father's family for a short time before moving back to different areas in South Africa, settling in Kenhardt. Genevieve lived all her life in Bloemfontein with her parents who, despite the differences between their families and societal expectations, have remained married. Although she was raised in a suburb that was formerly a Coloured-only area, there are many people in the community who identify as Black and Indian. When Genevieve's Motswana father first moved to the town as a migrant worker 30 years ago, his arrival was met with petitions. The community wanted him gone, refusing to let a Black man live among them.

Genevieve didn't really think that her parents' being from two different ethnic groups, Motswana and Coloured, was strange in her community and particularly at school among her middle-class counterparts. For a long time, she didn't realise that she was mixed, and it certainly was not clear in her own mind whether she was Coloured or Black. But apartheid's phenotypic obsessions still permeate South African society, and Genevieve would be required to answer questions such as why her hair had more kinks than her mother's hair, or why she did not speak Setswana like her father. She only really started thinking about her identity as she reached her teenage years, not unlike Sandra Laing.

It was also a teacher, a Black woman, who pushed and prodded like an apartheid-era population registration bureaucrat. She took Genevieve's racial interrogation further than anyone had done before. She asked Genevieve what she was and, dissatisfied with her answer, insisted that the 15-year-old could not identify as a Black South African, which is an identity that Genevieve uses alongside identifying as Coloured. Given her looks, the self-appointed racial expert reasoned, Genevieve would come across as less confusing to others if she simply identified as Coloured.

A more painful realisation followed. At a family braai, Genevieve's uncle – her father's brother – remarked that she and her mother were 'the Coloured side of the family'. It was then that Genevieve slowly began to realise that her father's family did not consider her as Mostwana either.

These incidents were not only a form of rejection for Genevieve, forcing her to choose a side, they are also examples of how Genevieve, born into a new South Africa, is being denied the ability to self-identify and embrace all aspects of her identity. It is alarming that, decades into a democratic South Africa, it remains difficult for people to self-identify without the baggage of racial classification conventions. Genevieve has always been surprised by how brazenly people not only question her about her identity, but also tell her what she should identify as based on their assumptions about biology, language, the patriarchal norms of taking on one's father's name and cultural identity, and any number of other factors they deemed important.

The insults and microaggressions Genevieve suffered in parochial Kimberley are amplified when she moves through cities like Johannesburg and Cape Town. There, the audaciousness expands with the city's sprawl. She talks with bemusement about how she has been told in big cities that Coloured people have no culture. This tickles her in some ways because her mother's family and experience in Kenhardt allowed her to firmly locate her own Colouredness in a deep sense of culture and tradition, in a history older than South Africa itself. Genevieve has experienced Colouredness as deeply cultural. Although she was not raised in the small Northern Cape town her mother is from, she talks fondly about the food, culture, songs, sights and sounds she associates with the time she has spent with her grandmother, and how she appropriates so many lessons she learnt there about values, being a strong woman and respect for others. She describes the sing-song way in which the accents of the Nama people in Kenhardt are distinct, loaded with beauty and meaning. The way people speak Afrikaans and English has undertones of the traditional Nama languages that carry much of their culture. The people of Kenhardt keep livestock, from chickens and turkeys to goats and cows. In towns like these, the pastoralist roots of the 'Bushman' people are evident. Genevieve describes rites of passage like the 'Hok meisie'[10] ceremony, which signifies young girls' coming of age. She is proud of her heritage and considers the cultural experiences of her mother and grandmother as a big part of her sense of self.

The cultures of Coloured people are varied. For some Coloured people, Colouredness is based on communities who invented shared culture after the Group Areas Act forced them together. For others, their culture is the preservation of ancestry, practices and lifestyles that predate apartheid and colonial disruptions and naming conventions.

For the apartheid regime, Coloured may have been what was left after White and Black were determined, but for those who have lived with this label for over 70 years, it is so much more than just the space between Black and White. Not all Coloured people are of partly European descent. There are people who are Coloured today because their families are descendants of the Nama people. Others are descendants of enslaved Malay brought by Dutch merchants between 1652 and 1915, when the enslaved Malay trade finally came to an end. Others still are the children of enslaved Mozambican, Malagasy, Angolan and Ghanaian people brought here to build a country.

Identifying as Coloured is more complex than having a racially mixed heritage: Colouredness is a spectrum of identities with varied origin stories that intersected during apartheid to create a cluster of complex communities brought together by historical circumstance. While Trevor Noah is undoubtedly of mixed heritage, then, to assume that this makes him Coloured is to forget that being Coloured needs a strong cultural component and sense of community.

4. MUSICAL ROOTS

Tessa Dooms

I was no more than four years old when I first sang the song 'Thank you, Lord, for Your Blessings' by Jeff and Sheri Easter. The melodic tunes and harmonies were a chord that bound together my little family of five. As the youngest of three children, the *laatlammetjie*, I was born into a home held together by Christianity and music. Elliot Dooms, my father, was a preacher. My mother, Irene Dooms, was a dutiful and committed church sister. Both were not only members of our church community, but also a father and mother to many in the church and our Eldorado Park community. My parents belonged to the community. They were then, and remain, the first people called in cases of sickness or death. Our home always had additional people to feed for Sunday lunches and Christmas meals. My parents were rarely home, constantly in service of others in need.

When he was at home, my father's place of solace was the room that he and my mother share. We often heard him strumming gently on his guitar while singing hymns in his usual hushed tone. My mother had, and still has, an unrivalled vinyl record collection of exclusively Christian music. She owned every Jimmy Swaggart record and is still one of the proud owners of the original Boney M. Christmas album. Sunday mornings were accented not only by the aromas of the beginnings of a 'seven colours' lunch that we would eat immediately upon our return from church, but also the sounds of Jimmy Swaggart bouncing through the airwaves, announcing to my sleepy self what day of the week it was.

I cannot imagine a Sunday morning, growing up, without music. But that was not the only time music was an integral part of our morning routines. I will never forget the small, consistent and endearing birthday ritual my parents made sure that we never missed, even as we entered adulthood. For as long as we lived at home, on the morning of a birthday in the household the rest of the family would wake up before the crack of dawn to rouse the birthday girl or boy with the most soulful and melodic rendition of 'Happy Birthday', sang in harmony. Ruth, my eldest sister, and I shared the soprano. Phoebe, the middle child, sang a high-pitched tenor. My mother mastered the complicated alto. As expected as this 'surprise' was every year, it made us feel special and cared for every time.

We also took this act on the road. Along with musical parents, I was born with musical siblings. Ruth and Phoebe may not have been impressed with my vocal cords as the crying baby who had intruded upon their world, but they were forced very early on by my mother to teach me to hold a note in our harmonic trio. Rehearsals were most often held in the car en route to church. Captives in the back seat, my sisters and I would not be able to escape my mother's meticulous ear for a false note, sitting less than an arm's length away.

By the time I'd become a chatty three-year-old, I was ready to take my training to the stages of churches across Coloured communities that included Eldorado Park, Riverlea, Newclare and Noordgesig. As the fifth member of the group, who never practised his deep tenor but always contributed it impromptu on any stage, my father lovingly called us 'Irene and the girls'. We were the opening act before every sermon he preached. And on the days when we anticipated being the musical item at church, my mother, sisters and I would practise our harmonies all the way to church.

Our first, and most enduring, musical offering was 'Thank you, Lord, for Your Blessings'. This was more than an anthem; it was our family's main theme. My father and mother had met and come together in a patchwork Coloured community to form a family. As a base, they used religion to create a common cultural reference for shared values, norms and a way of life that would provide us with the semblance of a coherent origin story. In a time when apartheid forced marginalisation and restrictions on our identity and opportunities, God and Christianity helped them make sense of their circumstances, and they in turn passed on that faith and its melodies to my sisters and me. They gave us reasons to feel grateful for the little we had and hopeful for the future, in spite of the history that constrained us. If Christianity was what gave us a script for our lives, music became a tool for bonding and finding ways to live in harmony that were much needed in our family and community.

I was born in the 1980s, one of the most turbulent times in South Africa's liberation history. The words to the song 'Thank You, Lord' were an acknowledgement of struggle as well as a decision to cling to hope. My parents were always at pains to remind us to count our blessings; to consider that we had, by way of our family and church life, some basic comforts that other people lacked. They reminded us that, while we were victims of an unkind regime and world, we could find safety in the comfort and love of our family. Hence, my family and I sang about focusing on the things we had and could control, as opposed to what we could not change.

Karl Marx, the German philosopher and social thinker, describes religion as 'the sigh of the oppressed creature, the heart of a heartless world, and the soul of our soulless conditions', viewing religion as a drug the masses used to escape their realities.[1] Marx was not entirely wrong. In my family, music offered an escape. Not one that minimised recognition of the impacts of our oppression, but an escape into hope, which focused our attention and efforts on finding joy and purpose in life in even the smallest possible pockets. It certainly infused a lot of heart and soul into efforts to make the best of sometimes dire economic and social ills in our communities and, with hindsight, historical and personal pain that often went unattended.

Our family's story is not unique in Coloured communities. Whether through the sombre hymns sung during Anglican Mass, the up-tempo melodies of the Baptist choirs or the happy-clappy gospel groups in evangelical churches, Coloured communities have always been abuzz with music and emotion on Sunday mornings; this is a theme that permeates many aspects of Coloured lives and has come to define Coloured people's relationship to music.

It was no different in the home of Zarcia Zacheus, in the little North West town of Bloemhof. A South African songstress and jazz talent, Zarcia is Coloured. Her roots are more musical than my own. When her parents moved to Johannesburg, Zarcia was born and became a part of an extended family of Zacheuses. Her immediate and extended family were both filled with wildly talented and passionate musicians. In Eldorado Park, the Zacheuses are legendary. Whether as individuals, groups, or a choir – yes, a choir – of relatives, their talents are recognised and celebrated in the community. Zarcia's mother was a music teacher. Zarcia recalls how, as a shy and socially anxious child, she would hide behind her mother when asked to greet people, even those she knew. But when she'd be asked to sing a tune, she would transform. As she grew older, she realised that music was not just the family trade – it was an escape from her own fears, and it was through music that she learnt to express herself to the world.

Zarcia Zacheus performing songs from
her most recent jazz album in Eldorado Park.

Looking back, Zarcia understands now that music was an escape for so many children in Coloured communities, a collective escape through the radio, LPs, cassettes and, later, CDs. Even now, you can imagine a girl or boy plugged into their cellphone, listening to a mix of their own and their parents' escapist songs.

Then and now, parents, constrained by limited finances, used music as a generally inexpensive pastime that children could engage in to keep them out of trouble. 'You didn't need money to sing,' Zarcia exclaimed as she realised how innovative Coloured parents were being by encouraging their children to join choirs, start singing groups and enter one singing competition after the other as a way of doing something constructive. I believe one would be hard-pressed to find a Coloured child raised in the 1990s in the communities surrounding Johannesburg who had not partici-pated in – or at least attended – a 'Putting on the Hits' singing competition. Even leisure was most easily found in the free access to music on the radio. What is thought of today as those lazy, soulful MetroFM Sundays remind me of the old-school R&B and jazz 'numbas' that collided in the air as you walked down any street in a Coloured community on weekends. Loudly booming from each house was a different but complementary tune that offered a feeling that went beyond leisure. It was a feeling reminiscent of a community whose existence may be hard to see through cultural attire or shared symbols, but could, like those frequencies, be felt in the air and deeply in our hearts. Connection. Culture. Creativity.

Through singing, Coloured people make meaningful connections with others and learn new skills. Singing invites people into a shared experience as listeners or to join as singers and musicians – to add their talents and skills to a collective experience of music-making, minds and souls finding each other in shared expressions and meaning, emotion and release. It is where people find a sense of purpose and it represents some of the most positive reflections of Coloured life, the capacity of our communities to create beauty. My niece, Seth-lynn, is 20 years old, born after apartheid – and identifies as Coloured. She is also a talented musician. Seth-lynn attends the National School of the Arts and, while she has friends from different backgrounds too, her group of Coloured friends realised, one day, just how much music connects them. That day, they started a jam session. Although they had all been exposed to musical traditions from around the world, when they decided to play the music of their childhood they all had exactly the same references – even though they had been raised in different communities, meeting only when they started attending a cos-mopolitan high school. Seth-lynn, firmly an ama2000, born in 2003, and her peers were being brought together by music made well before their time. Their shared references were hits like 'My Girl' by The Temptations,

Marvin Gaye's classic 'Let's Get It On' and, of course, Michael Jackson's hit song 'Man In the Mirror' – typically African American soul and jazz classics from as far back as the 1970s and 1980s, and into the gospel 1990s era. This was the music their parents and grandparents jazzed to at parties, chilled to on a lazy Sunday afternoon, celebrated with at every wedding, reinforcing a real or imagined connection between African American and Coloured people.

Seth-lynn Strachan playing the piano for her family.

These 'born-free' Coloured musicians from different religious, geographical and language backgrounds realised that when they used the words 'old-school music', it evoked the same feelings of nostalgia and joy. It meant referencing the same songs and artists, and talking about the same kinds of family events and customs. They were more connected through song than ever before.

Perhaps the pride that Coloured people take in their ability to create music and art poignantly reflects the need they once faced to create identity, family and communities under the brutality of colonial and apartheid rule. The origins of African American 'negro spirituals' are often associated with the momentary escapism and mirage of freedom that singing from deep in one's soul brings, as was the case with enslaved Africans en route to the shores of the US.[2] I can only imagine the sense of community that humming and then singing new songs in perfect harmony created, on ships and later on the plantations that would become the graves of so many Africans enslaved during America's settler colonial conquest.

Having studied music history at the University of the Witwatersrand in the early 2000s, Zarcia makes an astute observation about the links between African American experiences and use of music and Coloured experiences. Like the hymns and songs sung by Coloured communities birthed in disruption, displacement, dislocation, slavery and the loss of identity, the negro spirituals were a sigh of an oppressed people needing release and yearning for a better tomorrow. Zarcia reminds us that behind the beautiful melodies are messages of pain and deep sorrow. Coloured people cannot sing lyrics to 'Oh What A Beautiful Morning', a song by Gordon MacRae, in bliss like our White counterparts. No – our songs are about brokenness and pain and, at best, struggle and hope in the midst of hopelessness.

Folktales about the role of negro spirituals suggest that songs like the famous 'Wade in the Water' were not only useful as a collective reminder to endure suffering, but also a coded message to the enslaved that it was safe to escape through waters near the plantations. With that in mind, the words of one of its verses, 'Didn't my Lord deliver Daniel? / And why not every man?', are more haunting as a reminder that all these people wanted was to be treated with the dignity that others were afforded.[3] Similarly, when Coloured communities sing hymns such as 'So Baie Diep Haal Hy My Uit' (loosely translated as 'God has brought me out of such deep troubles'), they lament a position in life from which only God can save them.

Escape. The need to escape. The desire to escape. For many Coloured people music represents a connection to a shared history of struggle. Music brings people together and for Coloured people it has always been a way to connect with themselves and one another. For example, Zarcia and I share common childhood experiences. On a monthly trip to town to buy groceries, Zarcia's family happened upon a store that had an organ for sale that the entire family loved. They huddled together in the shop to establish whether each member was as interested in the purchase as the next; her father decided that a plan must be made to ensure that the organ became part of the musical family.

My family has its own organ purchase story, in the form of a large acoustic piano that we called an organ. One afternoon my mother and I were already packed into the car when my father announced that he had a surprise for us. We drove to what my mother recalls as a place near Pretoria, to the home of an elderly White couple who were selling a piano. I was in awe: this was no simple Casio keyboard that we knew from the church band. To us, this piano may as well have been a baby grand. We sat in the lounge, each getting an opportunity to show off our skills on it. My father wanted to be sure that we all wanted the piano and would treasure it as much as he would. It was a family decision – a bonding experience and an addition to our home that would make it happier and more harmonious. Being able to take home the piano was a fun surprise for my sisters, who by then had both begun piano lessons and could read music. This was a treat we could all share.

Music connects Coloured people not only to one another, but also to a vast history of struggle against oppression, indicative of the Black experience. African American sociologist W.E.B. Du Bois, in his 1903 book *The Souls of Black Folk*,[4] suggests that the best way to determine who, among all the people of the world, fits the definition of the word 'Black' is to trace the origin story of the people with a history of oppression at the hands of White people. He calls this a shared history of struggle, which connects all Black people of the world to a political identity associated with unequal and unjust power relations. Although apartheid's tools of divide and rule included having Coloured people internalise the idea that there is a benefit to distancing themselves from being Black, the affinity of Coloured South Africans to African American culture and history shows that we have always, albeit tacitly, identified with Blackness. Yet, even though Coloured communities share a history of oppression and a nostalgia for the same music, the anti-Black sentiment among Coloured communities towards other South African communities who identify as Black is a shameful part of our history and experiences. Coloured identity, particularly during apartheid, became reliant on a form of self-preservation that required a rejection of links to Blackness to become more palatable to an extraordinarily powerful White regime. While this is shameful, it does not help for us to attribute blame to our parents and their parents without empathy; they made survival decisions in the face of growing uncertainty and institutional racism, an experience not limited to Coloured people then or now.

The power of music as a form of expression amid racial injustice is a common feature that connects various groupings of Black people in South Africa – as far back as the musings of Tiyo Soga in the late 1800s,[5] songs as powerfully timeless as 'Senzeni Na?', and more recent chants rising from the #FeesMustFall movement and the students' revolutionary call to decolonise the national anthem by dropping the stanzas that celebrate the settler pilgrimage of the Voortrekkers. All are part of a repertoire of expressions that are an undeniable mark of political struggle by Black South Africans.

Interestingly, with the exception of artists like Abdullah Ibrahim and Don Mattera, very few instances of music emanating from Coloured communities as part of political struggle are known or celebrated. In the wake of the 1976 student uprisings, Abdullah Ibrahim organised an illegal benefit concert, an act of defiance of the apartheid regime that had forbidden mixed-race bands to perform. His now legendary song 'Mannenburg', which is also the name of a predominately Coloured township in Cape Town, exploded as a default anthem for struggle and Black resistance from Cape Town to Soweto. As a family in exile, he and his wife Sathima Bea Benjamin continued to use music and their public profile to remind the world about the injustices in South Africa under apartheid. While most music that is known to have sociocultural significance in Coloured communities relates to religion or pop culture, their use of music is in similar ways a reflection of the people's times and struggles.[6]

African American musical culture, at the height of the civil rights movement in the 1960s and 1970s, birthed a version of folk or American Roots music that sought specifically to conscientise and unite Black communities. This stretched across a range of genres, including jazz, gospel, pop and blues, created by extraordinarily talented musicians who aimed to attract attention to a cause greater than themselves.[7] More pronounced is the fact that Roots music for African American people is about their roots in Africa and the history of Black struggle. These roots are intertwined with the roots of many people of African descent, dislocated physically from their lands and heritage.

One colourful and complex example of this intersection is the annual Cape Town tradition called the Tweede Nuwe Jaar parade, performed by the Kaapse Klopse. Directly translated from Afrikaans to English, the parade is called the Second New Year parade and its performers are Cape Minstrel groups, mainly from Coloured communities. Traditionally held on the second or third day of January, Tweede Nuwe Jaar is a colourful and musically exciting event that sees minstrel bands from across the Cape arrive in bright and multicoloured costumes. The troupes wear uniforms that look like sailor suits, formal suits, or marching band suits after they have been splashed with neon paint or rolled in sparkles and feathers. It is an explosion of colour, music, creativity and joy.

As children in Coloured communities, we longed to attend this spectacle. For Coloured communities outside Cape Town, the opportunity to see Tweede Nuwe Jaar even once in a lifetime is a dream. It is a spectacle that is a tangible expression of many aspects of Coloured culture, affirming many parts of our lives. 'Coon culture', as it is casually referred to in Coloured communities, is a turn of phrase that was not strange for me to hear as a child. But the more I understood about its roots, the more I understood its meaning. A meaning rooted in pain, not pleasure.

The meaning of Coon culture and the link between Tweede Nuwe Jaar and slavery in the Americas jumped out at me in the days after the 2023 Tweede Nuwe Jaar celebrations. I met Gregg, an American man born in Grenada, days after he had experienced the parade for the first time as part of his holiday in South Africa. Gregg's eyes widened as he spoke with a mixed sense of awe and horror at not only the idea that the festival draws on American minstrels, but also our casual use of the words 'Coon culture'. I looked at Gregg and was taken back to my Atlanta experience of saying the word 'Coloured' to an American audience for the first time. It was culture shock, a collision of worlds so far apart but so connected and similar that made for moments of confusion and clarity about how connected histories of Black struggle truly are.

Gregg's bewilderment was not misplaced. The Cape Minstrels are rooted in slavery and racism. That is a fact. The shared history of slavery in the Americas and South Africa is credited in part with a sharing of sensibilities between contexts. Slavery forced together enslaved people from various backgrounds. Music and theatre were ways to find common expression as the creolisation of the Cape began. Sharing in song was a form of bonding but also a form of escape from the harsh realities of being captive, and dressing up further heightened this form of escapism. While jazz and gospel were expressions of struggle, minstrel culture is one of escape. This became an actual celebration of escape in the late 1800s when formal slavery ended and freed men and women could celebrate occasions like the New Year in their own ways and on their own terms. The advent of goema music, characterised by the beating of drums by the newly freed people, continues to be a big part of the Cape Minstrel parades.[8]

One of the most politically incorrect references the Tweede Nuwe Jaar draws from is American minstrels of the early 1800s. This was a culture of White American theatre and music, based on the mockery of Black people using Blackface. It was a musical culture designed to ridicule, humiliate and dehumanise enslaved Black people. It is also how the racial slur 'coon' gained traction in popular culture. It is a characterisation of Black people, particularly enslaved people, as lazy, childish, silly and even happy to be oppressed. The practice of American minstrel culture made its way to the Cape as early as the 1870s when a wave of minstrel societies formed there. New life was breathed into the culture in the 1960s through a popular American minstrel group called the Ethiopian Minstrels. In the same era of the cultural exchange between South Africa and America of jazz and gospel as part of Black struggle and civil rights traditions, the minstrels took root as well. This cultural exchange was a complex one, made possible by the shared history of slavery.

The Cape Minstrels are hard, then, to disentangle from the roots of Africans who were severed from their roots through colonial rule, slavery and apartheid, even as they stand on the land of their birth and ancestry. Coloured communities need to come to terms with the idea of being rooted in Africa and the broad history of Blackness that extends far beyond the racial politics of South Africa.

It is worthwhile to argue whether the Cape Minstrels' continued existence reinforces a racist past. The way in which the practice has evolved since 1994, however, makes a case for their continued political struggle, despite the practice being weighed down by so much racist historical baggage. The apartheid government targeted the Cape Minstrels and curtailed their activities. So, as part of the transition to a democratic South Africa, in an act of reclamation, Coloured people used the minstrels to signal their hope for change. In 1993, many minstrel groups united under the theme 'Peace in Our Land'. The troupes used the song 'Gimme Hope Jo'anna', first popularised by Eddy Grant in the 1980s, as an apt way to make a political statement. The origins of 'Gimme Hope Jo'anna', however, were meaningful for the minstrels as the song was an adaptation of an old folk *ghoemetjie* called 'Give me Hope Johanna'. Unlike the popular use of Jo'anna as a reference to Johannesburg, in its original form Johanna in the song was mixed-race little girl, navigating a postcolonial world even before there was apartheid, as the product of miscegenation in a country that feared racial mixing. In the original lyrics of the folk song 'Give me Hope Johanna', Johanna is praised for telling people in South Africa that they did not have to be White to be right. The song further urges Johanna, was as a person of mixed blood, to be hopeful that South Africa could be governed by people who are not White – and could be governed for all people.[9]

Almost thirty years later, hope for the future is the thrust of the carnival. Despite the Cape Minstrels' use of jarring language and problematic tropes, their mission to take cultures of pain and turn them into cultures of hope and joy is a firm part of Cape Coloured cultural contributions to the nation.

The music of the Cape Minstrels is not the only music genre that shares a history with the Americas and, indeed, with Black struggle. In Cape Town in the 1980s and into the early 1990s, Prophets of Da City, a hip hop collective affectionately referred to as POC, burst onto the South African musical stage. Theirs was a version of politically charged music reminiscent of a combination of American-conscious rap, popularised by artists like Killer Mike, and local political music produced by the likes of Miriam Makeba, Hugh Masekela and Abdullah Ibrahim. By then, the music had evolved from being about the displacement of forced removals to being about life in the ghettos created by the Group Areas Act. POC's unique sound was drawn from Coloured culture and the grit and colour of the Cape Flats. When DJ Ready D met Shaheen Ariefdien through the underground hip hop scene, their unique talents and political activist roots spawned a movement of Coloured rappers willing to speak out about the need for political change and to battle against social ills in their communities.[10]

The resulting music reverberated through Coloured communities, and even among international audiences as they toured. Tracks like 'Understand Where I'm Coming From', which pays homage to struggle heroes such as Steve Biko, Oliver Tambo and Chris Hani, became hits as their lyrics empowered. Their sounds offered deep descriptions of the state of township life: riddled with poverty, violence and crime in the context of a government that did not care. These songs were the soundtracks to the lives of so many young people in South Africa – not only Coloured people, but Black South Africans. POC's music crossed from areas like Elsie's River to Khayelitsha, defying apartheid's efforts to divide and becoming the soundtrack of a shared history of struggle.

To me, POC signified a moment when music made Coloured culture visible and legitimate, a positive contributor to change in South Africa. It was a reclamation of space by a group of people who had been so easily overlooked – considered, at best, as having no recognisable collective existence, and at worst as a people with proximity to oppressive Whiteness, which came with certain benefits.

Coloured musicians reclaiming cultural space is something that is close to Zarcia's heart too. As a jazz artist, she intentionally chose that genre for its connection to her upbringing and its somewhat chaotic musical style that defies the classical conventions set by European music icons like Mozart and Beethoven. No rules. Freedom. These are the ideas Zarcia associates with jazz. Unsurprisingly, jazz has its origins in the American South – New Orleans in the 1910s. In a post-slavery era, what better way to revel in one's freedom than through a combination of leisurely sounds that riffed freely and unpredictably from one note to the next?

One night in 2019, in the dark streets of downtown Johannesburg, Zarcia's music transported me to what I imagined the dark, underground jam sessions were like in the 1910s, sessions that gave us the beauty that is jazz. The room was small, smoky and low-lit, with a spotlight on Zarcia and her band of three musicians. The songs from her then recently released album, *Therapy*, also transported me back to Eldorado Park when I was a child, with her sounds striking chords in my soul. Nothing, however, could have prepared me for the realisation that the most Coloured-sounding tune of the night was slowly unwrapping itself to reveal the most soulful rendition of Tina Turner's hit song 'Simply the Best'. I was moved to tears. How could a pop/rock classic from so far away and so long ago remind me so much of home, and make me feel so much more like myself? After the gig, I remember telling Zarcia that she was truly the embodiment of what we mean when we say we are our ancestors' wildest dreams. I could, in that moment, imagine generations of Coloured people and their ancestors feeling seen and acknowledged in the space of a four-minute-long song about rapturous love. Zarcia's rendition was slow and sensual. Unlike Tina Turner's version, which draws the listener's ear to the chorus, Zarcia's honed in on the beauty and meaning of each verse. It evolved Tina's passion from a love that shouts loudly to the world to a love that whispers tenderly into one's ear.

There is need for a return to Coloured identity and expression through music, for a renewed opportunity to showcase the talents, unique experiences, cultural nuances and aspirations of Coloured people. Instead of hiding behind our pain, anger and frustration, we must claim full right to be a part of South Africa. I believe this is possible through song, dance and art. Zarcia particularly notes the importance of singing in Afrikaans, not only to reappropriate the language as part of the history of Coloured identities, but also to usher in an era of Afrikaans music by Coloured people that transcends struggle and asserts power.

Yet there is, and has always been, more to Coloured experiences than expressions of pain and struggle. There is humour, complexity, energy, strength and warmth that comes with being Coloured, and this deserves a place to shine as brightly as any other people's stories. This return is perhaps best captured by the lyrics for 'Hey Ouens' by a 1990s Durban-based group called Kulud (featuring T.R.O.). Like a Coloured anthem of the 1990s, the lyrics of this song made many Coloured youth feel seen and heard. From the references about 'wy-ing to Wrap it Up', a famous place to buy bunny chow in Durban, to the inclusion of a childhood township game 'Aqua-della-mmm-ahhh-what-se-jika, Jika-jika-jika-valour', this was a song about the fun parts and the inside jokes of Coloured life. It is an effortless mix of Afrikaans and English in colourful slang. It's an endless string of made-up words like 'kuza' to mean 'support', *dala* mainly as a threat to do what you must, and 'Tchawla', which I remain convinced was invented on the spot to rhyme with *dala*. The boundless creativity and energy in 'Hey Ouens' are the perfect metaphor for experiences of Coloured joy.

Beyond the pain and resilience, Coloured communities are bold and beautiful, so the song is not wrong to declare boldly that 'Bruin-ous, bruin-ous / We are the main ous!'

5. *HUISKOS*:
IDENTITY ON A PLATE

Lynsey Ebony Chutel

Somewhere in Noordgesig, one of Johannesburg's oldest and most storied townships, their scent winding through the narrow passages of the semi-detached *treinhuise*, ginger and garlic are sizzling on the oiled base of a warped weekday pot. In Durban's Sydenham, with its steep hills and sliver of ocean too far in the distance, in a narrow kitchen packed with family heirlooms and towers of Tupperware, on the stove, bay leaves, curry powder, elachi, jeera and dhanya dance on the sweet, translucent onions, the come-hither call that it's time to eat. In Lavender Hill, where the backyards cram up against each other on the wrong side of Table Mountain, the sugary base of a tomato *smoortjie* sprinkled – or doused – with curry powder tickles the nose as its surface bubbles and plops like lava. In Douglas, you can hear sneezes from the clouds of White pepper that turn green beans into *groenboontjies*, adding to the Northern Cape heat. At the end of a gravel road in Koffiefontein, the homely cubes of beef, slaughtered just the day before, swirl with carrots and onion. And somewhere in Sandown, amid its fine dining and international flavours of fast food, the nostalgia of pilchards has come for a visit.

These osmic identities waft through Coloured homes all over the country, from townships to suburbs, increasingly, across South Africa. They could also, in truth, all come from one street, as a testament to the diversity of Coloured identity. In any culture, food is a marker of community. Recipes carry our memories; ingredients carry our stories of struggle or wealth. *Huiskos*, quite literally 'home food', is the meal we come home to.

Often, when that stinging criticism is levelled that Coloured people have no culture, I know it is not true by virtue of the plate of food lovingly and uniquely put down in front of me at family gatherings. Like any culture, we have borrowed, we have reinvented, but we have also preserved our identities on that plate. As a people who are defined by a mix of cultures and histories, our *huiskos* is a clear representation of this.

In conversation, sharing our favourite foods is a way to connect and show our friends and family who we are. On the playground, every child thinks their mother's cooking is the best, particularly when last night's leftovers are in their lunchbox. As we grow older, the meal our mothers threw together over and over, that Tuesday and Thursday staple that we dared to complain about but only to siblings and friends, becomes a treasured memory we recreate to remind ourselves who we are. For me, it's dhal. My aunt used it to thicken a chicken stew to feed my three growing male cousins, my older brother, my uncle and his daughter, my mother and I, all squeezed into our three-bedroom council house. Boiled eggs were added to the mild lentil curry for a midweek meal that would stretch from dinner to everyone's lunchbox sandwiches the next day.

As our fortunes changed and the house emptied out, I wanted nothing to do with chicken anything – not curried, not stewed, neither oven-baked nor even deep-fried, with or without the skin. As for lentils, even as vegans made them trendy and pushed up their price as they lectured us about their recently discovered nutritional value (something poor people of colour have always known), I would not budge – not for pink lentils, nor brown ones, not even for the larger orange lentils lurking behind the chickpeas in health-conscious meals at trendy bistros around Johannesburg. Yet now, in my own home, I turn to that lentil-and-chicken stew as a balm for the relentless contemporary capitalism that prizes profit and convenience. I make my own and have learnt to come close to my aunt's recipe, even with Woolworths lentils. But it tastes best when cooked by my Aunt Joan, in my mother's house in Eldo's, with an unwritten recipe perfected to make it go as far as possible without losing flavour, as she did all those years ago.

Huiskos is the seat of a memory for most cultures. It is not only in the recipes passed down from one generation to another, but in the flavours and aromas that bring connection and a sense of identity. Try as we might to describe it, *huiskos* does not have a specific flavour – instead, it is the amalgamation of our shared histories dished onto a plate. Yet, as all these smells from all these kitchens show, there is no single food of which it can be said: this one thing is Coloured cuisine.

As I chop the ingredients for a controversial debate, now is as good a time as any to confess that I have only ever eaten bobotie once, as a tourist atop Table Mountain. It's an unfair critique because it was probably watered down for the sake of tourist palates, but I did not care for it. I am open to anyone willing to convince me otherwise – after all, who would say no to a dinner invitation? – but it did not stir in me a nostalgic longing, let alone an identity crisis. I can still identify as Coloured and not like bobotie. Identity is complex. What's more, as I dared first to whisper and then more loudly (possibly obnoxiously) to confess this to others, it turned out I was not the only Coloured South African not to have eaten, much less cooked, bobotie. Did it make me less Coloured? Or somehow shake my claim to this already fraught racial-classification-turned-identity? Or could we finally start having a conversation about the myriad Coloured experiences across South, and southern, Africa, and stop flattening the experience to a single story? Could we re-examine the stories we tell ourselves, the recipes we hold dear, to reconstruct Colouredness and make space for a little more nuance, a little more complexity? A balance of flavours, to borrow from the culinary world. I have since enjoyed a deconstructed bobotie on a vineyard outside Cape Town, but this had less to do with finding home on a plate than with exploring how South African chefs were reinventing classics.

Bobotie still deserves a place in the culinary archives of Coloured cooking, even as we deconstruct it. It is a classic South African meal, and its unique flavours of sweet and savoury are the hallmark of the Cape Malay cooking that has become familiar in homes around the country. Its story is quintessentially South African, capturing the history and complexity of Coloured identity. The first bobotie recipe is believed to have been written in a Dutch cookbook in the early 17th century, but its origins are Indonesian. *Bobotok*, or *botok*, is a Javan dish, made from the flesh of coconut with vegetables and spices such as chilli and basil added to the sweetness, all steamed in a banana leaf.[1] It arrived in South Africa with the enslaved Javans brought to the Cape by Dutch colonialists. It's a testament to, and a tragedy of, the story of colonialism and the erasure of its victims that we do not know who the innovative enslaved cook was who looked around this alien landscape and found the ingredients to recreate his or her own comfort food, a dish that must painfully have reminded those who ate it of a home they were ripped away from and would never see again. Centuries later, that recreated comfort food has since gone on to become something of a national dish in a new land and for a new people.

That forgotten story and the survival of the flavours of *bobotok* or *botok* are also a reminder of a common thread that runs through Coloured identity: celebrating some ingredients at the expense of others. The Cape's enslaved population was made up of people from Africa too, from Mozambique, Angola and Ghana, where there are also unique culinary expressions of identity. While enslaved Malay people were allowed to keep their religion and some of their identity, thanks to colonists' modest respect for Islam, enslaved African people were treated as a lower class of slave – their names were changed, their faith lost, their identities stolen. This is perhaps why foods like *xima*, the soft corn-based porridge that is the staple of the country that is now Mozambique, never became part of the recorded diet of enslaved people who were later categorised as Coloured. Or perhaps its similarity to *pap* meant that *xima* melted into the South African diet, an example of our connectedness before the false separation imposed by colonial borders. But it's more likely that, as racism and the colourism it created began to take hold, *xima* would have exposed a proximity to Black South Africa that would have made it a liability for Coloured South Africans eking out a separate identity according to apartheid law, at the expense and rejection of an African identity.

Despite its power to define a whole family's destiny, racial classification was, as we've seen, also a nastily arbitrary system. When genetic markers like physical features were not enough, it relied on what the apartheid government decided were markers of Colouredness. Food, alongside language and, more ridiculously, hand gestures and mannerisms, were all used by apartheid-era population registration bureaucrats to determine whether one was Coloured or Black. Officers would ask people what they ate for breakfast or dinner, or how they cook their food, as a signifier of culture and therefore race.

In a 1956 appeal to the Race Classification Board to have her husband's race reclassified from Native to Coloured, a woman named Martha

Goliath gave evidence in favour of her husband Jacob Goliath, with records showing that she told officers,'*Middae eet ons vleis, rys en groente,*'[2] (In the afternoons, we eat meat, rice and vegetables), to prove his proximity to Europeanness. This decision was made over and over by people forced to forget much more than the food they grew up with – perhaps even to reject the meals their mothers or grandmothers made for them and the memories that went with them. Often, it was a deliberate decision, made to create a clear division between Black and Coloured, us and them. It was also a decision that was rooted in economic pragmatism – being Coloured brought advantages. Either way, it is evidence of how White supremacy has erased the cultural ties it finds inconvenient.

But White supremacy does not always win. Sometimes, it is sweetly subverted and a cultural staple bubbles to the surface. Koeksisters arrived in South Africa as *stroopkoek* or *oliekoek*, directly translated as 'syrup cake' or 'oil cake', a yeasted dessert deep-fried and drenched in syrup. One of the earliest recipes, found in the Dutch recipe book from 1668, *De Verstandige Kock*, harks back to a Persian recipe in *A Baghdad Cookery Book*, written 300 years earlier. At the time, Dutch cooking was believed to be greatly influenced by travels to the Middle East, and the syrupy balls of dough were brought along[3] by Dutch settlers to other parts of the world. *Stroop-koek* or *oliekoek* arrived on the east coast of North America, in what is today Canada and the United States, where it is believed they evolved into doughnuts. In South Africa, they took on a unique plaited form, believed to have been a result of influence from Scottish and Swedish settlers. They in turn took inspiration from *De honesta voluptate et valetudine*, one of the first cookbooks ever written, originating in 15th-century Venice. That little ball of sweetened dough is a tasty piece of evidence of how the foods we take for granted, like doughnuts, are in fact a global artefact of cultural exchange – and sometimes even appropriation, when one considers the power dynamics of taking recipes from a culture without acknowledging that culture. But what happens to that little ball of dough in South Africa I regard as an act of survival and subversion, spicing up and sweetening the bitter taste of oppression as a reclamation.

As the delicacy became popular in the colonial households of the Cape, enslaved Malay cooks are believed to have held on to the spicy influence of the original Persian recipe, which would have been closer to the flavours they carried with them from the faraway homes they would never get to see again. I wonder how they kept the spices, though. Given the cost of cinnamon and cardamom at the time, would they have swiped some from the mistress's table? Skimmed some of the cardamom off their masters' meals because, well, his bland palate wouldn't know the difference? It goes without saying that slavery was inhumane and brutal, so there's a comfort in imagining an enslaved cook hiding some spices for herself, taking whatever joy she could. We have only our imaginations for this, but we can tell from the recipes that came from these cooks that they were innovative, and had a sense of humour, despite their dire circumstances. In later cookbooks, specifically *Traditional Cookery of the Cape Malays*, published in 1954, the difference between boere koeksisters and *bollas* (unplaited koeksisters) seems to be as simple as the instruction 'Make bollas exactly like kosiesters [*sic*], but add cinnamon', attributed to a woman identified only as Galiema.[4]

Today, I'd like to think that every block in Coloured communities has a Galiema, an aunty known for her koeksisters. Their recipe has been passed down, written nowhere but in memory. Almost every aunty has a trick or secret that makes her koeksisters or *bollas* unique – a hint of aniseed, perhaps, or a naartjie peel, or very likely both. You won't hear the secret from me. But what I will share is that, if you're smart, you'll get your Sunday morning order in on Friday already. By Sunday morning, orders of dozens and dozens of koeksisters are making their way to homes, to the local shop, or to being doled out in the churchyard after the service. The community's designated koeksister aunty would have fried and *strooped* (syruped) to order the night before or in the early hours of Sunday morning to ensure that an age-old tradition continues.

It doesn't take a trained chef to see how the dish has evolved. I'd known koeksisters all my life – well, at least I thought I had – until my family stopped at a *tuisnywerheid* (home industry) one day for a roadside snack and out of sheer curiosity. There, in a fridge *nogal*, were little twists of dough, dipped in sugar and labelled koeksisters, baked by a local *tannie*, a white Afrikaner aunty. Boere koeksisters are small and pale, and dipped in so much syrup that they are sticky and sickly sweet, the syrup totally infused into the dough. They have a hard shell and a soft inside, no extra toppings, and are served cold. It's no wonder Woolworths and its legendary cold fridges have capitalised on them, selling them by the dozen along-side malva pudding and lemon cheesecake. There is also a *tannie* in each town who holds her recipe dear, a recipe that has been passed down from generation to generation and is savoured by her family too. But some-where along the line – experts think it was in the early 20th century but are unclear about the pastry's exact evolution[5] – the deep-fried joy we have in common took on a very different nature.

Coloured or Malay koeksisters, or koe'sisters, are made with a dough that is spiced with cinnamon, nutmeg and sometimes cardamom until it is a deep brown. A more traditional recipe calls for mashed potato to be folded into the dough. Once risen, plaited and deep-fried, it is dipped in a sugar syrup, floated next to the cinnamon sticks and star anise that give the syrup more depth of flavour. Then, still dangerously hot, the *gestroopte* koe'sister is rolled in desiccated coconut and served warm. Sometimes, a paler but still puffier koeksister is made in Coloured homes, but in this lighter version the aniseed flavour is strong, lifting the ground ginger in the dough, delivering the same flavour punch. And yes, you can buy unsyruped koeksisters in bulk, freeze them and *stroop* them at your own convenience, especially when you're far away from home on a rainy Sunday morning.

Both evolutions of the koeksister are delicious, but only one tastes like Sunday morning to me. We may never know when exactly this split occurred, but on either side of this yeasty divide it is often the only koeksis-ter each side has known. While they may not be sold in large supermarkets like their paler counterparts, Malay koeksisters have prevailed in Coloured communities, and have been adopted in some Indian South African com-munities (as Coloured communities have taken on biryani as their own). As they've gained more visibility in the mainstream media, the dropping of the second 'k' – a nod to Coloured accents and likely the result of the evolution of the word from the Dutch word *sisser*,[6] meaning 'sizzle' or 'hiss', the sound the dough makes as it's dropped into hot oil – has come to be used as a signifier of culinary and cultural difference.

A re-embracing of cooking has coincided with the greater grasp of iden-tity politics. Across the industrialised world people are returning to the kitchen, taking back their nutrition from big corporations. The COVID-19 pandemic encouraged millions to bake bread – sourdough, banana or corn – and every week, disembodied hands on social media videos promoted four-ingredient recipes of all kinds, from naan to fettuccine. For many, a return to the kitchen also meant a return to childhood recipes, a comfort when families were separated amid COVID-19 lockdowns and restrictions. But this rediscovery of home cooking has at its foundation a classist positioning of nutrition and memory. It suggests a completed cycle of the place of food in our lives, from childhood meals prepared by parents, to the aspirational yet dangerous indulgence of fast foods and sugary drinks, to returning to the kitchen with an understanding of nutrition and healthy eating. It suggests a budget that can afford to buy neatly packaged fresh fruit and vegetables, a selection of free-range meat and eggs, a globalised palate that can experiment with the flavours of various international cuisines. It drives up the price of staples like lentils and turns teff into a sought-after commodity as influencers discover a new fad and learn what people in the global south have always known. It also ignores the foods that have moved into low-income neighbourhoods as healthy food drifts out of reach and processed food corporations discover a new market, moving in with their aspirational marketing campaigns and low prices. In poor communities, not just in South Africa, distributors do not bother to explain the origin of their meat, nor do they even feign a promise that their produce is not laced with chemicals. The nutritional information is optional and, even when displayed, it is hardly noticed when families are simply trying to eke out a living.

These neighbourhoods don't stand a chance against the sophisticated industrial marketing machinery of major international corporations that position their brands as aspirational even as they offer little by way of nutritional value. The Golden Arches Theory of Conflict Prevention, a glib foreign policy thesis posited by *The New York Times* columnist Thomas Friedman in 1996, argued that there was a correlation between globalisation, capitalism and international peace. 'No two countries that both have a McDonald's have ever fought a war against each other,' Friedman wrote,[7] and the world ate it up. The theory made its way into foreign policy textbooks around the world and we embraced it here when, soon after Nelson Mandela became president, Ronald McDonald became an ambassador of sorts as McDonald's Drive Thrus popped up everywhere. Other brands followed; KFC ingrained itself into South African culture, eventually adapting its Streetwise Two meal to offer a side of pap, in lieu of chips – or, as the Americans say, fries. In 2023, the American chicken brand went as far as introducing its version of *sphatlho*, a beloved township sandwich or kota, setting off a debate about cultural appropriation and big brands starving corner shops.

We know now, of course, that a Happy Meal does not bring world peace and that urbanisation and corporate expansion not only forfeit nutritional value, but also plaster over history and culture with neon colours and catchy jingles. There's a violence here that the world has only just begun to reckon with, but perhaps in South Africa we should have known better how loss and disenfranchisement change the way we eat. But in adapting to that forced change, we can also find resilience, innovation and even more flavour.

What is perhaps one of the most iconic Coloured meals, the Gatsby, was born of necessity, loss and displacement. One day in 1977, Rasheed Pandy was faced with that age-old problem, 'What to eat?' All day, he and his friends Froggy, Boera and Hennie had been clearing a piece of land in the recently formed township of Lansdowne, to which the Pandy family would be forced to move, so that they could build on it. Pandy knew the community well: his father had run a butchery in the area for years, and Pandy, wanting to strike out on his own, had started a business that was close to his heart and his taste buds – a fish-and-chips shop. That's what people loved at the time, and it's the food Pandy had always loved, sneaking to the Portuguese fish-and-chips shops even as his father warned they didn't do halaal over there.

On this particular day, the shop was already closing and Pandy and his friends had been working hard. Pandy looked around his fish-and-chips shop kitchen for something to feed himself and his friends. There was nothing much left, except some polony, some chips in the fryer and a jar of the atchar his father made that Pandy always kept nearby. He slapped it together – the chips, then the polony, and then a slather of atchar – on a few leftover Portuguese rolls.

Froggy, the first to taste the meal, stuffed it into his mouth and, through chews, said it tasted like something the Great Gatsby would eat. 'Larnie, this is mos a smash, man!' he declared as he bit into the culinary experiment. 'It's a Gatsby smash!'

It wasn't quite the miracle of the loaves and fishes, but that quick chip-polony-atchar combination created a unifying cultural marker. Pandy, ever the businessman, decided to make a few more of these new Gatsbys the next day, putting them in the window beside the fish and chips he was known for. Few bit; the sandwich just wasn't popular in a market that liked the familiar comforts of the old neighbourhoods' childhood homes from which the Group Areas Act had moved them.

But then came hip hop and the emboldened, more globalised generation born on the Cape Flats, for whom the Gatsby was home. By the 1980s, the Gatsby had evolved, growing from the smaller round Portuguese roll to a baguette-inspired footlong roll that easily fed four. Even its very breaded encasing is a testament to the complexity of Coloured heritage, and how, as it encounters other cultures, it borrows from them to stay alive. Rather than an act of appropriation, the Gatsby itself is about how a displaced, disenfranchised culture nourishes itself to survive.

By the time 1994 brought democracy, young people were flocking to Pandy's shop and the Gatsby had gone national. In the intervening years it made its way to Johannesburg, where it goes by the name of 'AK', a reference to a Kalashnikov rifle, or AK-47, on account of the long baguette into which it grew. This in itself is a reflection of how violence plays an outsized role in the stories we tell about ourselves.

The Gatsby's very ingredients locate it in the township. These have evolved to include steak, mince curry, or a Russian (a salty, spicy sausage), and sometimes even a confusing leaf of iceberg lettuce, but with the original chips, polony and atchar all still stuffed into it. These ingredients are also put into a quarter of a loaf of unsliced White bread to make another township favourite: the bunny chow. The bunny chow was borrowed from indentured Indian labourers in KwaZulu-Natal, who quite literally made an edible lunchbox and a South African icon. Atchar, a spicy pickle, is also traced to South Africa's Indian community, but a version of this pickle, atchara, exists in Malaysia too, to which many Coloured South Africans can also trace their roots. This cross-pollination of ingredients continues across South Africa's townships. Atchar, chips, Russians and polony are the same basic ingredients of the kota, or *sphatlho*, as it is made in Soweto, which, like a bunny chow, is stuffed into a quarter of a loaf of bread that fills a schoolchild's stomach all day. Kotas are also inexpensive and accessible in the neighbourhoods that were created through displacement, reminding us about our common experiences as people of colour in South Africa.

Still, it is now impossible to reference polony, the processed meat in the centre of Gatsbys, kotas and school sandwiches all over South Africa, without mentioning the listeriosis outbreak of 2017 and 2018. It was the world's worst such outbreak[8] and led to the deaths of 180 people, most of them in working-class communities who buy bulk packs of processed meat to get by. It played out in the public sphere, highlighting the class divisions, still stratified by race, that endure in post-apartheid South Africa. The Gatsby can feed a whole family on a payday Friday. It also reflects the innovation of working-class cooks, particularly Rasheed Pandy on the Cape Flats – but indicates the food choices poor communities have to make and the direct effects of the Group Areas Act.

Steven de Klerk, home from boarding school. My great-grandmother, Johanna van Vooren (née Nyawo), sold *mosbolletjies,* sweet soft buns, to make extra money to feed her family.

Born of an Indian father and a Cape Malay mother, Rasheed Pandy's own food culture is a melting pot of histories. His grandfather worked on the ships in Durban with his uncle. One day, while cleaning and fixing a ship that had docked at the harbour, they just never got off as it sailed away. Looking for better prospects, they arrived in Cape Town as stowaways. Once in Cape Town, the Pandy brothers began building their lives by marrying Cape Malay women. They did this intentionally to ensure that their children could buy property in a city that did not allow Indians property rights. The brothers and their new wives settled in Salt River, their kitchens combining the smells of Indian and Cape Malay cooking. A curry-and-bredie mix is still one of Rasheed Pandy's favourite meals and his father, he recalls, was an 'exceptional' cook who had an innate understanding of the balance of flavours.

As their businesses and new identities flourished, the family moved to Claremont, where Rasheed was born. The Pandys lived there for 30 years before a VW Beetle with a GG number, a government-owned car, plate started circling the block. It was a well-known apartheid tactic, an early-stage enforcer of the Group Areas Act. The circling Beetle was meant to intimidate this family of colour and force them to leave what had become prime property in Salt River, reserved for White people. Eventually, as the forced removals spread, officials in that VW Beetle got out of their car, walked right up to Rasheed Pandy's father and gave him two options: 'Sell, or we'll chuck you out,' recalls Pandy. His father held on stubbornly, but his mother, fearing violence and retribution, looked around at the other families who had lost everything under the new Act and persuaded him to sell. They sold the plot for just R4 000 to a White Rhodesian family fleeing the coming independence of Zimbabwe. They found a plot in Lansdowne, one of the relatively more affluent areas that seemed to promise some stability in the face of displacement. To build a new house there, the family spent R20 000 – losing out after all.

Still, like Black, Indian and Coloured South Africans everywhere, the Pandys made a life for themselves in this new township. These were still places of sorrow, but they were made hopeful by resilient families who made a home from the unjust lot they'd been dealt by the apartheid government. Now, three decades into democracy, Pandy's shop is an institution and a line of customers stretches around the corner for the original Gatsby. It's hard to separate the bitter history from this culinary landmark. While Pandy, like so many other Coloured people of his generation, made the best of a terrible situation, the enduring legacy is impossible to ignore – so obvious in the snaking line for social security grants not far from Pandy's shop.

In some ways, the Gatsby shows the enduring effects of the Group Areas Act and how the Act shaped South Africans' sense of identity. The Act legislated some of the most intimate experiences of South Africans, bringing public policy into private spaces and interactions through a series of blandly worded amendments. In many ways, the rainbow nation identity South Africa has tried to cultivate is a response to these enforced divisions that remain impossible to break down. Take Heritage Day, for instance. In South African history, 24 September has had several iterations as a public holiday. It was originally Shaka Day, to commemorate the death of King Shaka in 1828, but the apartheid government refused to acknowledge the day. Then in post-apartheid South Africa, a compromise was reached that would mark the day without reference to a specific ethnicity in a country that was trying to build unity. The result is an annual public holiday, Heritage Day, on which "everyone" wears 'traditional' clothes and cooks their heritage's signature dish. By the mid-2000s, that day had taken on another form: Braai Day, the brainchild of Jan Scannel, a White South African who wanted a unified culture to take precedence over the disparate histories he saw being celebrated.⁹ He saw burnt meat coming to signify a unified country, with the late Archbishop Emeritus Desmond Tutu becoming Braai Day's patron. Sure, South Africans of every race really like meat, but you'll rarely find them sitting together at the same table.

In a country where the geographic and cultural lines of the Group Areas Act stubbornly persist, the family recipe can be an act of defiance. In Durban's predominantly Coloured neighbourhood of Sydenham, the Van Wyk family serves a meal that is distinctly Balinese. The Van Wyks' ancestors came to Durban via Indonesia and, while classification as Coloured flattened that history, the family have held on to their origins through food. They cook an adaptation of a Balinese dish, *karswa*, passed down from a Balinese grandmother. They use spaghetti instead of noodles, which was easier to come by in the average South African township supermarket. The spices and ingredients they now use – elachi, jeera and sour milk or *amasi* – make the dish seem like a Durban curry, but even in its adaptation it resembles an Indonesian dish. The Van Wyks' recipe is part of a collection of recipes, *African Salad: A portrait of South Africans at home*, by photographer Stan Englebrecht, who traversed the country collecting South Africans' handwritten recipes that spoke of who they were, their past and their ambitions for the future. In recounting their family recipe, the Van Wyks spoke about how they adopted an Afrikaans surname to survive apartheid, only for it to feel like a burden in post-apartheid Africa.[10]

Further away, in Griekwastad, Aron April modernised his family's simple potjiekos with a glass of Coca-Cola to bring a tanginess to the meat as it cooks in a *drie-been* (three-legged) pot on an open fire. But in modernising one part of his family legacy, April has decided to return to the past, by letting go of his surname and the legacy of apartheid that it represents. For decades, the Aprils of Griekwastad and the Karoo were known as the Beesvel family, on account of the animal-skin shoes Aron April's great-grandfather was known for making. In learning his family lore, Aron April later learnt that the family's surname was in fact April, and in 2002 he successfully managed to change it and reclaim his past.[11]

When that past collides with the future, it becomes an opportunity to imagine who we are and who we can be. In Franschhoek, chef Reuben Riffel has used memory to claim a space on the global culinary circuit. At the eponymous restaurant, alongside oysters with a yuzu gel sit samosas with a mango chutney, and bobotie that is infused into a spiced lamb neck served with apricot, slow-roasted fennel and grilled zucchini. And of course, there is malva pudding, but it is elevated with a unique rooibos ice cream and poached guavas. Riffel's restaurant doesn't cater to the everyday South African pocket, but it doesn't have to. In a global food culture that is challenging the centrality of European cuisine and introducing new cultures to the world, this homage to Riffel's mother Sylvia and the flavours of working-class Franschhoek brought to the wine town's affluent main road is a triumph.

All these histories make Coloured cuisine hard to define, which is why the term *huiskos* feels so apt. There are certain foods and flavours that are distinctly ours, that we can lay claim to, but there are also differences that we should not paper over to create a national identity. There are many ways to be Coloured, reflected in our flavours. For me, the most dominant flavour is nostalgia and familiarity. As a student in New York, I tried to recreate the flavours and dishes I knew. Kielbasa, a Polish sausage, stood in for Friday wors but the baked-bean gravy just couldn't be recreated, despite the variety of beans I found on American shelves. I was thoroughly spoiled when my aunt spent too much money to send a package of four tins of Koo Baked Beans. I prized those tins, eating them slowly to prolong the courage they gave me to navigate an alien, and often unforgiving, city.

This is a familiar feeling in a city of eight million, the yearning for home. Everyone comes to New York with their dreams in one hand and memories in the other. South Africans are there too, congregating at Madiba's in Brooklyn. Here, an imported can of Cream Soda is priced the same as fine South African wine, and the décor is a sort of post-apartheid amalgamation of pop art Mandelas and Nguni patterns. I laughed at the menu's insisting that Greek salad was South African because South Africans, inexplicably, always have it as a side, but it was right. Polenta, it turns out, makes a decent replacement for pap, and somehow they'd got the wors right. At Madiba's, to be South African is to have a braai, and while that does feel quintessentially post-apartheid South African, it's also the easy answer to the question of what is home. Like the rainbow nation, it requires no excavation, no hard truths, it's just an easy, replicable recipe. It works, though, and we embrace it because it's easy.

One snowy Sunday – in February, when the darkness comes much too early – I wandered the streets, missing home in a way that a Skype call would not fix. Trudging through the snow on a street in Hell's Kitchen, I smelled the sweet and spicy aromas of home. But it wasn't South Africans who were making them: it was a Malaysian restaurant. I spent more than my scholarship stipend would allow, that day, on the flavours that felt closest to home, using the emergency credit card my mother had given me. Thankfully, there were cheaper options that got me by on most other days. Sometimes it was roti-and-lentil curry from South Indian restaurants and, after a while, *arroz con pollo*, chicken and rice, at a Dominican diner in Washington Heights started feeling like home. Most times, though, it was the biryani from a Moroccan vendor on 110th and Broadway – whose generous portions fed me for two days for $5 – that kept me not only fed, but also fulfilled.

Christmas has always been an occasion for my large, rambunctious family of food lovers. From the stoep of our old house in Utrecht in northern Kwa-Zulu-Natal, lost through dilapidation and the Group Areas Act, to the

Siblings, cousins and friends gather to celebrate a birthday party on the voorstoep
in Utrecht, KwaZulu-Natal, in the late 1970s. Martha de Klerk, home from
a shift as a hospital cook, prepared the spread and treated the children
to sweets and drinking straws.

apartheid concrete block house with its bucket toilet in Utrecht's Coloured
township White City that my family was moved to, to the home on a small-
holding my family painstakingly built after apartheid, we always eat together. As our family has grown, the table has quite literally become longer
and the rituals have evolved. We no longer slaughter a sheep, but we do
plan the menu weeks in advance. Over the years, as we have climbed out of
poverty, our Christmas lunches have come to include trays of lasagne and a
fig-and-parma-ham salad nicked from a Jamie Oliver recipe served alongside old favourites like tongue and potato salad. Cheesecake and berry
compote have replaced custard and jelly, but we always say grace and count
ourselves lucky that we are able to sit down to another meal together. It

isn't Coloured cooking, not in the limited, sometimes glib way we've come to think of Coloured food, but it is ours, and reflects who we are and how our collective identity has evolved. The spices remain the same, but the ingredients have changed to reflect where we have come from and where we are going. Some of the recipes are written in a hardcover exercise book, stored in the dining room server with the Christmas cutlery, but most are committed to memory, and lovingly but chaotically passed down, with measurements and ingredients shouted across the kitchen from aunts to nieces and now great-grandsons in the late-night Christmas Eve rush to get lunch ready in time for the next day.

In many ways, a plate of food is as much the seat of memory as a photo album. A *skaapboud* roast and crispy potatoes with a side of peas on a Sunday will forever remind me of my grandfather Sidney de Klerk; tripe curry, Uncle Steven; meatloaf with a hint of red wine, Uncle Stanley; turmeric rice, Uncle Charles. Milk tart belongs to Aunty Ruth, and anything else sweet, from butter biscuits to Christmas fruit cake and a family pudding we've nicknamed pie-de-lie, is Aunty Muriel's preserve. My mother Lorraine has dominion over anything with yeast, particularly vetkoek, and my aunt Joan, well, everything, because she is the family's designated head chef, so her hand is in all our food memories.

And as for my grandmother, Martha – she is simply *huiskos.*

6. *AWÊ! MA SE KIND*:
FINDING OUR MOTHER TONGUES

Lynsey Ebony Chutel

The hymns were mournful in Setswana, the voices rising over the packed church. Familiar *koortjies* (choruses), sung in Afrikaans, brought comfort. The liturgy, read in English and chanted in Sesotho, brought a message of solace to the widow, weeping quietly in the pew. An isiZulu chorus, started spontaneously by colleagues remembering a friend, began in the silence. The eulogy and tributes, English peppered with Tshivenda, Sepedi and Xitsonga, celebrated a life from a childhood in small-town Limpopo to an adulthood in big-city Gauteng. When we buried Uncle Eddie at the St Catherine of Siena Catholic Church in Eldorado Park's extension eight, we said goodbye to him in every language he spoke, a polyglot grief that reflected who he was.

Edward 'Eddie' Thomas was born in Uitkyk One in Seshego, where as a boy he learnt, as he played, Sepedi, Xitsonga and Tshivenda in that natural way children integrate until adults separate them. He learnt English when it was time to go to primary school. High school took him to Johannesburg, to the Babel that is Alexandra township, where his keen ear picked up even more languages and some *tsotsitaal*, too. Then there was Daveyton, more words and even more friends. By the time he began working as a bus driver, there were few people he would pass and not crack a joke with in their own language. Passengers hopped on and off his bus, leaving even more phrases and figures of speech that Uncle Eddie soaked up. By the time he had worked his way up to the role of supervisor in the Johannesburg city council, Uncle Eddie could speak every one of South Africa's 11 official languages, woven through with the slang and patois of each. As

Edward 'Eddie' Thomas as a young man, posing
in a photo studio in Johannesburg in 1974.

the post-apartheid municipality in Johannesburg and Gauteng rebranded itself several times over, with new logos and corporate visions and mission statements, Uncle Eddie was able to navigate these new names and structures because he had built a genuine connection with the people with whom he worked. He was naturally charismatic, and still learnt to charm everyone he met in a language they knew.

Uncle Eddie was my uncle in that wonderful communal sense that makes someone not need to be a blood relation. He was married to Aunty Ruth, also not my aunt by blood but my mother's good friend who worked with her as a nurse for years at Coronation Hospital, now the Rahima Moosa Mother and Child Hospital. They were family to me in that way that strolls after church on Sunday, a pop-in for tea, or big birthday celebrations turned friends into family. Our families also shared a history of transplantation, from rural homes in verdant hills to Eldorado Park's narrow streets and cramped council houses.

Uncle Eddie was old-school, tall, handsome, dapper, with a twinkling sense of humour. He used his pension to travel the world and, absolutely unsurprisingly, picked up some German in Europe. Aunty Ruth, who married him when she was 45 and he was 54, giggled like a schoolgirl in all the years they had together. He was an adventurer, but also a steady and undeniable presence, never fighting for attention, simply commanding it.

As his loved ones mourned him, I began to understand how this presence and charisma had come to be: it was connection. Through a childhood that defied apartheid's concocted and manipulative divisions between Black and Coloured, with family on both sides of the colour line, Uncle Eddie had learnt to speak all 11 languages and moved between groups of people, across race and class, with an ease that was the very thing the apartheid system hated and tried to prevent. His own mixed heritage, and later his bus trips and truck rides between towns and townships, allowed him to move between the worlds that the system tried to cut off from one another. And while he always knew exactly who he was and what he stood for, this was not defined by the classification code in his ID number. It was perhaps this fluidity, this ability to make anywhere feel like home, that made Aunty Ruth fall for him. That, and the fact that he was tall and handsome and charming, of course.

Yet where Uncle Eddie had picked up all his languages, Aunty Ruth had lost one of hers and rejected another. The fourth daughter of a Zulu mother and an Indian father, Aunty Ruth spoke only isiZulu as a child. Orphaned as a baby, she was raised by her Zulu grandmother, Gepasi Emmy Sibisi, in Emmaus, a map-speck of a town in western KwaZulu-Natal, somewhere on the road between Pietermaritzburg and the Free State, with the Drakensberg and Lesotho in view. Aunty Ruth remembers a happy childhood in Emmaus, her grandmother ever-present. That's why she didn't question it when her grandmother would wrap her hair and nose in scarves when they went out – it was just what they did. When her grandmother told her to feign a toothache if anyone in town asked, she obeyed, thinking nothing of it. But they were not playing dress-up. The bandages were Ruth's grandmother's way of hiding the features – the curly hair and sharper nose – that would give away her heritage. It was either that or have the government

Sisters Ruth and Emily posing in the yard of the boarding house
where their eldest sister Margaret worked in the mid-1960s.

take the little mixed girl away from her loving Zulu grandmother.

But it is impossible to wrap a little girl in bandages forever, to hide what
and who she looked like. Soon, apartheid-era social workers made the
discovery and took all four girls away. Her grandmother fought to keep
them, but she was no match for the system. Aunty Ruth was placed in St
Monica's, an orphanage in Durban for children who had been abandoned
or removed in part because of their race. A few years before Aunty Ruth
arrived, the courts had placed Bessie Head in that red-brick home. Head,
whose mother was committed to an infirmary for relations with Head's
Black father,[1] would go on to become one of the continent's most beloved
authors, but her years at the orphanage and the rejection of being a mixed

child in a segregated system would continue to haunt her.

Ripped from the only home she knew, Aunty Ruth slowly forgot her isiZulu. The sisters at St Monica's would allow the children classified Coloured to speak only English. Her sisters, who were too old for the orphanage, found work in a boarding house and tried to retain some sense of family. Young Ruth was allowed to visit them. It was the same boarding house where their late mother had worked; the owner had offered to be a foster parent. But it wasn't charity – the Budhal sisters were to be cheap labour. They were made to clean up after guests, but could only smell the food in the kitchen where they worked. Eldest sister Margaret scraped together cents from a second job to feed her younger sister. The boarding house 'foster mother' spoke Afrikaans, shouting orders and insults at the girls. Aunty Ruth, the youngest, stubbornly refused to learn Afrikaans. Decades later, when she found herself working as a nurse in Johannesburg's predominantly Afrikaans-speaking townships like Westbury, she could not pick up any Afrikaans. A mental and emotional scab had hardened over the language through which not even a nurse's compassion could break. Her isiZulu did not return either, lost in the recesses of her childhood.

When Ruth and Eddie married, Uncle Eddie found himself on the Coloured side of Union and Klipspruit Valley, the roads creating a false barrier between Eldorado Park and Soweto. The two townships had few differences; the few advantages that Eldo's had over neighbouring Pimville and Chiawelo, like the earlier introduction of indoor plumbing and electricity in apartheid block houses, are an example of the fight over the scraps that fell from the table of White South Africa. The two-room matchbox houses in Eldo's are a little bigger than those in Soweto. The streets a little wider. There are more parks with swings and civic centres per capita in Eldo's. There are also fewer doors in a row of council-built houses, and their roofs are triangular, not curved. Where Soweto had blocks and blocks of neglected hostels, symbolic of the displacement, exploitation and, later, violence that haunted it, Eldo's has that feature that has come to represent Coloured poverty and othering: blocks of dilapidated, crowded flats. Yet, until 1994, crossing the road that separates the two areas was taboo, a risk to see friends or family, or a deliberate avoidance of one group. The division was similar in Noordgesig, northeast of Soweto, facing Orlando to one side and Diepkloof to the other.

Ruth and Edward Thomas marry in the Anglican church in
Eldorado Park on 6 February 1999.

This division did not need to be policed. Instead, internalised racism and
prejudice ensured that many Coloured people continued to other themselves, even as they suffered the same forced removals and found themselves a stone's throw away from the very people from whom they worked
so hard to separate themselves. Many regarded their almost-neighbours
with suspicion and disrespect, keeping their distance to gain, and hold on
to, whichever meagre advantages that being classified as Coloured provided. This is one tragedy, and success, of apartheid. Another is the ease
with which it used language to enforce segregation. As communities and
cultures mixed in Johannesburg, the simplest way to enforce the farce of
'separate but equal' was through language.

To separate people, the apartheid government first had to categorise
them clearly. Among an ethnicity that is essentially defined by miscegenation, with opaque origins lost to a history of oppression, language is perhaps
the easiest unifier of Coloured South Africans, specifically the Afrikaans
language. Most Coloured people spoke it, the segregationist bureaucrats
reasoned, so it was used as part of the rubric of classification. Except that,
once again, the apartheid system fell short in considering nuance – or
simply didn't care. People in Durban, Pietermaritzburg and elsewhere

in KwaZulu-Natal cannot, and do not, speak Afrikaans, even if they've learnt it in school. It is always English, with a specifically Natal twang that overemphasises the letter T, giving it a soft, pillowy sound. There are also idiosyncrasies that vary from town to town, sometimes from neighbourhood to neighbourhood. You just know when you're talking to someone from Eastwood in 'Maritzburg. In smaller KwaZulu-Natal towns, Coloured people also speak fluent isiZulu, just as they speak isiXhosa in the rural Eastern Cape. But in the Coloured townships of cities like Durban and Pietermaritzburg, where competition for resources and labour meant that a close proximity to Whiteness and a perceived distance from Blackness was a boon, isiZulu is nearly as rare as Afrikaans – at least outwardly.

Historically, this preference for English in KwaZulu-Natal reflects the colonial power structure that shaped the province, once part of the British Empire. Wealth and power still reside in English, even as political power has changed. The British annexation of what was then called Zululand (although even that was a construction of western mapmakers) made it part of the port outpost of Natal in 1887, positioning English as the lingua franca. Not only was it the language of the administration, but it also remained the simplest way to ascend in status. Even as Coloured people in Natal spoke isiZulu and, in some small towns, Afrikaans, English was very much the language of power in the province, even under apartheid. My mother and her siblings grew up in Utrecht, a town so steeped in Afrikaner nationalism that it once declared itself a Boer republic, so that was the language they all spoke. At home, with a Zulu grandmother and Zulu caretakers, isiZulu, too, was the language of their childhood. But once they were ready for school, it was time to learn English. Their high school education – Coloured-only boarding schools in Harding in the Midlands, and then in Pietermaritzburg – reinforced English, its literature, religion and culture of respectability, and preserved the status quo of Coloured people as an in-between people.

Today, the province of KwaZulu-Natal tries hard to represent itself as a melting pot even as racial and ethnic fissures run fatally deep. The fragility of this melting pot became apparent during the 2021 riots, when neighbourhood watch groups turned themselves into heavily armed militias, pitting Indian against Zulu. The tourist brochure version of KwaZulu-Natal's history papers over how these divisions turned the verdant province red as the apartheid government and its political allies violently manipulated ethnic identity in the days before the end of apartheid. Stubbornly, despite isiZulu's ubiquity in the province and its innate poetry, minority groups like Indians, White people and Coloured people have not widely embraced the language, especially in the cities – a marker, perhaps, of old resentments and prejudice. When a White person learns isiZulu, he or she is celebrated and trotted out like a Wilbur in *Charlotte's Web*.

Ruth Thomas, then Budhal, showing off her Christmas dress with her sisters Margaret, seated, and Emily at a studio in Ladysmith, KwaZulu-Natal, 1963.

Afrikaans is met with even more resistance, despite its inclusion in the national curriculum. There still seems to be something in the breeze, wafting in over the Indian Ocean, that prevents people from Wentworth to Woodlands from learning Afrikaans. When it is spoken, it's done with great effort and a lot of laughter. Afrikaans surnames are anglicised, and in that unique east coast accent with its soft Ts and long Ls they almost sound believably British. Still, even there, where Afrikaans is rarely heard,

Coloured people were perfectly happy to be called Bruin Ous, using the Afrikaans terms to signify a unified community. But the term 'Bruin Ous', at its most popular in the late 1990s and early 2000s thanks to a hip hop track that travelled everywhere, contested the very term 'Coloured', pushing up against the apartheid classifier in the search for a post-apartheid identity. It's interesting that a community who rarely spoke Afrikaans rallied behind an Afrikaans word; perhaps this speaks to the creation of a culture and the need to make a national connection.

For all its comfort as a common tongue for many Coloured people, there is an ambivalence about Afrikaans itself, and its place in South Africa today. The role of Coloured people in the very creation of the language – both historically and in the present – is also contested. That debate finds itself within a much larger national conversation about language and a resurfacing of ethnicity that is increasingly looking to the past, challenging accepted historical narratives and the creation of South Africa itself. If we were to use language to create a border around identity and culture, as has sometimes been suggested to rectify colonial geographic and ethnic delineations, we risk robbing that language and its people of their history and nuance. Language does not evolve in a straight line, in logical steps: the people come first, and then come the grammar rules. Language stretches and contorts as people describe their experiences, and give names to things, places and feelings as they discover them. This, of course, is not a neutral process, and power shapes that creation of language, regardless of the discourse that stems from it. Often, it is the oppressor whose words prevail but, between the lines, the oppressed have subverted languages around the world. When we accept the victor's tale or the loudest voices' version of a language and its creation, language becomes a tool of othering, manipulating ethnic identities and histories to create an us and a them. The official history of Afrikaans has done that, making it the tool of the oppressor and ignoring its evolution as a language of subversion and necessity for the Africans whose tongues fashioned it from Dutch.

When Africans first began to speak Dutch, it was for the purpose of interpretation in the early naiveté of the relationship between Dutch traders and the Khoe. Among the first speakers was Autshumao, the leader of the Goringhaicona clan who lived on the beaches of the Cape coast and first encountered the settlers. Autshumao had learnt Dutch and English after travelling with English sailors to Bantam, an English colonial hub in the Philippines.[2] On his return, his ability to negotiate with these new traders made him a rich man. But as the trade relationship continued to develop, the Khoe found that their transactions with the European traders were becoming increasingly lopsided. Here already, four centuries ago, the use of language tipped in favour of maintaining European power. There are few accounts of the Dutch learning the language of their Goringhaicona trading partners. Instead, in a world that was beginning to change irrevocably, the language that had created Autshumao's advantage also left him isolated from his own people. Trade soon turned to war, and his relationship with the settlers did not guarantee him his freedom – his former trading partners exiled him to Robben Island, as one of that windswept island's first prisoners.[3]

This relationship also cost Autshumao his name. For centuries, his name has been forgotten, with colonial historians and, later, apartheid-era history textbooks simply calling him the derogatory name 'Herry the Strandloper'. Even the recorded name 'Goringhaicona' was a mangling of !Uri 'ae ona. His fellow translator, Khaik Ana Ma Koukoa, was dubbed Claes Das,[4] his name too complex for incurious European tongues. Autshumao's niece, who also acted as a translator and became a doomed envoy between her people and the settlers, was named Eva. Her name was Krotoa, and the reclaiming of that name in post-apartheid South Africa has become a battleground for the retelling of the story of the Cape but also of the role of African women in those early years of colonialism.

The records we have of the lives of Autshumao, Khaik Ana Ma Koukoa and Krotoa are single stories, clerical accounts of their lives in relation to the Dutch settlers or the one-sided memoirs of ordinary, often mediocre, European men who have recast themselves as the heroes of conquest. Their stories are written in a language that was unable and unwilling to name and describe the dignity of the Africans with whom they came into contact.

We know little about the anguish of isolation they must have faced, the cultural schizophrenia of what we call code-switching today, as those first translators searched colonial Dutch for words to describe their culture, and their values. Anyone who speaks more than one language knows that language is more than syntax and grammar – proverbs are a short history, jokes are tales of survival, greetings are unifiers, and one gesture could be a whole poem. So much must have been lost in translation, and we feel that loss acutely now as we slowly start to understand that European languages overlook much of who we are as Africans. It is harder still for Afrikaans-speaking Coloured people, who claim a mother tongue that has tried to reject them, to recast itself as a White man's language, denying its origins for the sake of the White supremacist project of Afrikaner nationalism.

As the Cape Colony took shape in the early 17th century, graduating from an outpost to a thriving city, Dutch was the lingua franca, reflecting the political and economic power structures already entrenching themselves into the soil of the Cape and which endure today. Yes, the French Huguenots were not permitted to teach their language, but their culture endured in part because of the long, written history of the French language as well as the innate social standing of the French refugees who came to the Cape. When the Dutch East India Company (VOC) brought enslaved people to the Cape from Angola, Mozambique, Madagascar and Indonesia, it forced each one to learn Dutch at the expense of the language of their homes. Those born at the Cape spoke only Dutch. By the early 18th century, the population of these Dutch-speaking enslaved people equalled the number of European settlers. In a life that allowed little dignity, fluency in the language of the master and the mistress was rewarded with a trite gesture that gave them some pride in a warped system: the enslaved peoples who were allowed to wear hats were the people – privately owned – who were deemed acceptable to serve in the homes of, or close to, their colonial overlords.[5]

This loss – of names, places, histories and dignity – is why it is such a victory that South Africa is beginning to acknowledge that the language we know as Afrikaans today owes much to the enslaved people who spoke it. Much of the syntax, rhythm and even new words that differentiated Afrikaans from Dutch were formed in the mouths of enslaved people. It was the descendants of these enslaved people who printed the first Afrikaans text, in the 1840s, written in Arabic script. As the language broke away from Dutch and defined itself, it created a unifying identity not only for a generation of European settlers born in the Cape, but also for the descendants of the enslaved Africans and Asians who had adapted to life in the colony, despite its hardships. Afrikaans also became the medium of instruction in the Muslim schools permitted at the colony, and the language of sermons[6] in the mosques in the 1850s.

Still, this creolisation of Dutch into Afrikaans is one of several stages of the evolution of the language we know today. If adaptation and exploitation first necessitated the shift from Dutch, the Whitewashing of Afrikaans was driven by political power and White supremacy. There was a growing need among White settlers to separate themselves from the enslaved and servants – the Black and Brown people – who had quite literally built not only the Cape, but also the language that was now being used to create a sense of independence. This separation would require severing any ties between Afrikaans as an African European language and the enslaved people who created it.

As we've seen, to succeed, racism must create an us and a them, must separate master and slave and declare the superiority of one over the other. Academically, it isn't hard to understand, but psychologically and emotionally there is a brutal intimacy to the racial violence and malice of the purification project. Imagine a group of people ripped from their homes, their families, their histories, robbed of their languages and their names. Now, picture those people raising the children, feeding the families and building the homes of their kidnappers and oppressors. Imagine, then, the resilience and creativity of these people, the ancestors of Coloured people, in taking a language used to subjugate and disempower them and turning it into something that is their own.

Creating a new community as a matter of survival, the enslaved people of the Cape subverted the Dutch they were forced to speak and added their own words, still in use today: the 'baie' in 'baie dankie', derived from Malay to mean 'thank you very much'; 'piesang' to describe an exotic new fruit, the banana; and 'piering', a saucer, also Malay. The division between White settlers and African and Asian enslaved people was elastic and the language reflects the complex proximity of this. Dutch children raised by their enslaved nursemaids began to sound like their surrogate mothers, mixed marriages were increasing and cross-colour liaisons, often exploitative, were even more common than formal marriages. This simultaneous proximity and rejection between Coloured and White in language, race and, of course, political and economic power created a social orphanhood – a people not allowed to hold on to who they were, but not free to create a new nation.

Just as Islam inspired the first written Afrikaans for the enslaved and people of colour, there was a growing need to translate the Bible for poor and working-class White people who had been born at the Cape and no longer spoke High Dutch. In 1875 the Genootskap van Regte Afrikaners, the Society of True Afrikaners, was founded, and became one of the first projects of Afrikaner nationalism. The society was the start of a rebellion against British colonial rule, but its founders, including Stephanus Jacobus du Toit, a Dutch Reformed Church minister, also articulated the need to move away from 'Hottentots Afrikaans' and rediscover the 'civilised part of our people'.[7]

The Genootskap van Regte Afrikaners quickly evolved beyond grammar rules to become the first modern political party in South Africa, the Afrikaner Bond, in 1880. The Bond joined forces with the South African National Party, the earlier iteration of the National Party. The Bond understood that language ties a people together, and just who would qualify as belonging to that people became a point of contention. Was the Afrikaner community a linguistic or a racial community? It was CJ Langenhoven, the early-20th-century lawyer, linguist and later poet whose words still shape our anthem, who answered, Afrikaans 'is the one and only White man's language which was made in South Africa and which had not come ready made from overseas'.[8] As Langenhoven drifted into journalism and then politics during a time when the once-wealthy town of Oudtshoorn endured economic collapse, his sympathies towards poor White Afrikaners grew into a fervent nationalism in which he argued that this section of society's inability to speak High Dutch should not be seen as a marker of class, but rather as the making of new Afrikaner identity.[9]

Again, it seemed the colonists were robbing the enslaved and disenfranchised of their identity, just as they had under the VOC. It also set off one of the first rebellions against Afrikaans and the lopsided Genootskap between Coloured and White. Dr Abdullah Abdurahman, the founder of the African Political Organisation (APO), a Coloured political movement founded in 1902, called on Coloured people to reject Afrikaans and learn the more universal English. Yet Afrikaans endured among Coloured people for issues linked to class, culture and history. The APO's own newspaper, *The APO*, was published in Afrikaans, still the language of a majority of its readers, and featured a column called *Straatpraatjies* (street talk), a political take written in the vernacular of working-class Coloured people and peppered with English words used to skewer the Afrikaans political elite. The Afrikaanse Nasionale Bond, a rival Coloured political group founded with the sponsorship and influence of White Afrikaners, was so irked by the audaciousness of *The APO* that it started its own newspaper, *The Clarion.*[10] The APO also preferred the term 'Cape Afrikaners' to 'Coloured', an early sign of the deep ambivalence that Coloured people would have towards this word. The bilingualism of Straatpraatjies itself reflected the contentious relationship that Coloured South Africans would have with Afrikaans and the White people with whom they shared the language – although some would call this a tussle, rather than a sharing.

This relationship meant that even if Coloured people remained 'lesser', South Africa's White leadership were themselves ambiguous about their relationship with Coloured people. On the White side, it created a political and cultural paternalism, and on the Coloured side, a deep resentment and sense of rejection. But it also created a false sense of superiority over Black Africans.

As the National Party consolidated its power in postcolonial South Africa, winning the 1948 election, Coloured people still had the vote, although in a limited franchise. But the party regarded the voting Coloured political elite's preference for the United Party, regarded as orientated towards English and internationalism, as a political threat, and quickly sought to neutralise it by stripping Coloured men of the vote, removing them from the parliamentary voters' roll by 1956.[11] That right was only restored in 1994, along with that of the rest of South Africa's Black voters.

As Afrikaans holds on to its place as one of 11 official languages in post-apartheid South Africa, we ought to examine the existing fissures in the communities and identities this language created. After the bloodshed in its name, it's hard not to consider that it was rather generous of a post-apartheid government, itself made up of people who had suffered deep trauma in Afrikaans, to allow it to maintain its position. Of course, the reconciliatory government of Nelson Mandela would not paint over every Afrikaans sign, but that's not an impossible idea.

I always feel that historical ambiguity pulling at my chest when the issue of 'Die Stem' is raised. I personally enjoy the rise and fall of the verse, like the peaks and valleys it so beautifully describes, and in my own naive rainbow nation hopes I want to hold on to our multilingual anthem. But in my own love of a polyglot anthem, I have to wonder about the place of the seven other languages left out of the anthem, and the enduring power of the languages that still enjoy pride of place. But the words themselves, written by language activist CJ Langenhoven, are a tribute to the Voortrekkers and the Great Trek, an act of dispossession that has been Whitewashed as the courageous journey of pilgrims. How do the victims of apartheid sing about unity in a language that was once used as a whip and a shackle?

One of the darkest periods of South Africa's history was the 1976 uprising against Bantu education, specifically the use of Afrikaans in Black schools. In an education system already designed to be inferior, this cruel edict from the apartheid government would not only further entrench the oppression of Black South Africans and reinforce Afrikaans as a language of subjugation, but also put an already undignified education system even further out of reach. In rebellion against Afrikaans, township after township erupted into protest, with children in school uniform running from police with whips and fanged dogs or in Nyalas firing the live ammunition that killed Hector Pieterson and other children. The violence of 16 June 1976 is not limited to a single day: for some time, Security Branch officers harassed and tortured children, unseen snipers picked people off in the street as a warning to others, and young people disappeared, fleeing into exile or being murdered before they could. How does one reconcile using Afrikaans in post-apartheid South Africa with the fact that it was once the language of death?

This fight against Afrikaans awoke in the young Coloured activists of the time a need to separate from the paternalism of Afrikaans as a linguistic community that created a false proximity to Whiteness. When Worcester-born student activist Cecyl Esau saw the images from Soweto, it galvanised in him the need for a united struggle against apartheid.[12] The demand for a fair education coming from Soweto resonated with Esau and other students. On the segregated campus of the University of the Western Cape, an increasingly conscientised Esau resisted the curriculum and structure of what he and fellow activists called a 'bush college' created to limit their future. They pledged their solidarity and joined the protests that were by then nationwide. Esau was arrested in August of that year and detained for 76 days. He returned to campus and activism, but was determined to oppose the apartheid government in Afrikaans, his mother tongue, severing it from the Afrikaner nationalist project to spur Coloured resistance. He and other members formed the Cape Youth Congress, which would eventually form part of the United Democratic Front (UDF). In 1983, he squeezed into a small car with fellow students and activists Cheryl Carolus and Joe Marks, and drove up and down the N7, to Springbok, Upington and then Kimberley and Beaufort West, to spread the message – often in Afrikaans – of hope for a multiracial democracy.

But 1976 would not be the first time the apartheid government would experiment with, and eventually implement, Afrikaans as a medium of instruction. The policy had already been piloted and had proven success-ful in Coloured schools since the 1950s. The bilingualism of Coloured students in the Cape during and before this period was given as an example of the success of culture over medium of instruction, pointing to the continued dominance of Afrikaans despite the introduction of English – an argument that overlooked the language's socioeconomic power. Critics of the push to force Afrikaans to become the medium of instruction quick-ly saw the policy as the subjugation of one group over the other, including over Anglophone South Africans. As one critic argued in opposition to the National Party policy in 1956, exactly two decades before the violent student uprising against the nationalisation of this policy:

> What is being attacked is the use of Afrikaans as a political weapon not only for supremacy of one section of the *Herrenvolk* over the other section, but, worse still, for its use as an agency of domination over the millions of Non-Whites in the country. [13]

The enforcement of the policy in Coloured schools led to an exodus of Coloured professionals, particularly to Canada. Yet, despite the stages of political rejection of Afrikaans in the 1950s and the uprising in the 1970s, Afrikaans continues to be spoken by Coloured and Black South Africans. The culture and community that the language has created has endured de-spite this Whitewashing, in part because of the true history of the language.

The distinctive lilt of Afrikaans in Namaqualand and words like[14] *ghoung (to hold onto), xhommmaggageit (to be untidy)* and *t'joenie (a kind of meat cut)* are living witnesses to the remaining Khoe and San peoples. Refugees of a colonial war and survivors of a smallpox epidemic, they migrated deeper into the Karoo to escape the Dutch and carried their language with them as the bond of a new survivors' community.

As we reckon with the fractured community that Afrikaans has created, we must also grieve all that has been lost to Afrikaans. Centuries after the deaths of Autshumao and Krotoa, the last speakers of the N|uu language are in a desperate race to record it before they die. N|uu, along with Khoe-khoegowab and a mix of other languages, was spoken by the indigenous Goringhaicona or !Uri'aelona clans. Centuries later, just as the VOC had done before, the White owner of the Northern Cape farm where Katrina Esau grew up threatened to shoot her and her family if they dared speak N|uu to each other. Today, Katrina Esau is in her eighties, and among the last N|uu speakers alive. She is intent on spending what she calls her last years preserving[15] the language through film and written projects. Along with the recording of the language is a recollection of the practices and customs of the N|uu, such as how the old clans did not create shame around menstruation.

Esau and others have also become linguistic activists, not unlike CJ Langenhoven, lobbying for the recognition of indigenous San and Khoe languages as one of South Africa's official languages. Their hope is to have N|uu afforded the status and protection of South Africa's other languages. But again, the political power of language is on display, and a minority community far from the country's political centres has little of this power. The selection of South Africa's 11 languages at the expense not only of Khoe and San languages but of others like Lobedu, too, shows how the rainbow nation's reconciliation project has also papered over history and nuance for the sake of unity. Tragically, the Coloured experience is not unique.

That's why projects like the *Trilingual Dictionary of Kaaps* are so important.[16] Still in its nascence, the project is one of linguistic activism that is pushing for the recognition of Coloured contribution to Afrikaans, but also the reclamation of a dialect that shaped the language. A dialect that draws on all the languages of the indigenous tribes and enslaved people of the Cape Colony, Kaaps predates Afrikaans, and possibly even Kaaps-Hollands, a localising dialect of Dutch that emerged and which some Whitewashing linguists point to as the only origin of contemporary Afrikaans. Today, the words and syntax of the language still exist in working-class communities and townships around the Western Cape. These communities, descendants of the Cape's displaced indigenous people and the enslaved communities of the former colony, still live with disenfranchisement, not just economically but culturally. Kaaps is an enduring unifier, the history of its people wrapped into the dropped syllables or extended vowels of its speakers. But it is not *suiwer* (pure) and has been dismissed as slang for decades. The manner in which Coloured people at the Cape and elsewhere speak has been mocked, regarded as the tongue of the uneducated and uncultured.

The trilingual dictionary – a project by the Cape Town-based non-governmental organisation, Heal the Hood Project, alongside socio-linguists from the University of the Western Cape, and with assistance from anthropologists from the Center for Race, Ethnicity, and Language at Stanford University – will record and could formalise the language in much the same way as the first Afrikaans Bible did nearly two hundred years ago.

My own memories, like those of many Coloured families, are all in Afrikaans, like the Black-and-White nostalgia of a photo as I live my own life in high-definition, multinational English. The stories we heard as children, which began with *'Toe olifant nog koning was'* – our 'once upon a time', translating to 'When Elephant was still king' – were all in Afrikaans. I have always spoken both, though English has taken primacy. In primary school in Eldorado Park, by our first year we had read about Mo the Monkey and his friends in the readers prescribed for Grade 1 (then Sub A) learners. By Grade 2, we were reading *Boet en Saartjie*. There was one English class to every three Afrikaans classes, and English-speaking children were called high-buck, or better than, already showing the class divide along language lines and the receding of Afrikaans from the futures of Coloured people. Now, most schools in Eldorado Park are English, yet Afrikaans holds its place in the family home, with Coloured people, particularly from that transitional generation, switching between the two. Still, that generation now chooses to put their children into English-medium schools to ensure their future and their ability to navigate the country.

But in our continued yet conflicted embrace of Afrikaans, could we as Coloured people be limiting our own sense of community and identity? From its inception, as creolised Dutch, Afrikaans has always favoured White South Africans. An imposed language, adopted and refashioned out of necessity, it is still the language of subjugation. The language's own struggle for independence from Dutch has been enabled by its rejection and oppression of the people of colour who speak it. The Afrikaans language, older than South Africa itself, is the story of how our country came to be, told through the tongue of European oppressors. In this telling, it inherently disempowers people of colour. As we recast Afrikaans as a truly African language, one that Africans had a hand in creating, what defence is there for the torture victim who remembers every syllable a Security Branch officer spat at them in Afrikaans, or for the student recalling the profanity of the sjambok-wielding police officer chasing them down? If we forget the central role that Afrikaans played in the violence of Afrikaner nationalism, these personal and national traumas will never heal.

When it comes to Afrikaans as a tool of oppression, Coloured people may no longer be downtrodden, but how rare it is to turn on the television and hear Afrikaans spoken as Coloured people speak it to one another. Unless it is in some sort of documentary, usually centred on society's ills, the Afrikaans that Coloured people speak has been stripped of the lilt or *brei* that makes it a tapestry of its diverse histories. I assure you, no Coloured family speaks the way *7de Laan* mother and daughter Charmaine and Vanessa speak to each other. The popular soap opera flattens any cultural nuance and robs us of South Africa's real diversity. Then again, the show's handling of race is even more ham-fisted, and it would be impossible to enjoy the distinctions of the language without a reminder of how these came to be.

Yes, it is only a soap opera, but imagine how much richer it would be if the show were honest about the class and historical differences between its cast of characters, exploring those elastic but effective separations first seen in the early years of the Cape but this time when we are all much clearer about how we got here. What if South Africans made a show that was honest about the racial and class differences that still endure, and wove it into the intrigue and silly romance of soap operas – after all, isn't that exactly how South Africans live?

It may sound like a lot to ask of a soap opera, but it's a reminder that the stories we tell ourselves – and others – about who we are and how we got here are important. If Afrikaans continues to function at the expense and exclusion of the people who helped create it, should it still be allowed to call itself *Afrika*ans? Does it still get to enjoy the warm embrace and deference of being one of South Africa's official languages? Even today, as it did during its infancy more than two centuries ago, it continues to position itself as a language that is being persecuted, but has little room for acknowledging its own role in subjugation. When protestors argue for the preservation and protection of Afrikaans, whose Afrikaans are they fighting for?

Perhaps, rather than waiting for an answer, Coloured people should examine our own creation and embrace of an identity that is stuck in an ambivalent relationship with White supremacy. We should interrogate the primacy of Afrikaans as a unifying tongue, or the one that holds so much of our recorded history, at the expense of the languages and cultures that make us who we are. Embracing everything we are, introducing ourselves in all the languages available to us, is an opportunity to move, like Uncle Eddie Thomas, easily between worlds. Afrikaans should not be shunned – but when we speak it, whose story do we remember?

7. *KERKSUSTER* OR *STRAATMEIT?*

Tessa Dooms

I was in Standard 1 or 2, what we now call Grades 3 and 4, only 9 years old, with a bed full of teddy bears and a preoccupation with imaginary friends, when I first actively had to choose between presenting myself to the world as a *kerksuster* or a *straatmeit*. I was on the playground with a group of boys. As boys do, they began to tease me. In Coloured communities, it is expected not only for boys to tease and taunt girls, but also for girls to accept it. Girls are always watched closely for their reactions: they will either retreat sheepishly or, invariably, get angry and simply cry. But sometimes, when it all gets too much, Coloured girls drop any sense of demureness and fight back. And so the stereotype of the angry Coloured woman is born.

In the popular imagination of many South Africans, a Coloured girl is aggressive, loud and even dangerous. There is an unspoken assumption that Coloured girls are raised to fight, encouraged to be aggressive and rewarded for being loud. The truth is far more complicated. Coloured girls are presented very early in life with a choice between being a good girl or a bad girl. A girl who chooses to accept her fate or fight for her rights. A girl who is righteous or rebellious. You simply do not get to be both.

So, I found myself on a playground in primary school being taunted by a boy during first break. We were playing, as children do, when Leonard, a boy I considered a friend, decided to make me the butt of his jokes and the subject of the other children's ridicule. While he never got physical, his taunting was close, personal and public. He made jokes about my appearance and abilities. Nothing was off-limits. As my humiliation built, so did my anger. I wanted to respond from that place of anger, but how could I?

I was Tessa Dooms, a girl from a Christian home. The daughter of parents known in the community for being kind and gracious. Would I graciously retreat, or rudely respond?

This is one measure of what it meant then, and continues to mean, to be a *kerksuster* or a *straatmeit*.

Being a *kerksuster*, an Afrikaans word loosely translated as 'church girl', is about more than church. It is the caricature of a Coloured woman as a wholesome, family-orientated pillar of the community worthy of respect and honour thanks to her restraint in the face of hardship, which often includes violence. A *kerksuster* is respectful. Not necessarily quiet, but a woman who represents the moral high ground. A woman who errs on the side of a submissive posture towards men, even if she is naturally the more dominant person. If she leads, she leads from behind, and operates behind the scenes. Being behind the scenes also includes an expectation of being in places like the kitchen, cooking. The homemaker who quietly ensures that the household is in order for the benefit of the men, children and community – and, in the ultimate irony, a woman who, despite accepting her role as one of submission, is proactive at problem-solving, determined not to be a complaining or nagging woman but one who can be relied on as a pillar of the community.

Straatmeit, an Afrikaans word that has no simple English equivalent, is a somewhat vulgar term used to describe a girl or woman associated with behaviour that is only fit for the streets. In colloquial terms, it may be said that a *straatmeit* is a woman with no house-training. But like the *kerksuster*, the *straatmeit* can also be respected and honoured. If the *kerksuster* is respected for her ability to retreat, the *straatmeit* is respected for her audacity and fearlessness, often in the face of extreme violence. There is less expectation of a *straatmeit* to be respectful. Respect of a *straatmeit* is earned, not automatic. This is a woman who has chosen to fight. Fight disrespect. Fight social norms. Her fighting spirit is a badge of honour. She fights because for her the alternative is intolerable: a lifetime of constantly being a victim or being invisible. A life in the shadows, doing the heavy lifting of building families and communities without much respect and in the face of patriarchal oppression. *Straatmeit* is a label that brands women as those who are good at being bad. It becomes a label that is hard to shake, once given. And it becomes a self-fulfilling prophecy.

All Coloured girls and women, at some point, are faced with the choice between these tropes of respectability.

Until that moment on the playground with Leonard, I was a *kerksuster* by default. Being a good girl was an accident of birth as the youngest of three good girls who came from a churchly home, raised by a mild-manned preacher for a father and his calm, dutiful wife, my mother. Until then, I had followed the unsaid script: retreat, do not react, and definitely do not attack. I do not recall, until that day, ever having uttered a profane word, certainly not at another person. But that afternoon, Leonard's making some people laugh at the expense of others brought me to an identity crossroads. I remember consciously making the choice to take the road less travelled by Coloured girls 'like me' and to shout out one of the phrases most infamously associated with Colouredness: '*Jou ma se poes!*'

Yes – I said it. I said it as I chased him around the playground, yelling it at the top of my lungs even as I ran. '*Jou ma se poes!*' is a harsh phrase, a vulgar interpretation of yo' mamma jokes. It uses the equivalent of the C-word in reference to someone's mother, the ultimate offence. It is a phrase that has become a staple of colourful language in popular Coloured culture.

Hearing those four words coming out of my own mouth eventually stopped me in my tracks. I imagine that those around me were equally stunned. But, in the moment, I could think only about myself. What saying those words meant to me. What the words themselves meant for me and my sense of identity as my parent's child. My anger at Leonard faded and confusion set in. Had I, in a single foul-mouthed swoop, switched from being a habitual and legacy *kerksuster* to being a *straatmeit*? Was it a one-way switch? Is this how I would now always be perceived by those who had seen it happen? What kind of Coloured girl was I?

Tracey-Lee Miller, a Coloured woman born and raised in the Cape Flats in the 1980s, admits that she too has grappled with that very question. She is a smart, thoughtful and ambitious woman whose life has taken her down many unconventional paths – for a Coloured woman, that is. She has travelled the world, been wildly successful and also hit rock-bottom. She has been married and divorced. She is also raising two extraordinary daughters, Lela (15) and Liso (10), who are both just as smart but also incredibly intuitive and wise far beyond their years. As a single mother,

Tracey has done well to build a life in and outside of Coloured communities, a life in which her girls could grow into people who have a sense of identity and community.

I met Tracey when I first moved out of Eldorado Park. I had moved out of my parents' home to take up my first job as a junior lecturer in the small, predominately White and Afrikaans student town of Potchefstroom. We met on a community website called 'Bruin-ou.com', a platform that encouraged Coloured people to build new forms of community through dialogue about the serious issues South Africa was facing and the hidden issues that Coloured communities face: self-identification, stigma and fostering a sense of belonging. This was the goal of its founder Charles Ash, originally from Durban, who started the website after moving to Johannesburg in the early 2000s to connect his new sense of Coloured community with his community of origin.

No longer surrounded by Coloured communities daily, I found myself missing home. Not only my family home, but also the laughter that comes from Coloured people's use of language. The inside references to music that only Coloured communities easily get. I missed Coloured culture, the absence of which I felt so acutely in suburban Potchefstroom.

If ever I was confused about the idea that Colouredness is a cultural experience embedded in communities, the fact that I had found a virtual Coloured community while not physically living in one was all I needed to convince me that being Coloured is less about biology than about socialisation.

When I first encountered Tracey, I remember being struck by how a Coloured woman could come across as so smart on the one hand and so irreverent on the other. She was like no Coloured woman I'd ever met before. Until then, to my mind, the *kerksuster* versus *straatmeit* question was binary. You were either one or the other. There was simply no way to have traces of both in your conduct and how you presented yourself to the world. Yet, there was Tracey, in her joy, her assertive energy, her contradictions of deep faith and spiritual curiosity, and her bravery to go, unapologetically, after the things in life she wanted. Tracey challenged all my long-held notions of what I thought Coloured women could be.

When I met Tracey, she had just signed up to meet her would-be husband through a public radio dating show. On the show, you met people through radio interviews, anonymously, and would then only meet them in person at the altar. Tracey never did get married through the show, though. As the show approached its end, a man she had previously had a relationship with heard about it and showed up to propose to her at work one day. They married traditionally instead, and later divorced.

Tracey began her journey into Coloured womanhood as a *kerksuster*. Her family and community responded to people who went to church very differently from people who did not, she recalls. There is a level of status automatically afforded churchgoers in Coloured communities, which has very little to do with faith and belief. Church and religion have for a long time been, and continue to be, a proxy for good values, family values and a strong commitment to being in service of the community. There are many stories in Coloured communities of families whose children would be sent to church alone if the parents – in most cases, fathers – did not attend. Churches are central to the socialisation of children, not as good Christians per se but certainly as upstanding members of Coloured communities. The more zealous a churchgoer, the more respect is accorded.

Tracey explains this seemingly unearned respect by linking it to a perception that people who are religious have a special relationship with struggle. To her mind, they are seen as those in the community who have overcome life's struggles through faith. The *kerksuster*'s high level of faith is regarded as evidence of having transcended suffering. A bizarre chicken-and-egg scenario is at play here, making it hard to determine whether religion is the source of the ability to overcome or the reward for overcoming. What is clear is that struggle and suffering are assumed to be a standard part of Colouredness. And whether it is the chicken or the egg, religion symbolises the ability to come out on the other side of those difficulties a better person. This narrative makes religious people role models in a community beset by social ills like economic marginalisation, social exclusion, alcoholism, violence and other struggles.

The social value of religion in Coloured communities is undeniable. My parents, when establishing their family in the 1970s, used religion as a social and cultural lodestar to merge their varied and somewhat fractured family traditions. Both of my parents had non-traditional or disrupted experiences of family. Neither was raised by a present father, and both lived without their mothers for long periods of their childhood. The traditions associated with a two-parent household were foreign to them. So was the idea of common culture. Apartheid had disrupted culture in both my parents' lives, leaving a void they needed to fill.

Religion was used as a proxy for culture. In the process, however, they found a true sense of spirituality that anchored their beliefs. Instead of relying on my father's childhood norms rooted to Motswana culture or my mother's proximity to Zulu culture, the values my parents chose to anchor family to were Christian morality and the church's social expectations. This included devotion to God and a commitment to community, centring love and sharing with others, conservative sexual practices like abstinence before marriage, and, one of the most important in my household, modest dress for women. My parents took very seriously the Bible's instruction in Deuteronomy 22 verse 5, which says that a woman should not wear clothes meant for a man. In practice, this meant that wearing pants of any kind was prohibited for women in our church, and was strictly enforced in our home as girl-children.

In the almost forty years of my life, I only have one recollection of seeing my mother in pants. She purchased a pair for a family holiday in 2010. They were brown, loose-fitting cargo pants that she would also use on another holiday for swimming in the ocean. I was the first girl, in fact, to wear pants in the family, at the tender age of six. My parents' last – and late – child, I somehow convinced my mother that I needed a pair of jeans because they had pictures of Mickey and Minnie Mouse on them. My mother innocently agreed. I remember coming home from shopping on that day much too vividly, considering that I was only six years old.

We had a post-shopping practice at home of modelling our new clothes immediately after they were purchased. This was particularly for the benefit of my father, a chance for him to see (explicitly) and approve (tacitly) our clothing choices. My pants debut was met with shock – not only from my father, who reserved comment, but also vocally by my sisters, who were 11 and 12 at the time and had never imagined that wearing pants was possible. There I was, gleeful as a cat who'd stolen milk, in my first-ever pants, unmoved by the disapproving looks and obvious ire of my sisters. So committed were my parents to raising *kerksusters* that my wearing that one pair of pants would not translate into my sisters' wearing pants for at least another decade.

This was such a contentious issue that throughout their teens my sisters would borrow pants from school friends and cousins, until finally, at the age of 21, Phoebe, the middle sister, bought pants when she started working. It was her money and thus her choice.

Tracey, similarly, remembers that religion was a proxy in her life for social status as a girl and, later, a woman. She found great comfort in her spirituality and her conception of God, but she also found identity in a church community that affirmed her. It was a deep sense of commitment to her faith that made her feel protected and secure. And this allowed her to give freely of herself in service of others, both at church and in the community. Being Sister Tracey, as she was affectionately known in the community and particularly at school, was a role that she took to heart. Tracey's identity, like that of so many Coloured women, became closely linked to extending herself in service of others. She participated as a children's church teacher and later a young lay preacher. She led small church social events and projects for social upliftment. Doing good and being good to others meant sacrificing things that gave her personal pleasure or gratification. It was a sense of pious responsibility over the desire to explore pleasures and passions.

When other girls, whether erring on the side of *kerksuster* or *straatmeit*, were dating and exploring even innocent flirtations, Tracey was wilfully unaware of her attractiveness or potential to be attracted to others. She distinctly remembers the moment in high school when, in her effort to help a teacher write on the board, a boy noticing her legs for the first time exclaimed, *'Kyk Miller se bene!'* ('Look at Miller's legs!').' Because of her stance at that moment, her legs were peeking out from underneath her otherwise long and matronly skirt. The attention, and the realisation that she, a good and chaste girl, was the object of her peers' desire, was the start of a conversation about chastity and the meaning of virginity that would have extraordinary results.

Once she was alive to the relations between boys and girls, Tracey quickly realised that not only were boys treated differently from girls, but girls were also held to higher social standards than boys. While a boy was allowed openly to exclaim something that showed his sexual or romantic attraction, like that boy in class had done to Tracey, a girl's doing that would result in her being labelled anything from 'forward' to 'easy', 'loose' or 'promiscuous'. A man's status is elevated by being sexually free, while a woman's worth is diminished by even the thought of private expressions of sexual liberty. Thus, Tracey discovered that a woman's sexuality is not her own to enjoy. Her sexuality could be enjoyed by men who desired her, or managed by parents and other adults who approved of her, but was not hers to experience on her own terms.

This was most obvious when it came to the hot topic of her virginity. Men who desired her saw her virginity as a conquest for affirming their manhood. Her parents and church community saw her virginity as a sign of their own success in raising her to be a respectable woman. In both cases, her virginity had become a prize, even though she was never cast as the winner.

At the age of 18, Tracey took the unconventional and brave decision to change this and, for the first time, claimed power over her choices, her body and ultimately her identity. She approached a man for sex, choosing the place, the time and the circumstances. Unlike the narratives she had been told throughout her life that sex was about marriage or love, for Tracey, that day, sex was about identity and stepping into her power to make decisions about her life.

For Tracey, this radical act of choosing to define herself was the beginning of a lifetime of choices that not only defied the false dichotomy of good and evil, *kerksuster* and *straatmeit*, but was also an empowered decision to break free of the burden of performing piety, sacrifice and struggle for others while refusing labels of shame and disappointment.

The cage of expectation was broken for Tracey in one act of choosing herself. But did this mean that she could no longer identify with Coloured womanhood? Maybe so; perhaps the act of choosing oneself was always going to be a step too far for a culture that has allowed women to wear responsibility like a badge of honour. How could it be possible to choose yourself, your needs or desires, when an entire community expected you to choose them every day? As sisters, neighbours, aunts, wives, mothers and eventually grandmothers, women are defined by their relationships to others – and, as gender roles are defined over time, by the service they are able to provide.

What type of Coloured woman could you be without the people who define you? As a single, childless Coloured woman in my thirties, I have grappled with this question endlessly. Being unmarried and having made the decision not to have children, I routinely describe myself as a selfish person, even as I am presented with evidence of the many ways in which I extend myself to my family and community. But I cannot overcome the internalised judgement that tells me that I have chosen, and continue to choose, myself above all else – a choice that few Coloured women can, or do, make.

Surely, like our mothers and grandmothers before us, women like Tracey and I could find fulfilment in our lives even if we deviated from the *kerksuster* script we were expected to follow? To raise my sisters and me, my amazing mother Irene Dooms, whom I regard as the most selfless person I know, worked in the same industry, doing a similar job, for almost fifty years. She began working at the tender age of 14, after being tasked with helping her mother raise and care for her younger siblings. Her work in a printing factory, however, is hardly the work she is best known for. I have always known my mother to be a talented creative. If life had allowed, she could have made a successful career of singing, baking, sewing, or eventing. Instead, for the sake of her family, she chose the stable, albeit sometimes exploitative, conditions of factory work. Irene Dooms understands sacrifice.

Religion played an important role in determining the course of my mother's life amid great struggle. It was her guide and her comfort as she took the responsibility of parenting her younger siblings, even though she was still a child herself. She and her twin sister Iris were the heads of their household at age 15. My mother knew little stability growing up. In Witbank, where she lived with her grandparents in a Coloured township, her grandfather was not always kind. In her pre-teen years, she and her siblings came to live with their mother in Kliptown, Johannesburg, where she worked. When my mother was a teen, her parents reconciled. Her father, a Zulu man who lived in Ezakheni in the heart of modern-day rural KwaZulu-Natal, had written a letter to her mother, asking her to return to their marital home. Many of the teenage children remained in Johannesburg to complete school. This is how my mother and Iris became the main breadwinners and caregivers to their siblings.

One day, one of my mother's uncles, a man prone to partying in backyards and shebeens and drinking his fair share of alcohol, came home and announced that he had been fired. His knee-jerk response was to use the last of his money to drown his sorrows and so off he went, in search of the next bottle. But instead of a hangover, he returned with a small booklet titled 'What should I do to be saved?' The Christian pamphlet had caught his eye on his way to a party, handed to him by a man on the street.

He told my mother and her twin sister that they should attend church with him in Kliptown. The decision to attend church changed my mother's life forever. For her, church provided much-needed community and a grounding sense of values. Becoming a *kerksuster* gave my mother the tools to form a cohesive vision of the kind of woman she wanted to be and a community of support to help her become that woman. It introduced her to friends who have become lifelong sisters – and her husband, who has become an anchor, the person with whom she could build the stable family life she was denied growing up.

My mother is the most natural caregiver. As a mother, aunt and grandmother, she takes pride in her role as a homemaker, nurturer and provider. She was a mother well before she gave birth to my sisters and me, a role she was thrust into by circumstance and for which she was not equipped when she first had to take it – but one that she used the discipline, values and norms of church life to help her craft.

Tracey's mother was much the same. She was an intelligent woman, who reports having had great mathematics and science acumen as a schoolgirl, but she never pursued studies or a career that utilised those skills. What she did was serve her husband, children, family and community with care, wisdom and kindness. Tracey often wondered if her mother had ever truly answered the questions in her own mind about which path she would have followed if only she could have chosen for herself. The truth is that choice is a luxury very few Coloured women can afford, thanks to the structural challenges that come with belonging to a marginalised racial and ethnic group in South Africa. And being a woman is, in itself, constraining.

Tracey uses a striking metaphor to describe the condition of carrying the expectations, needs and aspirations of other people in the way that women in Coloured communities often do, in large part at the expense of their ability to explore their own joys: beast of burden. In nature and society, beasts of burden are animals like oxen, mules and horses. Animals marvelled at for their beauty and celebrated for their strength, but best known for their utility in carrying the burdens of others. This description is disturbing in the ways that it is accurate. Having mothers

Tracey-Lee Miller's eldest daughter, Lela, enjoying lunch with her mother.

in our homes and communities who are willing to share our loads is something for which we all, as children of Coloured communities, count ourselves endlessly fortunate, because we do not often enough reflect on the interpersonal costs of such a life.

Coloured women are stereotypically known for being loud, tough, rough, or even violent; but perhaps, whether we are talking about the *kerksuster* or the *straatmeit*, we fail to look beyond the personas and see the enormous personal sacrifice of their having denied themselves the simplest act of choosing themselves first.

What does this all mean for future generations of Coloured girls and women?

Tracey is raising two girls of her own, now. Unlike our generation, they are not being raised in communities that are overwhelmingly Coloured.

While they have clear ties to Coloured identity and culture, having consistent access to cultural experiences that cross ethnic and class divides lends itself to a sense of identity building that does not limit them to the choice between *kerksuster* and *straatmeit*. Tracey describes her parenting as an act of 'winging it'. After having chosen to break free of the types of socialisation that framed her childhood and experiences of parenting, it is unsurprising that she is having, intentionally and innovatively, to walk a new parenting path.

What guides Tracey's decisions about how to raise her girls is a commitment to parenting from a place of love and not power, a place of freedom and not restraint. Tracey wants her daughters to feel safe enough to choose their own paths, knowing that she will protect them from the judgement others may impose and that her role will forever remain one of support rather than imposition.

With no children of my own, I reflect on this perspective while thinking about my nieces. What our generation – mine, my sisters and Tracey's – wants for them is a life with more choices and less fear. A life with more opportunities and uncertainty, but less regret. A life of more freedom and many more chances to fail in ways that are safe enough for them to be able to get up and try again. For a new generation of Coloured girls who will grow into womanhood today and in the future, I write this letter to you not as an oracle but as someone who reflects on the things I wish were said to our mothers, to their mothers, and to me:

For Kullud Girls

You matter.

Even if you choose not to read another word of this, I want you to know and believe it when I say that you matter. Every talent, every gift every ability, every skill you have not only makes up your matter but makes you matter. You are more than what others say you can be. You are more than your education and more than your chores. You are more than your relationships with family, friends, or lovers.

You can be whatever your heart and soul tell you to be; there are no limits to what is possible. If you close your eyes today and dream of a future you don't know, it may seem like a dark void with no world outside yourself that colours your imagination, or perhaps you may only see a predictable future characterised by the lives you've seen lived many times before by your mothers, their mothers and their mothers' mothers.

Your greatest gift is the gift you can give to the world – the ability to change the course of your life as often as you need to, to ensure your own growth and your place in the world. Your future is linked to that of your community and your country, but you must remember that the only and best way to serve others is first to tend to yourself.

Take time to get to know yourself.

Take time to understand your brokenness, your pain, your cracks, your bruises. Take time to understand your strengths, your abilities, your desires. Take time to understand your wants, your needs and the things you're most fulfilled by. When all is said and done, remember that you matter. You are more than adequate. You should never feel the need to prove that you are worthy. You never have to strive to please others. The only person you owe the best of yourself to is you. As you travel life's journey and discover more about yourself, allow yourself to walk through doors that are unknown, to do things you may not understand at first. Trust yourself to learn, to grow and to build your own life. When all is said and done, you are the best life companion that you could possibly have. Always remember that your first responsibility is to yourself, and the fruit of that labour will be a gift to the world.

8. OF MEN, *MANNE* AND 'MOFFIES'

Lynsey Ebony Chutel

Aubrey Carolus wanted better for his family, a better life, better dreams, and a better beach day one sunny Sunday in the 1960s. Instead of the polluted Kalk Bay harbour reserved for Coloured people, where the social ills of violence had already begun to spill onto the beach like oil from the dockyard, he and his wife Margaret set aside a few cents from their three jobs for the extra train fare that would take their four daughters to the more scenic Clovelly beach. They would pack a whole roast chicken, and crackers that would be soggy and cheese that would be hard by the time they got there. The *geskroeide* blanket used for ironing would be pitched to form a tent, and the youngest would fall asleep on the suitcase they carried all this in. Aubrey Carolus didn't know how to swim and was still traumatised from having had his head shoved underwater as a child, a shock tactic to teach children either to swim or to fear the water. But he wanted something more for his daughters. He wanted them to be fearless. He wanted them to embrace the ocean, gently introduce them to its majesty, so they could learn to love it and enjoy it like he never quite could. So that Sunday afternoon, he carried his second eldest, Cheryl, into waist-high water and held her as the water lapped gently against her.

Cheryl Carolus had a feminist father years before GirlDad became a celebrated meme. None of Aubrey Carolus's daughters ever wondered about her innate value as a human being. The Carolus girls were encouraged to be smart and precocious. They would avoid a hiding if they could rationally explain why they had done something naughty. Their father played with them, too. He and Margaret would play school, with their daughters as the teachers. When they gathered wood for the Dover stove in their two-room house, their father would chase rabbits and catch snakes with his daughters in a field that has long since been built over. He would walk them the nearly 3 kilometres to the nearest park and play, really play, with them. One day, he converted an old fridge into something of a bobsled and dragged it to the park for all the neighbourhood children to slide in. Their home was not overly political, but the words 'baas' and 'kaffir' were not thrown around as glibly as they were in other homes on the Cape Flats. Their value would not stem from the colour of their skin or the texture of their hair, but rather from their character, their integrity and their courage. Aubrey and Margaret did their very best, working days and nights, to make sure that apartheid's social hierarchy would not break into their home and sully their values. But while Aubrey could protect his domain inside his cosy Cape Flats home, outside, the apartheid system was determined to show him who was *baas*.

That Sunday on the beach, Cheryl Carolus, still a little girl and not yet the anti-apartheid activist we know, would have one of her earliest encounters with the apartheid security state. As the family relaxed in their bathing costumes, beach sand sticking to their wet legs and the taste of salt from the air and roast chicken in their mouths, two men in grey suits and vests unsuitable for the beach disturbed their idyllic picnic. They came over to the Caroluses and called Aubrey aside. Young Cheryl watched as what looked like a heated exchange began between the three men, with her father eventually capitulating. He walked away from those men in suits defeated. He didn't say much but packed up his family and their picnic. Only later would Cheryl learn that the police had threatened to arrest the whole family for bathing on what had been designated a Whites-only beach.

Men like Aubrey Carolus suffered apartheid's thousand little cuts through bitter humiliations each day, at work and even at rest, with all the dignity they could muster. Not only were their movements restricted – where they could live, work, swim – but the system also curtailed their ambitions. There was only so much you could provide for your family within the system. Through the homes it designated and the menial labour system it entrenched, apartheid deliberately created poverty among South Africans of colour. We know now that poverty not only has physical effects on its victims, but also emotional and psychological consequences that play out as undiagnosed depression, anxiety, violence and addiction.

It created a generation of men who were made to feel constantly inadequate and who never actualised. And to remind them of their place in society, White men, women and children would call grown men of colour 'Boy', sometimes 'the boy', with little value beyond their cheap labour. And they would bring them to heel, for the 'boy' always carried with him the threat of violence and a lack of civility and the only way to protect White society from it was to make sure he remained in a place of servitude.

At home, these men, bent by the system, would in turn replicate an environment of oppression and instability. The patriarchy that shaped and powered apartheid would be recreated in the homes of Coloured families, even as they tried their best to keep the system's grey-suited enforcers out of their homes. Often, alcoholism would help them forget the humiliation, but would create its own chaos and poverty in their homes from Friday to Sunday. On the flipside, it also created autocratic disciplinarians who ruled their homes with an iron fist, instilling the fear they lived with into the fibre of their families. Their rejection by the system made them possessive over what they had, whether women or children. Sometimes, things turned violent; despite the feminism Aubrey Carolus instilled in his daughters, Margaret became the object of his rage and resentment. Cheryl Carolus recalls how he beat her, despite their deeply loving relationship. He only stopped when the strong, athletic and already rebellious Cheryl threatened to beat him up herself if he laid one more hand on their mother.

'Toxicity of Black masculinity in general and under apartheid in particular [informed] what the gender stereotype of what a good man was supposed to be and my father didn't match up to that,' Carolus says now, able to regard her father's experience with the hindsight of history and examination. Carolus's father not only contended with systemic racism's rejection that kept him as a printing assistant who made extra money as a gardener and through other odd jobs, but he had also suffered the rejection of his own father. Carolus's grandfather, Andrew Hlongwane, lived up the road in Gugulethu but had little to do with his son, the child of a Coloured woman. The Hlongwanes rejected this mixed boy and would not allow him to take up the status of the eldest son of a Xhosa household, much less allow him to marry a Coloured woman. The rejection his mother felt was in turn rained down upon her daughter-in-law, judged a harlot because she was pretty and wore lipstick. Margaret's parents also rejected Aubrey, disappointed that their straight-haired daughter had married below her station.

This swirling toxicity of sexism and colourism, and rejection and insecurity, infused into the joyous childhood Carolus experienced also fuelled an anger. It was made worse by a system that reduced her to her skin and her hair, the opposite of who she was raised to be. It would push her into politics, then to the Black Consciousness Movement, student politics and the United Democratic Front, and then to the forefront of South Africa's liberation struggle and the national project to rebuild South Africa. To look back on her own childhood, and the complexity of the apartheid system, is to allow anger and joy to live side by side, to be saddened about the lost opportunities but also grateful for the ones gained. It is a nuance that the apartheid system rarely afforded Black and Coloured lives, and it is a nuance we still struggle to find in a country that is disappointing itself, not living up to its own aspirations to provide for its citizens.

The complexity of Aubrey Carolus's experience played out over and over in other Coloured households. It forms part of a picture of Coloured masculinity that continues into post-apartheid South Africa. Like much of Coloured identity, the making of Coloured masculinity cannot be disentangled from the making of Coloured as a race itself. 'God made the white man, God made the black man, God made the Indian, the Chinese and the Jew – but Jan van Riebeeck, he made the Coloured man,' was the early punchline that came to define how Coloured men were viewed.[1] There was little to laugh at, though. This 'joke' created the image of these mixed-race men as symbols of promiscuity, depravity between races, a mistake. As former South African president Jan Smuts put it in a lecture at Oxford in 1929, 'The mixing up of two such alien elements as White and Black leads to unhappy social results – racial miscegenation, moral deterioration of both, racial antipathy and clashes, and to many other forms of social evil.'[2]

In his thesis 'Coloured Men, *Moffies,* and Meanings of Masculinity in South Africa, 1910–1960', Cody S Perkins tracks how the tropes in which Coloured men are still trapped evolved alongside these men's racial identity.[3] Being Coloured is about, as sociologist Zimitri Erasmus puts it, 'living an identity that is clouded in sexualised shame and associated with drunkenness and jollity', a gender and racial identity rooted in

South Africa's slave history, colonialism, apartheid and, of course, White supremacy.[4] As cheap labour, Coloured men were described as lazy, incompetent and inefficient, a good enough reason to keep their wages low and to ensure that poor Whites were preferred candidates for becoming the *voorman* (foreman). As their numbers grew they became a menace, skollies who terrorised good White families and their own neighbourhoods. The word 'skollie' went as far as becoming a media characterisation that fuelled the call for the isolation of Coloured South Africans.

By the late 1930s, the menace of the skollie was reason enough to characterise areas like District Six as a hotbed of criminality, drugs and violence. During the Great Depression, the scourge of unemployed young Coloured men represented a threat to the city of Cape Town itself. Headlines in the *Cape Times* and *Cape Argus*, collected and resurfaced by Perkins's research, zeroed in on incidents of pickpocketing, muggings and public violence but made no space for the role that poverty and disenfranchisement played in the social ills unfolding in Coloured neighbourhoods. Instead, these only strengthened the case for segregation, to keep White populations safe. Public debate reeked of the same kind of paternalism espoused earlier by Smuts. When the threat warranted a parliamentary commission to solve the crisis (an age-old South African tradition), the editorial board of *The Sun* wrote in 1943, 'it is for the European to say what is to be the Coloured man's destiny'.[5] In an acknowledgement that it was the legacy of White supremacy that had created the conditions of criminality, the *Cape Standard* concluded that 'skollies are made, not born'.[6]

As the criminalisation of Coloured men became a political hot potato, Coloured politicians and activists began to take a stand too. This created a voice for Coloured South African men, but also relied on respectability and discipline as a solution. Scouts were introduced, and while the South African Boy Scouts refused entry to Coloured boys, the Church Lads' Brigade and the Muslim Lads' Brigade stepped in. Military training was espoused to make good citizens of Coloured boys. It also led to the formation of the Junior Cape Corps as an opportunity for reform, as a way of keeping boys on the straight and narrow.

These attempts at reform and respectability worked, and helped Coloured men hold on to the franchise, albeit in a limited way, until 1956. Through membership of clubs and of the church or mosque, they proved their civility, that they were upstanding men. Men who did not drink on the corner. Men who did not abandon their families. Men who were not skollies. Men who were not Black.

But it was on the sports field where Coloured men truly seemed to feel as if they transcended the limitations of their racial identification. On the pitch, or in the ring, all the masculine roles so carefully cultivated for respectability came to the fore. It was also an opportunity to challenge White supremacy. While they were not allowed to compete against White athletes, they gave feverish support to Joe Louis after he knocked out Max Schmeling in 1938 or when Jesse Owens took gold at the 1936 Olympics.[7] Sport-loving Coloured men looked to these international examples for affirmation of their identity. They also cheered for the Māori players of New Zealand's All Blacks from as early as tours in the 1920s, and at the 1996 Rugby World Cup.

Today, still, Brown men on the sports field are to be protected, held up as examples of respectability in a world designed to keep them downtrodden. Yet there are times when even this status fails to transcend the racial biases still inflicted by post-apartheid South Africa.

Among communities of colour, men speak of a universal experience of feeling undermined, a contemporary oppression that most often hides in the workplace. In environments where social capital is linked to race, Coloured men don't think they stand a chance, and their sense of being an outsider is felt deeply – through language, accent, office alliances, career prospects and all the other hierarchies through which modern capitalism has recreated ways to oppress those seen as the lower classes. That is why the sports field is meant to be a special zone, where ability should trump background. We know, of course, that the pitch is subject to the same limitations, but this is perhaps why, when someone who looks like us makes it to the top of the podium or hoists the trophy above their heads, it's a sign of hope that equality is possible.

It doesn't last, though, as Ashwin Willemse learnt on the set of a live SuperSport broadcast. Willemse is a warrior among Coloured sportsmen, a respectable man who would have been the prime example of the reformation that the sports field offers. He was part of the 2007 Rugby World Cup-winning team, and had a celebrated career locally for the Boland Kavaliers and then the Golden Lions. Willemse, the son of a teenage mother from a poor town had a seat at the table. As a retired player he transitioned to analysis, swapping the pitch for the television studio. There he was, on live television, sitting across from rugby legends Nick Mallet and Naas Botha, in May 2018. In the middle of his analysis of a Lions and a Brumbies match, Willemse went off-script.

'I've played this game for a long time, like all of us here,' he said, gesturing to Mallet and Botha. 'As a player I was labelled a quota player for a long time, and as a player I've worked hard for my own respect in this game. So I'm not going to be patronised by two individuals who played in apartheid, a segregated era, and want to undermine. So, I think for me, I've had enough, for my fair share.'[8]

It was a scene as dramatic as any surprise tackle. Willemse, still miked up, walked off the set, cables swaying, lights still on and cameras still rolling. Mallet and Botha looked amused and then stunned, and then continued as normal. The incident made more news than the game, bringing up rugby's consistent problems with race and representation – on the pitch, in team management and now in the television studio. Even in retirement, Willemse had to endure the racism of a sport that once symbolised the pride of Afrikaner nationalism. Despite his talent, his discipline, he was still just a quota player. Worse, he was a skollie made good, and would always be reminded about it.

Willemse was not a product of the elite feeder schools that breed Springbok players. He was a boy from Caledon, an Overberg town on the other side of the mountains, about 100 kilometres from Cape Town, where the highest hope for boys like him was to find a job on the surrounding farms or finish school and make his way to Cape Town. The worst, and common, fate was to fall into gangsterism and the province's pervasive drug trade – which happened when Willemse found himself a tattooed member of the Americans, running drugs and tangled in a life of violence and substance abuse. In his biography, he talks about the lows of this life, including a suicide attempt.

Despite his talent, Willemse describes his childhood in Caledon as one in which he rarely dreamt. Imagine, then, the resilience it requires to reconstruct your sense of self and shift from the proverbial street to the pitch, and to make a career out of your talent. Consider the imagination it took for Willemse himself to then go to university and become the first in his family to earn a degree. Then, go back to that studio, where all the outward signs tell you you've finally made it, only to be patronised by two White men who cannot even begin to understand your journey. One cannot underplay the role rugby played in saving his life, and the sense of achievement Willemse must have experienced not only in surviving, but also in excelling at the game that had become his lifeline.

In an interview[9] after the incident, Willemse described his own response and that of the people who came up to him afterwards to thank him for standing up to Mallet and Botha as 'legitimate pain'. It's rare to hear a rugby wing talk about pain that is not related to a sports injury, and the self-awareness of this moment makes it significant. Such empathy is rarely afforded to Coloured men, from within and outside the community. Success is a lonely road; often, it is easier to fall back into the accepted construct of masculinity – even if it poses mortal danger, there is company and familiarity along this well-worn path.

Just as colonialism and apartheid have shaped the racial identity of Coloured people, they have also shaped the masculinities of Coloured and African men throughout South Africa. Colonialism was, at its heart, a system of capitalism that relied on the exploitation of land and people who were regarded as lesser. In the society that grew out of this, African men were the servants, sometimes property, of White men. But work, even underpaid work in which one was maltreated, provided a sense of identity and pride in a system designed to strip this away. Coloured and Black men were an exploited labour class, but Coloured men had the twisted advantage of a slightly better education. Some were taught just enough for their skills to benefit White capital and act as a buffer to Black men on the factory floor.

When Coloured men were allowed to sit for an apprenticeship certificate in the 1950s, my grandfather Sidney de Klerk became among the first in northern Natal to have his talents formalised through a certificate in spray-painting and panel-beating. He seemed to have eyes that could detect the slightest shift in colour and light, and hands so steady that in another life he may have been an artist or an engineer. Instead, he worked for a car dealership, spraying the Buicks and Mercedes of the area's wealthy farmers. Soon, his work became so celebrated that men – 'White' men, to be clear – would come from across the province to have him work on their cars. It made the little garage in the small coal-mining town of Utrecht one of the most profitable dealerships in the region and it made the White Afrikaans family he worked for embarrassingly wealthy.

Brothers Christopher (left) and Steven (right) de Klerk pose next to the family car in the mid-1970s in Utrecht, KwaZulu-Natal.

The old Meneer and Nonna built the town's largest housing compound, collected a fleet of vintage cars and bought a holiday home in St Lucia, buoyed by the apartheid economy's inherent lack of competition. My grandfather, meanwhile, was forced to move his family from a crumbling but loving home at the foot of the mountain to a concrete block house with an outhouse and no plumbing, thanks to the Group Areas Act. The cars he drove his 12 children around in were hand-me-downs that he sentimentally named, hammered and tinkered with until they fell apart. Two-Tone was a 1939 Chevy Coupe that was as fast as anything – until she ran out of petrol, which happened often enough, and my grandfather would leave her sleeping right where she was and walk home, going back with a litre of petrol to wake her the next day. And Lucy was a Ford Prefect that eventually rotted and was dragged to the scrapyard.

Sidney de Klerk loved those ramshackle cars and seemed to form a hilarious bond with each of them. He formed a more complex relationship with the White family he toiled for, marked by his little rebellions and their grudging acknowledgment that they needed him, though that never inspired them to compensate him fairly. Always in grease-stained overalls, sometimes he'd be hungover, sometimes he'd threaten to walk off the job. He talked back to them, challenging them when and where he could. As a Coloured man, with skin the colour of milky tea, he had more leeway than the dark-skinned Coloured or Black workers, and he used this peculiarly colourist power to defend them where he could. He was belligerent in a way that few would dare to be; his subversiveness shows that he knew he was the talent, even if a system much larger than him stifled it.

But he always went to work, right up until the age of 70, walking from White City township through the spruit, his hands behind his back, always on time. Every day, he would rise before the chickens and methodically comb his thick waves into a side path; every other day, he would shave his beard in a basin in the backyard, using an amputated car mirror to guide his blade. At work, he was almost always excellent. A man of near-rigid routine, he would end the day with a few pints of milk stout, first at the *nie-blankes* bar in town, and then in an iron chair by his front door. On the weekends he would dabble in spirits, enough to get riled up, often, which would rile my grandmother up in turn. It was what all the men did. It was all their respite, a common respite across so many Coloured homes across the country. It was a never-ending fight, but it was largely the only fight. He never shirked his responsibilities and woke up every Sunday morning to cook as my grandmother went to church. His family never starved, his children all went to school and, when he could, he used his pension to build a home that was finally big enough – with two bathrooms, both inside the house.

For all his rigidity and belligerence, he was also much too lenient with his children, each generation being more spoiled than the last. Fish-and-chips Fridays, bags of sweets and raucous rides up the mountain that left dust trailing and giggling children in the back seat. And no, there were no seatbelts, but we always felt so safe, careening up a mountain. In a system that was inherently unsafe, he managed to make a sanctuary. He didn't say much, my grandfather, but he beamed with pride over his family. The older he got, the more easily and openly he cried. Perhaps it was because after decades of an unjust life, he could finally let a softness in.

Sidney de Klerk, wearing his panel-beater's jacket, stands near his son's first car in White City, Utrecht, KwaZulu-Natal in 1991.

Understanding masculinity in a context of subjugation demands more nuance than is offered by our dominating view of what we think a man should be. 'Hegemonic masculinity among the marginals is qualified masculinity. Being dissimilar to the hegemony of rich White men living in the centre of the Western world, the domination of men over women in poor countries is rarely effortless; it seems to demand more frequent and energetic assertion,' Kopano Ratele argues in *Liberating Masculinities*.[10]

These masculinities on the periphery came to be in a society where White men oppressed not only White women, but also African men and women, creating a masculinity that was borne out of, and is fixated with, responding to subjugation. Among Coloured men, a masculinity on the margins of the margins seems to have been formed. As is the case with political and linguistic identity, there is an orphanhood that permeates this sense of identity, and a need to create a sense of community and family.

In the absence of defined tradition as a conduit of culture – and therefore a platform from which masculine identities are expressed and passed from one generation to the next – in many Coloured communities, masculine identities are shaped by the environments in which they play out, for better or for worse. In neighbourhoods like the townships, created through violence and separation, masculinities were built on a rotten foundation – and not just among Coloured people. As early as the 1930s, as Johannesburg began to take shape as an urban environment, gangs began to form as a response to the harsh socioeconomic conditions that befell Black people even then. They emerged almost as an antithesis to the respectable, some would say subservient, man who worked for a pittance under the heel of White men.

Young Black men were outside the margins of society, struggling to find meaningful work. Those who were born in the city competed against new waves of rural migrants for work, and lost out. Employers who were already racist preferred to hire migrants because they were seen as more pliable and came at a lower cost. An increasing number of Black men were forced into an underworld to create opportunities for themselves on the margins.[11] This is a pattern that gave rise to the *tsotsis* of Soweto and the number gangs on the Cape Flats. It's a pattern that continues today and sounds the alarm for South Africa's inability to create meaningful employment for millions of men and women.

For men in particular, the desire to be a provider and gain respect through the ability to create, earn and parse resources is a trait that seems impossible to separate from expressions of masculinity and belonging. In the reams of research dedicated to understanding why young men and boys join gangs, there is also a common thread of creating community in that identity. Many spoke of the need to belong,[12] the reassurance of knowing that someone had your back,[13] and the ability to provide, through whatever means. For far too many it is a rite of passage, with or without consent. Joining a gang, or even petty crime, are seen as ways of leaving boyhood behind, of asserting power in a system by breaking its laws, challenging its rules, even if doing so is a threat to yourself.

Friends gather in a Reiger Park house at the end of the workweek in the early 1970s. Photo taken by Lorraine Chutel.

In a perverse way, gangs mimicked what life might have been like in a legitimate social setting, allowing opportunities to climb the ranks and accumulate social status. They were the subversive response to the 20th-century reformation efforts of the church, the mosque and the sports field. For many, they provided a sense of brotherhood, and even fatherhood. The price they demanded in exchange was another kind of violence and subjugation, oppression within oppression, that in turn exerted itself on women. It's why the alarming and heartbreaking rates of gender-based violence are the 'afterlife' of the violence of the street brought home. Much has been written about the identities that crime and gang life, in and out of prison, provide for Coloured men. In a way, even this research perpetuates a particular stereotypical narrative of Coloured men, as it has for African men in general. In their book *Men, Masculinities and Intimate Partner Violence*, Boonzaier and others make the argument to apply an intersectionality to men's lives, which is missing from research and the public conversation.[14] Not enough is done, they argue, to understand men's own understanding of trauma and how marginalised men see their own actions within the context of race, class, gender and history.

While we must guard against the 'But men also ...' argument that tips

129

over into blind, toxic victimhood, it is important to examine the stereotypes that Coloured men, like Black men around the world, seem to be incapable of escaping. So much of how we talk about men of colour continues to be influenced and shaped by White men and women. African men are hypersexualised or painted as mindless aggressors who must be tamed – a neat excuse for subjugation. So pervasive is this trope that it has reproduced itself in respectability politics, and it roots identity in a conservative and still patriarchal construction of what it means to be a man.

For the gangsters who have tried to turn their lives around, there is only death, sports or God. In Durban's overcrowded Wentworth, for example, gang membership is a way for teenage boys to construct an identity on the margins. The only entity more powerful than the gang is the church. Where the rule of law has failed, the church is seen to be the most viable way to regulate behaviour, pointing to these boys' need to find something outside themselves to save them from a deeply internalised identity constructed through good-and-evil, us versus them thinking.[15] Yet even when boys left the gang for the church, the attitudes that characterised their time inside the gang prevailed on the outside, particularly in church or in the mosque. Nowhere was this more evident than in their attitudes to women and their desire to police their partners' behaviour, even by threatening to use violence. In intimate relationships, the former gangsters could continue to exert violent power; their success as men was determined by their ability to exercise power over women and, in some cases, over men who are seen as weaker – particularly queer men.

Gang culture also recreated skewed gender norms, particularly in prisons. Prison marriages are a form of sexual, emotional and physical violence that has become an institutionalised power structure in the prison system, especially where the number gangs dominate. A new arrival or first-time offender in need of protection is vulnerable to becoming a wife, or *wyfie* (a female), and rape becomes the means by which to turn these offenders. Sometimes the act comes as sheer brute force, other times it comes as coercion in exchange for drugs and food, creating a dependency. In this marriage system, the wife performs what are viewed as the traditional roles of wife – cooking and cleaning a cell. The marriage ends, although rarely, when the man in the wife role is able to assert the violent tropes of masculinity and create his own self-sufficiency within the prison ecosystem.

Outside of prison, this violence is rarely spoken about or even processed. Instead, the shame often leads to re-offence, through revenge attacks or remaining at the beck and call of a prison boss and gang hierarchy.[16]

Terrifyingly, across Coloured townships in South Africa, gang violence has seen a post-pandemic resurgence. A combination of poor policing, the neglect of townships, and the poverty and joblessness exacerbated by the effects of the pandemic has driven young men back into gangs. In Gqeberha's Gelvandale, Westbury on the fringes of Johannesburg and other neighbourhoods around the country, boys as young as 12 are throwing up old gang signs from the 1980s, reviving a violent fight over turf and the drug trade. These gangs never went away, but during South Africa's more prosperous years there were more alternatives and boys dared to dream. Now, the clevas of the 1990s and 2000s – men who eschewed school for the streets, ran scams and crime syndicates, and flaunted their ill-gotten cars and clothes – are heroes once again, flashing money in communities where hunger is increasing. In these communities, the few sports grounds are desolate patches, the public pool has been dismantled and sold for scrap. The gangs that are resurrecting themselves prey on the sense of political and social isolation that these boys feel, the lie that they have been singled out and left behind by the post-apartheid system. But the apartheid system is no longer the singular enemy. Just as South Africa battles to construct its post-apartheid national identity, then, so too do men of colour. At times they seem at such a loss, little boys trapped inside angry men, unable to find themselves in a changing society. There is no doubt that South African men are suffering a certain distress, brought on in part by this transition. The result is an outward but also self-directed violence that continues to make just walking down the street unsafe for women, children and queer South Africans.

Men don an armour of their own as they move through the world. Apartheid has given way to a brazenly capitalist system, in which men's value to themselves and to women is expressed through material gain. Coloured men are not an exception here, nor is this a new phenomenon: 'being well-dressed remains an axis of meaning for some models of masculinity', as Kopano Ratele writes.[17] In urban settings in particular, masculine identity is tied to lifestyle products, a nod to the trope of the man as provider in commodity-driven capitalism. Like language and costume, certain brands have become aligned with cultural identity, often at eye-watering prices.

Jack Purcell, Sebago, Bally, Spitz, Lacoste, Ellesse, Versace – all names that roll off the tongue and are usually said with a combination of lust and bravado. These labels, and access to other signs of outward wealth, even if bought on credit, are the new signs of respectability. Yet again a community is created, this time around consumerism, and labels define who is the in-crowd and who is the out-crowd.

Over and over, Coloured masculinity has been linked to the status quo. In a community with little political power or cultural clout, being seen to create one's own identity through following the herd and actively submitting to tropes brings with it a sense of belonging that is so desperately yearned for. At times, this dress code of overcompensation creates a protective suit of sorts, commanding respect and signalling that Coloured men are not the *skollies* the world would like to believe they are. Some could argue that it is a form of wearing Whiteness, or at least the proximity to it. But as Ashwin Willemse has learnt, sometimes not even a green-and-gold blazer can protect you from the economic, social and sometimes physical danger posed by racism. However, in communities that are characterised by physical and emotional risk, that very sense of belonging is a hindrance to the self-discovery needed to create the non-violent, egalitarian and healthier forms of masculinity Ratele writes about, and for which I sincerely believe so many men yearn.

Leaveil Ward was taken out of his community in Heidedal when he earned a sports scholarship to Grey College. As the only Coloured boy in his Afrikaans-speaking class, maintaining his medium of instruction from Olympia Primary School, Ward began to live a double life on two very different sides of Bloemfontein. Travelling between the two worlds, he remembers the silence of the affluent, mainly White neighbourhoods.

'When you sleep over at your White friends, there's this sense of peace,' he recalls in an interview in February 2022. 'Then you go to your house and it's a different set-up. You know how it is in a Coloured house, sometimes there's music, sometimes there's drinking, sometimes there's *vloek en skellery.*'

As a boy he envied his White classmates' PlayStations and easy lives, but in adulthood he learnt that what he envied was his White schoolmates' stability and sense of self-determination.

'When you look back at it now, you can see why our lives have imbalances,' he says.

The son of a schoolteacher, Ward knew discipline and respectability in his home, but that is not a high enough wall to have protected any family from the commotion caused by apartheid's townships. When Ward first arrived at Grey College, with its sandstone pillars and curling Cape Dutch-style eaves, he felt alone and unprotected so he sought out community. In 1999, the school was 'very, very White'. He loved soccer, but Grey College's sprawling fields prioritised cricket and rugby. The first boy he tried to be-friend, who he thought was Coloured just like him, turned out to be White with a deep tan. His teachers were no longer familiar faces in the commu-nity who looked like his uncles and aunts, but were imposing White men, disciplinarians intent on maintaining the school's legacy and reputation through a changing South African landscape.

Leaveil Ward receives a sporting trophy at Grey College.

The little Coloured boy from Heidedal had to learn to move through this world. Sure, he was street smart, having grown up in a township, but Grey College quickly taught him that he needed a different kind of smarts. Even then, adorable and charming, he knew his skills lay in his ability to net-work; so, he moved between the English-speaking soccer boys and the Afrikaans-speaking rugby boys, cultivating an insider-outsider vantage point. His teammates became friends and he found role models among his stern teachers.

After matriculating, though, he struggled to find his place until he made the decision to strike out on his own. He worked for his father, who had started his own business, and studied online. But as a self-described 60 per cent student, academia didn't appeal to him and he would sneak away to train at the gym. He felt constricted by a life that did not feel like his own; a prescribed future hung over his head 'like a dark cloud', he said. 'It literally ate me up from inside.'

At 22, on a Tuesday afternoon, he dropped out of his studies. By that Friday he had moved out, determined to carve his own path, to find his identity. A familiar township cycle that spun on alcohol and consumerism began to suck him in, one in which little mattered beyond appearances. He felt like he'd disappointed himself, his parents, his very future, squandering their sacrifice and his opportunity at this prestigious Bloemfontein school. He spiralled further. But he broke free and found himself when he committed to the life he loved – the sports field, or a version of it. Ward became a trainer to elite athletes, among them an Olympic medallist, local celebrities and neighbourhood children who wanted more for themselves. Yet even though he has started his own supplements brand, Ward still feels that familiar pang of being undermined. Some clients – particularly White ones – question his expertise. Still, he is intentional about working with Coloured athletes, understanding their struggles off the field. The athletes he works with, also Coloured men, are held up as everyone's cousin when they succeed but abandoned when they're injured, walking a fine line in part because of their race, he adds. Among his own community, his desire to strike out on his own path has been met with scepticism. This, he says, is why he eventually moved out of Heidedal and why he's learnt to spend much time on his own, in silence, recreating the peace and privilege of self-determination he first encountered on the White side of town.

'I'm part of my community, but I'm not proud of my community,' he says in what feels like an act of rejection that few dare. It's a struggle that not only men face – anyone transcending a certain class feels it, and it requires a privilege that Ward says he would not have acquired without Grey College. Men like Ward are forced to risk isolation for the sake of survival. Where Coloured masculine identities have been shaped by the group – the communal experience of gangs or sports teams or respectable husbands –deliberately creating an individualised identity, as Ward has done, requires a rare vulnerability that South Africa has not yet allowed men, especially Coloured men, to have. Once again, sports is a lifeline. But this time, training is as much psychological as it is physical.

This recreation of the self that Ward experienced is a vulnerable process that requires time away to create a safe cocoon. So, it's been heartening to watch one of the best-known Coloured men in South Africa publicly share his journey, embracing his queerness day by day for the world to see. A performer for decades, Soli Philander's journey is well known. Coming out in 2017 at the age of 56, Philander has very publicly embraced a new identity, sharing deeply personal poetry and draping the odd lace shawl over a shoulder. Granted, Philander has always been an outlier, a performer whose eccentricities were embraced as part of the act. By embracing a queer identity, Philander may very well be sparking a conversation among old fans.

Philander, though, is an outlier for another reason: privilege allows a safety that few queer people have in townships. A marginalised identity in a marginalised community brings with it a lifetime of fear and trauma for many. Queer men may seem to be accepted within limited spaces, like the local hairdresser – and queer women, to an extent, as the 'butch' girl on the local soccer team – but this tacit acceptance comes with a trade-off. At best, if they are not entirely shunned, this acceptance traps queer Coloured people into an even more constricting stereotype than straight males, relegating them as a near-jester. At worst, it comes with sexual and physical violence at the hands of the very men who trade on heteronormative constructions of masculinity.

For as long as Coloured masculinity has tried to define itself as an antithesis to the craven, depraved forms of manhood created by slavery and colonialism, Coloured men have been eking out an identity on the fringes of this masculinity. The word 'moffie', so loosely thrown around in Coloured townships, is believed to have its origins on Cape Town's docks more than a century ago. In the early 20th century, Cody S Perkins writes, mixed-race homosexuals represented an exaggerated form of the deviance already associated with Coloured men. Gay men threatened the image of respectability and reform that the Coloured community was desperately trying to build as a form of acceptance and proximity to Whiteness. These men were not husbands and fathers, so they threatened the narrow definition of a respectable family. Seen as effeminate, they could not be sporting heroes, much less pastors or maulanas. But they were there, courageously embracing their visibility, despite the trauma inflicted by just walking down the street. Decades ago, gay Coloured men claimed their space, particularly on the entertainment stage, including in the early troupes of the Cape Minstrels and even as *voorlopers* in drag, leading the procession as an act of complicated cultural acceptance.[18]

Today, 'moffie' is still hurled as a throwaway epithet by family or strangers without any real interrogation of the damage the term causes. In spaces that are seen as acceptable for gay men to inhabit, the word even masquerades as a term of endearment. But even in this context there is a deep and violent rejection, an abandonment and orphaning that permeates the Coloured experience but seems much more acute in the queer community. There are also communities of queer men, however, who have subverted the word and created a family that cannot be ignored. This is a community that has created its own language[19] and culture and guards of their own history. That's why stories that eschew trauma as a genre, and instead aim to tell about the nuanced experiences of real lives, are so important – like Jamil Farouk Khan's story of being queer, Coloured and Muslim in *Khamr: The Makings of a Waterslams*.[20] In this memoir, Khan recalls a tumultuous childhood, an instability that would resonate with many Coloured families. The making of his boyhood and manhood was marked by his father's personal turmoil, which was at odds with the madrassah classes he was made to attend each day. As a queer man, he was damned by the Quran, but also by the lingering effects of apartheid.

And yet, as a testament to the intersectionality that is possible of Coloured masculinity, it was his father who provided the safe space that allowed him to come out. His grandfather's guiding words that could ring true for Coloured men across the country, straight or queer, *skollie* or *kerkbroer*, father, son or brother: *'Jy is nooit te sleg om goed te raakie, en jy is nooit te goed om sleg te raakie'* ('You're never too good to turn bad, and you're never too bad to turn good').[21]

9. ON THE MARGINS:
COLOURED POLITICAL IDENTITY IN SOUTH AFRICA

Lynsey Ebony Chutel

'Who goes there?' the British soldier shouted into the night, swinging his lamp to identify friend or foe, imperialist redcoats or rag-tag felt-hatted Boer commando that might be creeping over the hills of occupied Zululand in the dark of night.

Ouma Annie was neither.

Annie Penjaan's feet were swollen and aching, but they carried her to what she hoped was freedom. She walked under the cover of darkness, avoiding paths on which she could be tracked. The landscape was mostly foreign, far from her home of captivity, but she had her wits about her and resilience in her marrow. The hems of her skirts were covered in mud as she cut through the grassy fields between Paulpietersburg and Wakkerstroom, scaling hilltops after dark, hiding in the shadows of trees on the far edge of farms, to remain hidden. She could not risk stopping, she would not survive being caught. She and others like her had to keep going. In the background, the sound of war – cannon and shotgun blasts echoing over the mountain, and wagons rolling over uncharted terrain and even perhaps a bagpipe, played forlornly from the valleys of the Amajuba Mountains. She hid from the Boer battalions and the farming families who could spot her and recognise her for what she was – a runaway. Her head wrapped in a scarf, a shawl over her shoulders, her clothes those of the Europeans, she did not belong to the Zulu or the tribes of the hinterland. Her language, Afrikaans, made it clear to whom she belonged. She was property, not a person. Her only plan was to make it to the redcoats. In the chaos and death of the South African Civil War,

Annie and a few other enslaved Africans spotted an opportunity.

For as long as that war has been known as the Anglo-Boer War, the stories of women like Ouma Annie, my ancestor, have been forgotten. Enslaved people like Ouma Annie were not just the collateral damage of war between White settlers and a new set of White colonisers – their lives and freedom were at the heart of it. In December 1834, when the British abolished slavery in the Cape Colony, the descendants of the Dutch, German and French settlers would not accept such a drastic shift to their economic and political lives. These people, known as the Boers, had built their livelihoods on the free labour of enslaved people and the exploitative labour exchange with the already disenfranchised indigenous groups of the Cape.

Being a Boer meant little more than being a farmer, the descendant of Europeans, but born here in Africa; a community had begun to form, but politically it was still a relatively unencumbered signifier of identity. But among them were seeds of a growing sense of shared identity, one that was in opposition to the Natives they oppressed, the enslaved people they owned, and the British, who were now trying to enforce a new political system. What's more, this system would abolish a key part of the colony's wealth: the enslaved labour on its farms. If the Black and Brown people at the Cape were no longer enslaved, Boers would no longer be masters. They would lose profits and posturing. They rallied and protested, then packed up, hitched their wagons and began what has come to be known as the Great Trek.

As the settlers moved deeper into South Africa, they began to call themselves Afrikaners for the first time, a White tribe of Africa that had severed itself from European overlords and who would not bow to British rule. This early independence movement and its retelling in Afrikaner nationalist history overlooks the central role of racial identity and White supremacy in this secessionist rebellion, and its belief in servitude and the inferiority of people of colour that informed the creation of this new identity. When the settlers loaded their family chests into the ox wagon, they also took with them hundreds of enslaved men, women and children as property. Some ran away; many more feared not only the master's gun but also this new hinterland, alien in its dry scrub and flat plains and the treacherous crossings of its deadly mountain passes. As in any community enslaved for decades, the mental shackles were just as heavy. We have few records of the approximately 10 000 enslaved Africans, described as 'workers' in some sanitised texts, who trudged alongside their so-called pilgrims, but we can imagine what it must have been like. Some may finally have begun to call the alien Cape home, forming communities despite their captivity. But when the master said it was time to pack up and go, like yoked oxen they had little choice – displaced again.

As the caravans of wagons moved northeast, crossing the Karoo and through the flatlands of what would become the Free State and North West, the settlers also raided the villages they passed, kidnapping Africans and enslaving them, trafficking people as they went. Children and the young were particularly vulnerable to capture. They were beaten into submission, their names were changed and they were made part of the cargo that would travel to the new frontier. These children came to be known as 'Black Ivory', a euphemism[1] for treating people like commodities, captured and bartered as the Boer commandos did with elephant tusks. Sometimes they were acquired from African tribes who wanted to appease the throng of pale settlers making their way into their land. With slavery outlawed, these new captives became known as *inboekselings* or apprentices. After their capture in Natal in about 1839, eight-year-old Mozane became Valentyn, his brother Nzunzu became Kibit and their sister Lutika became Kaatje after they were handed to the Steyn family. The siblings' capture, their complicated relationship with the Steyn family and, later, their escape was recorded by a missionary, but thousands more were forgotten. British abolitionists overlooked the practice as a crude Boer labour law; these children served not only as unpaid labour, but later as a bulwark between the Boers and the African tribes they encountered.[2]

The grand narrative of the Great Trek continues to ignore these crimes. At the Voortrekker Monument in Pretoria, the intricately carved White marble frieze that tells the story of this journey from the Cape to Mozambique depicts battles and victories but never the enslaved who had no choice in this journey. It doesn't fit with the stated objective of the Great Trek, that a people ordained by God would cross into a new Canaan here in Africa. The Afrikaners drew parallels between themselves and the Israelites escaping slavery in Egypt. And yet they could not, or would not, see their own role as oppressors as they further removed a people already displaced by slavery, as part of their cargo. As the Voortrekker Monument rises up over Pretoria as a renewed symbol of Afrikaner nationalism, this wilful ignorance remains part of the story it tells.

Shame and trauma also kept the Black and Brown people dragged along on this journey silent. The only reason we know Annie Penjaan's story is because, until her death in 1959, 'who goes there' were the only English words she knew. Ouma Annie, my ancestor, was a joker, and one of the few details from the time that she did relay was how she and the other runaways played dumb to protect themselves. Inside British territory, the British quizzed them, asking them to reveal the positions of their Boer masters. Fearing reprisal in case the war went in the Boers' favour, they pointed in the wrong direction – or simply didn't understand what they were saying. Learning as little English as possible was also a survival tactic.

That daring escape would lay the foundation for a Coloured community in northern KwaZulu-Natal of which my family is still a part. We don't know where Ouma Annie came from or where she was captured. As a young girl, my grandmother Martha de Klerk, then Van Vooren, would never dare to ask how Ouma Annie, or Oom Danie, or Oupa Kiewiet or Ouma Katjie came to live and work on the farms of northern KwaZulu-Natal. My ancestors may have escaped the Boers to whom they had been tethered, but they were never secure, moving from farm to farm as *bywoners*, doing backbreaking work in exchange for lodging and food, moving with the harvest or at the whim of a farmer. With no land of their own after the war, they lived on White-owned farms in exchange for their labour and the opportunity to till a small portion of land and raise a few chickens and sheep, but never enough to threaten the farmer's wealth. *Bywoners* – farm hands – were often evicted over poor harvests or through plain spite. What we do know is that Ouma Annie was born in 1872 and Ouma Katjie, whose real name was Katrien, wore the White *kappie* (bonnet) that we now understand as the costume of agreeable enslaved people who spoke Dutch well.

The first few times my grandmother began to pass on this story, to my generation, she would always whisper the words, '*Hulle was seker slawe*' ('They were probably slaves'). When my grandmother, as a child, tried to ask, she was shamed. '*Hoekom wil jy weet? Wat gaan jy daarmee maak?*' ('Why do you want to know? What will you do with the information?'), the elders would answer, their shame silencing her into shame. In the retelling, my animated grandmother purses her lips as she imitates long-dead ancestors, her eyes widen as she says the word out loud – *slawe* – and for a moment you can see the inquisitive little girl still inside my whip-smart grandmother, her unanswered questions following her into a new century. But with each telling of this story, as her own grandchildren now quiz her about how we came to live among these rolling hills, she becomes more emboldened in her retelling. There are hidden interracial relationships, a changed surname, a family tree that abruptly stops. Not any more, though. At 95, re-examining her own history after the unravelling of apartheid, my grandmother was beginning to understand not only our family's place in the grand events of the Great Trek and the Anglo-Boer War, but also the personal tragedy of which the elders would not speak. Perhaps this silence, like Ouma Annie's playing dumb with the British, was also a survival tactic. To remember was too painful – and besides, who would listen, and what would it solve at the height of apartheid?

This marginalisation and political erasure is a familiar tactic employed against Coloured South Africans. Even more so is the false dichotomy that Coloured people face – to align with one side or the other, with little agency of their own. The British took Ouma Annie and the others in, but harassed them for intelligence about the Boers. Ouma Annie, out of fear, loyalty and scant command of the English language, gave little away. When the dust settled and the war was over, she and the others returned to a form of servitude as *bywoners* or were trapped in the *inboekseling* system. These early Afrikaans-speaking communities, found as far afield as Namibia and sometimes referred to as 'Black Afrikaners',[3] bore ties too close to the Europeans and were alienated from Native tribes, stuck in between.

Throughout South Africa's history, Coloured people have been played between two competing groups or used as a buffer between warring Europeans. After the annexation of Zululand at the end of the Anglo-Zulu War, one of the commissioners appointed to oversee the territory and settle land disputes, Lord Garnet Wolseley, divided the territory into what he called kinglets: thirteen territories, ruled by chiefs who were subservient to the British Crown.[4] Among those chiefs was one John Dunn, a Scotsman who became the first so-called White Zulu. Dunn's family arrived in South Africa and settled in the Eastern Cape. When his father was killed by an elephant, the family returned home, but Dunn married a Coloured woman named Catherine Pierce and joined an expedition to Natal as a big game hunter and mercenary, taking his chances eastward. In December 1856, Dunn was leading a commando of African and Coloured police-men in the British government's forces when he met King Cetshwayo in battle.[5] By then, he was frustrated with low pay and a low rank among the British, and King Cetshwayo, having encountered Dunn's impressive and self-interested negotiation, offered his former enemy a role in his court as advisor. For his defection, Dunn was rewarded with a heavily forested area full of wildlife, which he planned to exploit for the ivory trade. When the Zulu forces were defeated, Dunn's loyalties shifted again, and the land he was awarded became a strategic buffer between the British and the threat of the Boers in the Transvaal.

Dunn had the best of both worlds, and used this. While he enjoyed the protection of the British, he also cemented his position within Zulu politi-cal power, taking 49 Zulu wives and creating a buffer clan in what is now KwaZulu-Natal. It was a politically expedient move that would set up his descendants for decades. His grandson, Ernest David Dunn, was a member of the Labour Party in the apartheid-era Coloured Representatives Coun-cil. There, he represented 7 000 Coloured voters who still enjoyed a limited franchise, in general – and, in particular, the interests of the 400-strong Dunn community in the province. By the younger Dunn's own admission,[6] the Coloured Representatives Council was a 'rubber stamp body' and he ran on the ticket of opposing the very system within which he was trying to function. Still, in an interview Dunn revealed that his interests lay in maintaining separation, even if this limited his progress. As South Africa's transition began to appear imminent, Dunn was confident that his clan would hold on to power, telling researcher Al J Venter that he believed the Zulus under Buthelezi would not succeed in redrawing the province's borders in their favour, because 'these are not the same Zulus that fought valiant wars in the last centuries. They don't seem to have that something extra which made warriors like Tchaka [sic] or Dingaan'.[7]

Dunn's rather strident comments are made in the book *Coloured: A Profile of Two Million South Africans,* an exploration in the 1970s that sought to uncover where Coloured people stood in South Africa's chang-ing political landscape. The author, conflict journalist and researcher of Africa's military history, Al J Venter, travelled across apartheid South Africa profiling Coloured communities, from the fishermen of Saldanha to the 'basters' of Rehoboth in the Northern Cape, grappling with the central argument that '[i]f White South Africans cannot come to terms with this group with whom they share a common history, language and culture, they will never be able to deal with what has been called "the slowly awakening African Giant"'.[8]

Despite its overt paternalism and White supremacist foundation, Venter's work was for a long time the most comprehensive and detailed literary picture of Coloured people in South Africa, and his breadth of work should be commended. His overarching question belies the political buffer that settler communities had seen Coloured communities as. Sometimes it would find expression literally, as the spatial planning of the Group Areas Act showed, which often positioned Coloured ghettoes between White suburbs and Black townships. As demonstrated in the tricameral parliament, it was a bulwark of sheer numbers, until the Coloured vote was no longer necessary. And, as the purification project of the Afrikaans language showed, it was also rooted in a paternalism that stripped Coloured people of any agency by holding them in a place of marginal privilege compared to Black Africans – but still as one of the four classifications created by White South Africans.

Still, there were material, although meagre, advantages in this marginal identity. In KwaZulu-Natal, it was not just the Dunns but also the Fynns and the Ogles and the Nunns who formed their own clans, wedged between the British and the Zulu people.[9] Coloureds of Mauritian descent who were artisans and had converted to Catholicism earned twice as much as Cape Coloureds in the British colonies. In apartheid-era Johannesburg, for example, Riverlea may not have had a post office, but it had a postman in the 1970s – a step up from the Black townships next door. Venter describes the higher-class Bosmont as a 'Coloured Lower Houghton' in Johannesburg.[10]

For Coloured people, this created a political identity that was inherently rooted in marginality. This intermediate status in a racial hierarchy, combined with assimilationist aspirations, a desire to transcend stereotypes and a historical construction of an essentialist, race-driven definition of Coloured identity has created, as Mohamed Adhikari writes,[11] an identity that at its very heart battles with ambiguities and ideological conflict. Politically, it allowed Coloured people to claim a strategic position outside of the ambit of 'Native Affairs', which was to the benefit of some as early as the founding of the colony. Still, this position had little power. Those who tried to assimilate were rejected, but they would not risk associating with Black Africans. So, like John Dunn, the best option for those who enjoyed marginal privilege was to bow to White power[12] and focus on the incremental progress of their immediate communities.

This marginality is far more complex than being stuck between two worlds. Zimitri Erasmus's work uses the Caribbean experience to give a definition of 'Coloured' that is cultural, not racial, and – as a political identity – is shaped by colonialism, slavery and apartheid. It also allows identities constantly to evolve, making and remaking themselves within a growing understanding of the history of Coloured identity in South Africa and the differing stories that challenge a single narrative of marginality. Still, this marginality should not be seen as political impotence; if anything, it is 'in marginal social situations and among marginal groups that cultural innovation flourishes, precisely because they are beyond the hegemony of mainstream patterns and practices'.[13]

As some political leaders submitted to White power, others challenged this politics that suspended Coloured people in proverbial mid-air. In 1905, a British-trained physician from a prominent Muslim family challenged the limited prospects of Coloured people at the Cape. Dr Abdullah Abdurahman formed[14] the African People's Organisation (APO), which, as we've seen, ran a newspaper that spoke directly to the social, economic and political issues of Coloured people at the time and was bold enough to skewer the political elite in a column written by Abdurahman himself called *Straatpraatjes*.

The APO was not the first party representing Coloured issues, particularly the vote, but it resisted[15] the formation of the Union of South Africa that would shift the balance of power from the Cape to the Boer republics, resisted the pass laws, and fought to maintain some sort of Coloured franchise . Between 1909 and 1940, the group lobbied over issues such as education and unemployment, and established a labour federation, a women's guild and, notably, a teacher's league. But its inability to oppose the Colour Bar successfully weakened the party, according to Richard van der Ross's account in *In Our Skins: A political history of the coloured people*.[16] The APO quickly realised it could not survive without the collaboration of other nascent liberation movements at the turn of the 20th century and collaborated with the South African Native Convention, which later gave rise to the African National Congress. After Abdurahman's death in 1940, the APO was torn apart by a generational and ideological shift. When then minister of the interior Jan Smuts announced the formation of the Coloured Advisory Council, the old guard fell in line while others like Abdurahman's daughter Zainunnisa, who today is known as Cissie Gool, opposed it. A few years before, Gool had broken away as part of the National Liberation League, rejecting reformism.[17]

Thanks in part to Smuts and others' paternalistic view of Coloured people, the buffer they created and the veneer of legitimacy as a party that represented South African interests, the government of the time allowed separate Coloured parties to continue to function, although they were throttled politically. By the 1950s, as the formalisation of the apartheid system took hold and Coloured people lost the franchise, inward-looking politics would no longer suffice. Coloured political movements attempted to form a resistance, with the largest of these ethnic Coloured movements being the South African Coloured People's Organisation (SACPO). The group joined the Congress of the People in Kliptown in 1955, contributing to the Freedom Charter. But the group failed to mobilise, and with its leaders in exile it crumbled. Pro-Coloured parties fell away as Coloured people joined the ANC, the Pan African Congress (PAC) and movements that were better able to pivot from a narrow call for the franchise to a broader defiance campaign.[18] While limited Coloured political participation continued in various guises during apartheid, from the Coloured Advisory Council to the Department of Coloured Affairs, resistance continued. The United Democratic Front (UDF), a political umbrella movement of unions, civic organisations and student groups, filled the void left by exiled leaders to form a true grassroots movement. The brutality of the apartheid system had opened Coloured political resistance to true cooperation with groups whose identity lay in a shared experience of oppression under the apartheid government and the fight for liberation.

In post-apartheid South Africa, this resurgence of identifying with marginality has created a perception that Coloured people are more vulnerable under a government that is trying to dispense with White supremacy as a national policy. No longer able to access proximity to Whiteness, for whatever its meagre worth, the refrain 'not Black enough, not White enough' has become the common lament, as discussed throughout this book.

During apartheid, it was this, and an internalised racism, that allowed Coloured people to identify with the narrative of the coming Black government as the *swart gevaar* ('Black peril'). This sentiment allowed the National Party to hold on to power in the Western Cape in particular, and in Coloured townships around the country in general, in South Africa's first democratic election in 1994. Despite the party's egregious past as the political party of apartheid, and its history of Bills aimed specifically at neutralising Coloured political power and movements like the APO, many Coloured voters still identified with it. As the National Party disintegrated, the Democratic Party – and its current incarnation, the Democratic Alliance (DA) – has continued to capitalise on this political marginality. Though its leadership remains largely White, the party controls the Western Cape even as its Coloured townships remain stricken by poverty. While the wealth gap widens along racial lines in Cape Town, and gentrification – a new form of displacement – reshapes the city, Coloured voters continue to throw their weight behind the Democratic Alliance. (One should not, however, discount the failures of the governing African National Congress in the province.)

In the past several years, though, that strategy is no longer seeming to work. As identity politics increasingly begin to carve up South Africa's landscape, fracturing the politics of non-racialism and the rainbow nation, Coloured voters have also begun to retreat into movements that have Colouredness and its assumptions of political marginalisation at their core. In August 2020, 'not Black enough, not White enough' took on a decidedly modern interpretation, becoming #ColouredLivesMatter. At the centre of this new movement was a non-verbal teenager with Down syndrome. Nicknamed Lockies around the Hillbrow flats in Eldorado Park, Nathaniel Julies was known for wandering around the neighbourhood, where everyone knew him. He was also known as a dancer and would be cheered on the dance floor at house parties in Old Eldo's. But 2020 was the first year of the COVID-19 pandemic, and lockdowns were in full effect. So was the militarisation of the South African police service, which patrolled neighbourhoods to enforce a curfew. The military, deployed to support the army, had already killed a man in Alex – Collins Khosa. His name, too, became a hashtag, but any real justice was sacrificed for the state of emergency to contain the virus. The blue lights were known for being trigger-happy and unaccountable, so everyone obeyed them.

Everyone except Lockies, who did not understand the seriousness or the risk, and sneaked out after supper to get a packet of his favourite chocolate biscuits from the spaza shop next door. As he would often do, he wandered over to an abandoned truck at the foot of a block of flats and munched the biscuits.

A police car drove by and stopped in front of him. Instead of fear, he felt a thrill, remembering the time he'd got to ride in a police van when he'd got lost and the police found him and brought him home. His parents believe he must have moved excitedly towards them, not run away, as is the instinct of Black people – especially men – the world over. The last few moments of Julies's life are still shrouded in darkness, but neighbours heard gunshots; they said they saw police drag his lifeless body into a van. His parents identified his body, pockmarked by bullets, hours later, after a frantic search. The boy was dead, and the neighbourhood erupted in protest.

Julies's death capped off a period of vulnerability in the country, particularly in Eldorado Park. It had been a tough winter, chilled further by fear and confusion. The lockdown meant that the few who were working had lost their jobs. Anger already walked the streets of Eldo's, and it was compounded by the pandemic. Julies's death saw it explode. The rage and resentment spread beyond Eldorado Park, as it resonated with Coloured townships around the country. It evoked the global #BlackLivesMatter movement that had defied pandemic restrictions in the US to protest against police brutality, and had spread to Europe, where Black people were demanding that colonial powers begin to reckon with their past. In Eldorado Park, leaders saw it as a moment to demand change, to highlight their marginality and vulnerability. Even so, they would not be called Black, forgoing the hashtag #BlackLivesMatter for a localised #ColouredLivesMatter.

Local councillor Peter Rafferty found himself caught up in negotiations between the police, city leaders and angry residents. Naturally diminutive, his voice was drowned out by more radical groups with links to the Cape-based Gatvol, a grassroots organisation agitating for the rights of minority ethnic groups, particularly Coloured people.[19] When the protests broke out, Rafferty was in a council meeting. A DA councillor for several election cycles, Rafferty was growing increasingly frustrated with the party, which seemed only to pass by-laws and Bills that promoted White interests and brought none of the change to Coloured neighbourhoods that Rafferty, the high-school-prefect-turned-community-volunteer, had promised when he'd run for office under the DA's blue banner.

'I was a pawn,' he said in a recent interview. 'A voting cow, where the grass is, you go.'[20]

As the protest over Julies's death bubbled over, his party would not prioritise, he said. They would not see it as a Coloured issue, but rather as a reflection of the national failure of the ANC. For Rafferty, it was not only personal – he was losing credibility with the people who had elected him. He broke ranks with the DA, showing his disobedience by walking out of a council meeting when utterances by Gauteng Premier David Makhura and then member of the Executive Council for Safety and Security Faith Mazibuko, and Julies's death being initially characterised as resulting from gang violence, pushed the community's anger over the edge.[21]

'We are more than just drugs and crime,' Rafferty said in response to how quickly the trope of Coloured masculinity was rolled out in the aftermath of Julies's death.[22] At the time, George Floyd's name was on everyone's lips, even here in South Africa. His murder had struck a nerve around the world in societies where policy brutality enforces racial hierarchy. But in Eldorado Park, the police officers involved were Black and Coloured, and the victim was Coloured, yet the crimes were seen as the same. In a hint at the skewed racial nature of contemporary politics, the hashtag #AllLivesMatter began to appear beside Julies's name on social media. Coloured people who tried to align themselves with the #BlackLivesMatter movement, yet still refused to be seen as Black, were inadvertently promoting #AllLivesMatter, a hashtag that was being used for the very purpose of undermining the movement for racial justice.

At a meeting that brought together councillors and community activists from different parties and organisations, the hashtag #ColouredLivesMatter was settled on. The resistance to Black identity, even in a hashtag, is central to the marginality in which Coloured political identity plays out, and in which it has intentionally positioned itself. For years, the DA has been able to rely on Coloured people's commitment to their proximity to Whiteness as a cultural marker. It's why the DA, thanks to Rafferty, held on to Eldorado Park for years, until the 2021 local government election.

The murder of a non-verbal boy became the clarion call for Coloured nationalism and its consequences. We've seen this grassroots Coloured ethnopolitics before, and its dangers. In the early 2000s, PAGAD, People Against Gangsterism and Drugs, turned a vigilante movement into a terrorist organisation, using the fight against crime on the Cape Flats and presenting failures of successive governments to develop the Cape Flats as reasons to create a quasi-Coloured state that also targeted and bombed gay nightclubs.[23] Despite the jailing some of its of leaders, PAGAD not only survives, it continues to espouse fundamentalism and anti-queer sentiments.[24] More recently, groups like Gatvol, the civic group with sentiments of Coloured political frustration as its name, have rebranded to the Cape Coloured Congress, harking back to those early 20th-century movements as they establish themselves as a legitimate political party.

One of the parties to most successfully parlay contemporary marginalisation into the politics of the stomach is the Patriotic Alliance. This party is the reason why public spaces in Eldorado Park and other Coloured areas are painted bright green. The party was started by ex-convicts-turned-flashy-businessmen Gayton McKenzie and Kenny Kunene; in the wrestling-for-the-trough era of politics that became the legacy of former president Jacob Zuma, the two made what is with hindsight a very natural transition to politics. The Patriotic Alliance was formed in 2013 as a party that claims to be non-racial with centrist economic policies.[25] Yet it has in its rhetoric relied on an us versus them positioning to garner followers. More broadly, it has done this by appealing to South Africans virulent post-apartheid xenophobia and, among Coloured people in particular, it has made itself the Pied Piper of voters who see themselves as politically and economically marginalised because they were neither White enough for the old system nor are Black enough for the new system.

The strategy worked – by 2020 the Patriotic Alliance had correctly read the shifting alliances in Johannesburg's mayoral office, and manoeuvred so that the Patriotic Alliance's only councillor among 270 seats was appointed as the mayoral committee member responsible for economic development.

'I prayed. I said God, if we could just get the department of economic development, because all the jobs for our people are there,' McKenzie told a rally in Riverlea after the dexterous political move. 'All this vacant land and all these buildings that you see are with me now.'[26]

McKenzie and the Patriotic Alliance consolidated that power in the 2021 election; they may have won less than 1 per cent of the vote, but this is still a significant testament to their resilience given the 0.07 per cent they won in the 2016 election.[27] In the maelstrom of coalition politics that has created chaos in cities around the country, Kenny Kunene was, for a brief weekend in May 2023, acting mayor, and showed exactly the kind of anti-immigrant populism he would introduce if his power became permanent.[28]

This meagre election win was also enough to secure the party as a small opposition party positioned as a kingmaker in several councils, thanks to voters in Coloured neighbourhoods in the Northern Cape, the Western Cape, parts of the Eastern Cape and, of course, Gauteng. In the Central Karoo, McKenzie was able to parlay this into the mayoral chain for the region. In the Western Cape, the Cape Coloured Congress was able to convert the attention it had garnered during service delivery protests as the Gatvol movement into a political party that won 7 of 231 seats in the Cape Town city council.[29]

Back during the media circus of the Julies trial in 2020, Kunene became a familiar face among the court benches. It was no surprise, then, that Rafferty emerged as a Patriotic Alliance councillor in the next election after his using the hashtag #ColouredLivesMatter and his walkout from a council meeting led to his being sanctioned by the DA. His switch from blue to green worked, and Rafferty retains his ward in Eldorado Park – this time under a new political banner and with a stridence emboldened by the message of the Patriotic Alliance.

'I was called a Coloured nationalist, a badge I will proudly wear,' said Rafferty.[30] Using the hashtag was a conscious choice, part of what he sees is the need to change the national perception of Coloured communities. In using it, Rafferty wanted to articulate the frustrations of crime and substance abuse and joblessness that beset Coloured communities.

In less than a generation, Coloured political representation has abandoned the non-racialism of the UDF for an identity-based formula that seems to be working. The UDF was a mass movement born of a collective civic opposition against the apartheid government. In the 1980s, with political parties like the ANC and PAC banned, the UDF emerged as an umbrella movement of trade unions and students, church groups and other organisations, all searching for political dignity in an era that was dripping with blood. The movement was non-sexist, non-racist and rooted among workers. Many of its members were conscientised in the Black Consciousness Movement that had emerged a decade earlier through the writing of Steve Biko. It was a movement that sought to do away with apartheid constructions of race and racial classification, removing Black identity from the White gaze and unshackling from White oppression. Labels like 'Coloured' were seen as a burden in a movement that aimed to move towards a universal Black identity.[31]

The ideological underpinnings of the movement were rooted in the Black Consciousness Movement. This echoed W.E.B. Du Bois' definition of Blackness as a shared history of oppression at the hands of White people.

Under this definition, 'Coloured' would be an ethnicity, just as 'Zulu' or 'Tswana' are, rather than a separate racial classification. The Black Consciousness Movement directly challenged the marginality that had defined Coloured political identity since the APO and brought it in from the fringes, where it had been stuck between Black and White.

The Black Consciousness Movement gave author and activist Chris van Wyk a new language with which to describe himself and his world in Riverlea, the Coloured township surrounding the mine dumps of Johannesburg's gold rush. It also gave him a new understanding of his history, connecting his own story to a larger African historical narrative. For a people ripped from the continent in slavery, from their villages during the Trek, this must have felt like a political homecoming. It directly challenges the value of the proximity of Whiteness and White supremacy, and returns Coloured people to Africa. Thanks to the Black Consciousness Movement and similar pan-African political thought that prioritised intra-African connection and cooperation, the African experience no longer began when Europeans first arrived on the continent. Despite their defined classification and ethnicity that relied on the White experience and exploitation of Africa, Coloured people could be more than the products of slavery and displacement.

The Black Consciousness Movement inspired Van Wyk with the ideology and the poetry to reject the *amperbaas* status, the Afrikaans for 'almost boss' that encapsulates Coloured people's proximity to Whiteness, that so many in his impoverished neighbourhood held on to. In his memoir, *Shirley, Goodness and Mercy*, Van Wyk writes:

> The apartheid government has thrown all African people into a dish, a hellhole, a cesspit. The Coloured, on the other hand, have been thrown into that self-same cesspit, but upside down with our faces submerged in shit and Whites are holding us by our little brown ankles saying: should we or shouldn't we?[32]

Still, the UDF and the Black Consciousness Movement's universal notion of a Black identity privileged a certain Black experience, flattening the different experiences of Blackness even within the movement.[33] To be fair, in the midst of a political and ideological battle with the apartheid government, and without the subtlety and variety that contemporary identity politics has afforded us, the movement had not properly grappled with intersectionality. The Black Consciousness Movement's emphasis on Black unity and the UDF's focus on non-racialism did not fully account for the psychological success of the apartheid state's strategy to create a racial hierarchy. In response to this, to be ethnically Coloured and politically Black an opportunity to bring together duelling identities – identities that were for so long pitted against each other. It is a descriptor that I have come to rely on to navigate politics and identity. But it is also an answer that the relatively privileged can easily fall back on, while poor and working-class Coloured people are once again left feeling abandoned or exploited by the political system. A unified Black identity was a powerful resistance against the apartheid system, a common enemy. But what happens in the complexity of a post-apartheid system, when the competition for resources and scarce labour opportunities in the face of slow economic change begin to drive people back to the same insular and adversarial identities, just as they had in the early years of the Cape Colony? The answer to this will need more than Biko's Black Consciousness; instead, it demands an intersectional conscientising, this time driven by the need for healing and restitution that takes into account our multiple identities. If not, a future populist, ethnically driven politics could undo the gains of a multiracial anti-apartheid movement.

For some, the solution lies in reclaiming the past. On Heritage Day in 1996, Jean Burgess, a former UDF activist and member of the Black Consciousness Movement, first faced this disquiet about Coloured political identity and said that:

[a] Xhosa man asked me, in front of all the people in the hall, where my culture and heritage was … It made me feel like nothing. I couldn't answer him. I started searching for it … I wanted it so badly, I would have done anything for it. It's difficult to explain what it means to have one's culture denied.[34]

Burgess ultimately reclaims her identity as a Khoekhoe. She was critical of the Truth and Reconciliation Commission and of South Africa's land claims process as they neglected to address the historical suffering of the KhoeKhoe. Burgess went on to become one of the founding members of the Cape Cultural Heritage Development Organisation, founded within months of the experience in that hall. She has also declared herself the chief of the Gonaqua tribe, in a progressive, feminist reinterpretation of what precolonial leadership roles may have looked like.

Among Coloured people, these universalist approaches did not sufficiently address the marginality that still haunted political identity – which could be why groups like Gatvol and the Patriotic Alliance are thriving. For better or worse, it may also account for a resurgence of the San and Khoi identity movements. Recent years have seen a political revival of 'San' and 'Khoe as identities separate from 'Coloured', or as a replacement of this apartheid-era classification. Until 1951, the official categorisation of the San and Khoe, as well as other groups such as the Korana, Namaqua and those still derogatorily referred to as Hottentot or Bushman, were separate from the apartheid state's classification of 'Native'. For the purposes of the 1951 census, this changed and, save for people who identified as Griqua, all other tribes would fall under 'Native', which now referred to anyone 'who in fact is or is generally accepted as a member of any aboriginal race or tribe of Africa', according to the Population Registration Act of 1950.[35] That same Act defined a Coloured person as 'a person who is not a White person or a native'.[36]

As was common with the brutal bureaucracy of the apartheid regime, thousands of people faced a new fate. Many of the descendants of the Khoe and San had lived as Coloured people and enjoyed the marginal benefits of this, even as they rejected the classification of 'Hottentot' and 'Bushman'. Some, like the Griqua leader Andries Abraham Stockenström le Fleur I, tried to create a united Griqua nation that embraced the history of the early rebellion against the Dutch. This early expression of Griqua identity embraced categories that were deemed aboriginal or Native, and therefore Black. But to be called 'Black' would mean accepting a political step down, and so many accepted Griqua as a form of Coloured classification.[37]

Today, inspired by a global discussion on the role and rights of First Nations people, a revivalist movement has tried to position the Khoe and San as the rightful First Nations of South Africa. This embrace of new names, language and custom also answers a difficult question that Coloured people have struggled with in the new South Africa. They have also fuelled the argument for dropping the classification 'Coloured' completely in favour of one that celebrates San and Khoe heritage and seeks to situate Coloured people as the rightful indigenous people of South Africa.

Again, it is a Coloured identity that seeks to remove itself from Blackness. What's more, it papers over a complex history in an effort to create a single story that will fit into this reinvented narrative of marginality. Even that identity is fractious. A recently passed law, the Traditional and Khoi-San Leadership Act 3 of 2019,[38] could not garner unified support from public hearings, exposing instead the desperate need for a broader public conversation to begin to grapple with the matter of post-apartheid Coloured identity. The public submissions and the minutes of the meetings about the Bill showed the myriad issues that inform a sense of Coloured disenfranchisement.

For example, Francisco Mackenzie, chairperson of the Western Cape Legislative Khoisan Council, who identified himself as an 'authentic aboriginal Khoisan', questioned[39] the Bill's 'historical amnesia on the land grab from the Khoisan'. Jonathan Muller of the Gorachouqua Commission said the Bill should have been titled 'Traditional and Indigenous Leadership Bill' instead, to move beyond recognition of a tribe to acknowledgement of a position of Coloured people as First Nations peoples.[40]

Others rejected the Bill on the grounds that it represented the wishes of the so-called big five – the Khoisan, Griqua, Nama, Korana and the umbrella group of the Cape Cultural Heritage Development Organisation. Others, like the self-proclaimed Lowveld KhoiSan Council, wanted a Bill that prioritised cultural expression over bloodline, which can be hard to prove in a history of miscegenation. Others rejected it because it was anti-Christian, or anti-Muslim.[41]

To push the Bill through and deal with all these difficult questions, that old South African staple – a commission – was established that would begin the registration process of all Khoe and San groups active in South Africa, in a similar practice to the First Nations registrations in North America.[42] Even this registration process threatens to erase the very people it seeks to identify: if it is cast too broadly, it could nullify the very attempt to preserve Khoe and San identity; too narrowly, and it risks reproducing the marginalisation of the apartheid classification of 'Coloured'. The Act would also have far-reaching consequences for land ownership and administration, the Alliance for Rural Democracy argued before the Constitutional Court, citing that they had not been given the proper opportunity to challenge these aspects in part because of the chaotic passing of the Bill. Other groups, like the !Xun of the Northern Cape, were unable to access the venue for public participation. In May 2023, the apex court overturned the Bill, sending it back to Parliament.[43]

What's more, this process, and even the resurgence of identity-driven politics, removes Coloured identity from the bigger picture: the larger South African story. Instead of identifying with the national, structural failures of South Africa that continue to disenfranchise the majority of Black South Africans, not just Coloured people, there is further separation. The attempt to create a single Coloured voice, even if it is unified, risks further isolating Colouredness from Blackness. As my grandmother Martha de Klerk re-examined her own history by reading and watching documentaries and picking up hints of stories from around the world, she heard what sounded like the snippets of the stories she had heard as a child. This forced her to unravel the decades of lies and silence. Placing her personal experience within a larger context helped us, her grandchildren and great-grandchildren, better understand our place in post-apartheid South Africa. It's a journey I hope all Coloured people make – but as a collective, to come into the bigger South African picture and see how we helped shape it instead of trying to rip ourselves out of our own national portrait.

But it will be a hard road, and for many it is difficult to see beyond the current battles. In the aftermath of Nathaniel Julies's murder, his trial too took on cultural significance and saw expressions of misused identity politics. In the Protea Magistrate's Court in September 2020, as Julies's parents wept in the hard benches and journalists gathered to capture their tears, one man stood up shouting for Khoe and San rights. He was shouted down, but it was clear that, once again, this sense of political marginalisation had returned, and that Nathaniel Julies's tragic death was a vehicle for expressing the vulnerability and fractiousness of Coloured political identity.

10. RECLAIMING KROTOA

Tessa Dooms

I have often tried imagining life on the southernmost tip of the African continent on 5 April 1652. On the White, sandy shores of a land that boasted the beauty of mountains, lagoons, the blossoms of the pincushion proteas and the colourful delight of the fynbos, communities of indigenous African people lived, making the most of the land, resources and their human relations to form loosely connected groupings that walked a thin line between co-existence and conflict as they sojourned through and sometimes settled on different parts of what would become the Cape and the broader territory that would become South Africa. I imagine that those communities were not as distinct as they are in my mind now, in postcolonial South Africa, a mind that defaults to a diverse and divided society. I wonder how aware these groupings of people may have been of the differences between their origins, language, culture and value systems.

Patric Tariq Mellet's book, *The Lie of 1652: A decolonised history of land*,[1] provides us with a look into the barely known history of the southern tip of Africa before 6 April 1652, historically marked as the arrival of Jan van Riebeeck and the start of the Dutch colony that would change the course of southern Africa's history forever. Mellet gives us interesting insights into life in the approximately two hundred years that preceded active colonial domination. He describes an already established trade route between the east and the west where traders occasionally crossed paths at a budding refreshment station on the tip of Africa. Here, an already diverse community of traders and migrants from Europe, the southeastern parts of Asia, and parts of southern Africa like Mozambique and Mauritius formed a part of a social, cultural and economic developmental path managed in various ways by Khoe and San communities. A combination of pastoralist and fishing communities, the indigenous peninsula communities were a far cry from the unsophisticated and passive communities that precolonial anthropologies would have us imagine them to have been. This was, literally, just the tip of the continent.

The enterprising peoples of Africa were by no means incurious or averse to progress. The people of southern Africa very plausibly had a sense of community, a sense of belonging, a sense of purpose, a sense of history, a sense of a future that they were creating that wasn't contingent on colonial settlement.[2] The making of the Griqua people is an example of how colonial settlement has led to an emphasis on European anthropologies as the basis for defining the history of people native to Africa. Europeans encountering the KhoeKhoe groups is not the beginning of history for these groups. Indigenous groups had cultures, histories, leaders and politics long before settler colonialism. Yet for Griquas, their history is almost wholly described through the lens of Adam Kok, a Khoekhoe leader whose forging relationships with Europeans seems to have resulted in his personal freedom as a slave, and the Griqua community being allowed some autonomy in Kokstad, named after Kok, where they settled.[3] This came at a cost: the erasure of the histories of this subsection of KhoeKhoe people prior to the European encounter, as Griqua identity is framed as mixed-race, with its origins in international relations with European settlers. The complex history of a nomadic people, moving between the modern-day Western Cape, Northern Cape and KwaZulu-Natal, building community, working the land and engaging in trade, is reduced to a colonial history that centres the relationships with settlers as the origins of Griqua identity.

While history hails the likes of Bartolomeu Dias and Christopher Columbus as explorers discovering 'new worlds' in search of new frontiers of development, many variations of African communities were exploring in ways that have not been documented as mainstream and western histories. When the Dutch East India Company decided on colonial settlement at the 'Cape of Good Hope', it brought enslaved Malays who, like the Khoe and the San, would later be classified as Coloured people. In 2019 the Twitter musings of former Democratic Alliance leader (and ironically the former premier of the very Cape where colonialism took root)

Helen Zille defended, if not glorified, colonialism as not being 'all bad' because it ushered in development.[4] On the contrary, colonialism has erased the development arc it found in the Cape. It has also replaced the local people's development[4] trajectory with a new trajectory that privileges Europeans, oppresses native people and exploits those same people's natural and human resources for maximum colonial benefit.

The act of bringing slave labourers to the Cape begins a pattern of colonial conquest characterised by dispossession, destruction of livelihoods and slavery. The colonists did not, as we have been led to believe, find barren land and 'primitive' people. Colonialism was not a benevolent act. It was not even the equivalent of foreign aid or development work; it was development for some and destruction for many.

The colonists' narratives are limited to their being White saviours to people in need not only because their imagination does not allow them to consider that indigenous African people had a life before colonial settlement, but also because these narratives absolve colonialism and its beneficiaries from the damage done then and the legacy that lives on today. African people had culture before colonial settlement, had languages, had knowledge systems, and were creating a life and livelihoods with developmental potential that will forever be unfulfilled. The fact that we don't have that history documented as pervasively as European versions should not erase that history. It mattered then and matters now.

The history of South Africa we recount today is the history that began alongside colonialism, written by those who saw this land as little more than a colonial settlement. We must acknowledge that this does the history, the culture, the legitimacy, the ownership of land and the identity of indigenous African people (including contemporary Coloured communities) a disservice. Colonialism destroyed more than economies and natural landscapes. It shattered identities and histories, and the futures of indigenous Africans like the young girl history would remember as Krotoa. She was only five years old on 6 April 1652 but, within five years, she had become a noteworthy figure as colonial South Africa took shape. Krotoa's name and legacy, although lost for a period in history, has been reclaimed as part of political contestation for identity and legitimacy in post-apartheid South Africa. For a people searching for their past, Krotoa has become a re-emerging figure, an ancestor recalled.

My family home has always displayed a picture of my great-grandfather Johannes Dooms. The pencil-drawn picture is of a man with a slim face, sharp cheekbones and piercing eyes. Although it shows only his head and shoulders, I have always imagined him as a tall man. A man with a commanding stature. Importantly, I have always imagined him as a light-skinned man. The picture is not in colour, yet I have never considered that he was anything but light skinned. Maybe it's because I know that he was the youngest son of Theodore Dooms, a German man who arrived in South Africa in the aftermath of World War II, who met and married a Motswana woman as he settled into his new home in the warmth of Africa's southern tip. Maybe it's because some of his children, like my father's aunt Margaret, had light skin. Or maybe, and most likely, it's because I've been conditioned to see all memorialised Coloured ancestors as White or light. I do not recall ever being in a Coloured home to find a large, old portrait of anyone other than a White or light-skinned patriarch as the family's origin story and its pride and joy.

When I was a child, we'd visit Aunt Margaret Dooms in Vryburg, the small town in the North West to which our family moved when the forced removals started, whose home boasts a treasure trove of historical and political books about South Africa. Each time we were there one book would be pulled out by my now late great-aunt Margaret, or her grandson, my cousin, the now late Patrick Dooms. It was a small, slightly frayed, bound book written as a historical text that tells the story of how the town was forged. Aunt Margaret and Patrick would carefully leaf through it, showing us the young children our history. They would always focus on the passage in which Theodore Dooms is named as one of the founding fathers of the town.

The passage in that book was a source of great pride for me as a child for many reasons. First, it was an objective affirmation of my right to exist. My lineage was not theoretical – it existed as a story told by others. There, in Black and White, and in the memories passed down by the Dooms family. Theodore Dooms was also an important man in his community, so there was also status to the name I bore. Even today, in 2023, being a Dooms in Vryburg is a badge of honour. People today know and respect the Dooms family because of the long historical ties and the recent contributions to the town's development made by my grandmother's and father's generations.

With hindsight, what was missing from the origin story I was told was the Black woman Theodore Dooms married. The woman who was indigenous to the land. The mother whose womb birthed a lineage that includes my great-grandfather Johannes Dooms, my grandmother Onica Dooms, my father Elliot Dooms and me. I was an adult when I first realised that I did not even know my great-great-grandmother's name. I was in my first year of university when I was required to write a biographical analysis using a social theorist like Karl Marx or Max Weber. The assignment required me to interview a relative to provide a historical perspective I may not have known. I chose to interview my father, whose analysis of me was anchored on how he saw in me the heritage of strength and leadership of the many strong women in the Dooms family. He began to name them, and as he did I realised that in our family origin story I had never heard our African matriarch's name. In the story, she was always only the wife of Theodore. She was never even a name or a face, let alone a story.

Her name was Mammila Dooms, and she was the matriarch of the lineage I so proudly bear. Yet her place in my own origin story has been lost in the shadows of a European man who settled here and was given status and power in a land that was not his. My legitimacy in South Africa surely cannot rest more strongly on his presence than on my Motswana matriarch's.

Theodore had seven children with Mammila. It was, in fact, Mammila who raised the family in Dithakwaneng after Theodore all but abandoned the family to begin a new life as a White man without an interracial family. As South Africa became increasingly racialised, Theodore Dooms grew restless. He spotted an opportunity for upward social mobility based on his Whiteness and abandoned the Black woman and mixed children who had become a liability. He took a White wife and later moved to Pretoria. This left Mammila with the responsibility of raising their children and building a life for them as a single parent. Between patriarchy and White supremacy, I had forgotten to look beyond the written narrative and ask for the untold stories. I wish I knew more about Mammila's life. More about her history and character. More about her struggles. More about what gave her strength.

The only reprieve I give myself for not asking about the Black woman who had been invisible in my origin story is the presence of dominant Black women in the rest of my father's family tale. A woman may have been missing from the root of my origin story, but in the rest of the family tree all I can see are women. In fact, my sisters and I often remark that we have at times forgotten which of the Dooms women married and which remained single. This is because even the married women in the family would change their names legally but keep the name Dooms socially and colloquially. Now, Dooms women would not be made invisible in my lifetime. Many of them lived long lives, celebrating birthdays in their nineties and even over a hundred. They became leaders in community, politics, business and religion. Dooms women have created legacies of being tenacious pioneers. This description is not limited to Dooms women who were born into the family, but extends to those who took the name by marriage – like my mother, Irene Dooms. Even today, you would be hard-pressed to find a woman who has carried the Dooms name and is not noteworthy in her own sphere of influence.

Many Coloured families can tell stories of great matriarchs. Some in the past, but most in the past 70 years, the period since the making of Coloured identities through the lens of apartheid and the communities it forced and forged. These are women we have watched in our own lifetimes leading families and communities through hardship with great resolve. Yet a startling trend in our family is true of many Coloured families: the picture of the light-skinned male patriarch. This is not always a White European man, but sometimes a first-generation child born of a mixed marriage, the old sepia image overexposed so that the ghostly figure seemed even lighter, closer to Whiteness. We celebrate the women of our times for holding our families together, but our origin stories often credit men. This is the colonial legacy: Coloured people crediting the 'real' beginning of our nation to White or light-skinned men, while an unnamed, indigenously African woman has socialised the generation of people we have become in our various communities and in South Africa as a broader community. This realisation is only one example of how history mirrors the lived experiences of Coloured communities today. The life of Krotoa provides several more of these similarities, instructive for understanding the many undercurrents of social and political life in Coloured communities that we take for granted.

The story of South Africa as told through the narrow lens of the White gaze masks many of our history's legacies. One of them is the reduction of

Coloured identity and its existence to mixed-race relations between colonisers and indigenous people with little reference to indigenous people on their own, enslaved communities and other migrants who became part of the complex catchment of Colouredness. The consequences of this are economic outcomes that do not account for Coloured people as dispossessed landowners. Coloured people as victims of oppression in a local and global account of Black suffering. Coloured people as people whose histories and identities are not a product of race-based laws circa 1913 or forced removals. Like the story of Krotoa, the story of Coloured people is much older than the story of South Africa in western history books. Reclaiming Coloured identity is thus an important part of redress and development into the future.

In a 2005 journal article, '"Denying Coloured Mothers": Gender and Race in South Africa', Natasha Distiller and Meg Samuelson detail aspects of the life of Krotoa, the first known interpreter of the Cape Colony.[5] As the Dutch settlement started, Krotoa was identified by Jan van Riebeeck and his wife Maria de la Queillerie as a KhoeKhoe person who had become conversant enough in Dutch to be a good interpreter between the colonialist and indigenous Khoe and San people. The clever little girl had picked up their language quickly; she could be an asset, if not a civilisation project. She became a personal servant in Jan van Riebeeck's houschold, giving her quite a close proximity not only to information about the colony but also the cultural differences between Dutch ways of life and those of indigenous people. It is not clear whether she stayed in the Van Riebeecks' home, but her access to the norms and cultural values of the Dutch was part of an intimate education in Whiteness.

Krotoa was like many indigenous girls and women converted by Dutch women to Calvinist Christianity. Her conversion was in part because of her employment and economic ties to the Van Riebeeck household, and in part a product of a broader missionary approach to the colonial project that used religion as a way for women to develop bonds and social ties across racial and class lines.

This particular brand of conservative Christianity was the beginning of the establishment of the Dutch Reformed Church, which, much later in the passage of South Africa's history, played a crucial role in the creation and institutionalisation of apartheid as an idea and a legal practice. The

NG Kerk, as it's most commonly referred to, provided theological explanations for why racism broadly, and apartheid in particular, were morally justifiable. Similarly, for Krotoa and other early converts to Christianity in the Cape Colony, religion – through appeals to the existence of a particular conception of God and a moral code that was put forward as divinely superior to the morality of indigenous people – was used to normalise practices of racism and oppression as proof that some people were better than others. This use of religion as a proxy for morality, and moral differences as a proxy for the right to treat some people as less human than others, was not unique to the Cape Colony. The Puritan conquest of North America fuelled slavery and racism in the making of the US. Catholic and Calvinist colonialism in South America sought to explain oppression away and get oppressed peoples to internalise the reasons for their own enslavement by accepting racism as morally allowed, sanctioned by the Christian God. In South Africa, entire theological doctrines of separateness were practised within churches and used the Bible as a reference for ideas like separate nations and chosen peoples.

Krotoa, no doubt, became an insider and outsider to Dutch sensibilities. She was literally inside a Dutch home as an enslaved person. She had learnt the language and taken on the religious practices. Yet she remained an outsider, never fully accepted, even when she married a European man. Always judged, especially upon the death of her husband. Her sense of belonging to the KhoeKhoe community, and particularly its cultural religious life, was questioned, as she went back and forth between two very different world views.

We can never know how much her own Christian conversion influenced an acceptance of colonial racism, but it is said to have made her own KhoeKhoe people suspicious of her loyalties: her own people were not sure if she could be trusted to do what was best for them. This question of loyalty was crucially important; although her formal role was as a translator, it also made her an informed power broker between the colony and indigenous people. Krotoa's role was not simply that of a technocratic functionary – she was in a position to influence the quality and outcomes of negotiations between indigenous and colonial role players. This could affect economic outcomes, the social norms adopted for running the 'colony' and slave trade, and political power distribution as more governance structures were established in the Cape.

Krotoa was a brown-skinned Khoe-girl-turned-woman caught between worlds. Her experience of isolation at the Cape Colony 400 years ago mirrors the collective alienation of Coloured people experiencing contemporary South Africa. There is a similar sense among Coloured communities that other historically disadvantaged communities interpret Coloured people's position during apartheid with suspicion – as Krotoa's people did with her. It is true that part of apartheid's divide-and-rule project involved giving some classified groups incrementally more benefits than others, from substantive issues like access to education or better access to clerical jobs to seemingly petty and quite subtly dehumanising micro rules like wider streets and more trees in Coloured communities. Shared language, in the form of Afrikaans, and religion, in various versions of Protestant religion and even provisions for Muslim religious practices, made for a cultural proximity to Whiteness. This made people who identified as Black in particular suspicious of the motives and solidarity of Coloured people during apartheid. The idea that people who ended up in Coloured communities chose the benefits the system offered was, and often continues to be, overshadowed by the circumstances, instability and social costs that came with it.

Like Krotoa, not all the circumstances that led to Coloured people's proximity to Whiteness were a choice. Krotoa was still a servant, and still a child, when her interactions began, vulnerable to many abuses of power. The abuses that Coloured people suffered in the form of classification that often disrupted their family lives, that forced them off their lands and into new communities with strangers, were part of their story too. Identities taken and names changed to suit Whiteness in the face of threats of violence cannot be dismissed because of perceived and real privileges. It was complex. It remains complex.

Of course, there were choices Krotoa made. An important one was marrying a Danish officer in the Cape Colony. Krotoa, it seems, married for love, and had children with a colonist. But even this description of romantic love, in a context fraught with power dynamics, is complex. This moment creates more than proximity: it creates familial ties to Whiteness and its oppressions. In Coloured communities, it is impossible for many to deny familial links to colonisers, which mirrors my own family's uncomfortable history: a love relationship between a late beneficiary of the colonial project, my German great-grandfather, and the Mostwana woman he married and had children with.

For Krotoa, marriage and a family was not a guarantee of acceptance, respect or even being shielded from racism and oppression. The day Theodore Dooms left his Motswana wife and mixed children for a White wife and privileged community, he not only destroyed the family structure but also caused the physical and social displacement of his family. After Theodore Dooms left for Pretoria, Mammila was forced to start over with her children. In the village of Dithakwaneng, tribal authorities described the place where Mammila and her children settled as an island, a self-contained place for this family that was neither here nor there. Even today, the tract of land is still known as an island in the village. They did not live with other Coloured, Motswana, Xhosa, or White communities in the area; instead, they found themselves in self-imposed exile as apartheid took root in the 1940s.

Krotoa's social and political isolation was sealed by her own exile when she was banished to Robben Island. After the death of her husband, she found herself isolated, shunned and judged by both the oppressed and the oppressors. Krotoa was displaced socially with no man to attach her identity to in a highly patriarchal context. Her children were seen in the colony as a representation of the humanity of people who were not simply White, and she faced the anger of her own people, who saw her as disloyal. It is not hard to imagine that these factors, compounded by the economic hardship of raising children alone, led her to drink, further reducing her desirability in social life.

Krotoa died on Robben Island at the age of 31. Her death – lonely, rejected and with no clear sense of belonging – is a stark reflection of the soul of Coloured people during apartheid and in post-apartheid South Africa. When observing the social ills like violence, gangsterism and alcohol abuse in Coloured communities, it is easy to forget that these are stories of pain and isolation: stories of brutal enslavement, the violent rape of women by White colonial and slave masters, the shame of being mixed, neither one nor the other, being stripped of land and self-determination, having identities and families torn apart by White oppressors, all while experiencing very little empathy from Black communities whose experiences of oppression were – at least during apartheid – worse than theirs.

When Coloured people talk about feeling the exclusion that comes with being neither Black nor White enough, what they are really saying is that – in the midst of the unfolding sins of colonialism and the crime against humanity that apartheid was – the difficult, complicated and painful stories of their lives are not seen, acknowledged or validated by others, regardless of the side from which one looks. The overwhelming similarity between Krotoa's story and the story of contemporary Coloured identity is that, in all the making and unmaking of South Africa, voices, experiences and meaningful complexities have been largely overlooked, erased and made a footnote in histories past and present.

Four centuries later, Krotoa's memory and complex legacy is being revisited.

In 2007, I discovered the online community Bruin-ou.com mentioned earlier. In the age of the internet, a new form of reclamation and connection began. Charles Ash, who grew up in KwaZulu-Natal, felt burdened with the idea that Coloured people needed – and deserved – more representation in the mainstream media and online spaces. Bruin-ou.com was a refreshing space that invited a wide variety of Coloured people to share their experiences of, and perspectives on, issues from politics and religion to music and sexuality. To say that it was a diverse community is a gross understatement. I, for one, was often pleasantly surprised by how many different people, with very different backgrounds, use of language, food preferences and historical roots, represented themselves as Coloured people. But what was truly more surprising was how much we shared. Somehow, whether it was a Coloured person from a highveld township with mixed heritage, a Namaqualand Coloured person with roots in what is now the Northern Cape, or a Cape Malay Coloured person with slave ancestry, there would always be cultural overlaps. Between the stories of pickled fish and hot cross buns on Good Friday, reminiscing about jazzing to old-school, classic African American songs, debates about 'gladde hare' versus natural hair and stories about religious parents who would make sure that we abided by all the rules while they hid their 'nips' of alcohol from us, these diverse communities, created through accidents of history, had found common culture.

I enjoyed every minute of being a part of that community. For its time, it was revolutionary – an online community that was an expressly political project to unite and acknowledge Coloured identity.

At about the same time, in 2008, I first heard about the Bruin Belange Inisiatief (BBI), led by activists for Coloured people's rights like Ivor Opperman and Danny Titus. This group was determined to convene different people in Coloured communities to mobilise around social and political issues of mutual interest, and to approach government and other stakeholders about the inclusion of Coloured people in policy and programmes that were needed to advance the development of Coloured communities. Engaging with questions about indigenous people's rights to land to questions of representation in pop culture, the BBI was an important moment of Coloured communities' taking action to be seen as valid and legitimate role players in South Africa's history and future.

As it happens with movements, the BBI's voice faded but was soon replaced by similar initiatives in different parts of the country. In 2018, amid calls by the Economic Freedom Fighters, a political party, and others to rename Cape Town International Airport in honour of the late Winnie Madikizela-Mandela, Coloured and KhoeKhoe activist groupings in the Western Cape revealed that they had been lobbying for the airport to be renamed after Krotoa. Parties like the Independent Civic Organisation of South Africa (ICOSA) and the Griqua royal house argued that Krotoa was not only the symbolic mother of the Khoisan nation, but a symbol of all indigenous Bushmen people who were struggling for legitimacy outside of the Coloured classification that apartheid imposed on them, and against the increasing invisibility of their history and culture as part of the story of South Africa. This was about a much broader frustration among people who, through colonialism and apartheid, have become part of Coloured identities at the expense of having the fullness and richness of their lives and heritage acknowledged.

Fortunately, history is taking a turn towards an opportunity for reclamation for the Khoekoe, San and other indigenous people who have lost their identity to the making of Colouredness. No longer accepting labels given through colonial encounters or apartheid classification, these communities are reclaiming their birthright as the First Nations of Southern Africa. The fight to reclaim Krotoa as a symbol of a nation lost in the archives of history is evolving into a fight to reclaim political, social and economic rights. Struggles for political representation in Parliament. Struggles for land, and the economic and cultural benefits it promises. Struggles for language, and for languages to be added to the bouquet of official languages South Africa has adopted. Struggles for self-determination.

Perhaps Coloured communities' futures cannot be clear unless we reclaim our individual and collective pasts. For some communities, this means reclaiming precolonial and pre-slave histories on these shores and in lands afar. For others, it means reclaiming identities, names, languages and even family relations lost in the violence of slave trades, land dispossessions and apartheid classifications.

For some, like me, it means reclaiming all our own Krotoas. Reclaiming the heroic men and women and their choices, struggles, mistakes and abilities in the face of the colonial and apartheid encounters that sought to erase them and relegate their contributions to history to nameless shadows. For me, in reclaiming Mammila Dooms, my great-great-grandmother, I have gained not only an ancestor whose existence personifies my legitimate claim to this land, but a heritage of struggle that emboldens me to fight for the future of this land for generations to come.

11. RECLAIMING THE PAST, REINVENTING THE FUTURE

Tessa Dooms

Recently, my family went on its own journey of reclamation. Over the years, whenever we have all been in Vryburg at the same time, usually for a funeral or other occasion, my father would take us around the town to show us important landmarks and tell us stories about our family's history. On the eve of my father's 80th birthday he had the inspired idea that my sisters, my mother and I accompany him to Vryburg for a day trip solely devoted to a historical tour to close all the gaps in the family story. He needed us to know where he came from, he explained. As he reflected on his life, he wanted us to have a full appreciation for who he was and, by extension, who we were. We jumped into the car and headed to Vryburg once again, on a mission to discover the history we didn't know.

We started at the last high school my father had attended in Vryburg, Colinda secondary school. The school is located in Blikkies, the Coloured township. As we drove in, we were met with a driveway that led to the main school hall, flanked by the playground on one side and the administration offices on the other. The reddish-brown sand contrasted with the dull grey bricks and muted environment. My father recalls that the school looked much the same as it did when he left it, after he repeated Form 1 (Grade 8) because, although he passed all the other subjects, he failed Afrikaans – and so failed the year. Afrikaans was not a language my father was fluent in as a child in Dithakwaneng. He was a Motswana boy in a village where Afrikaans was spoken casually by White neighbouring children, who often had a better grasp of Setswana than he cared to develop of Afrikaans.

The Colinda principal met with us too. As many did in Vryburg, he knew the Dooms name and lineage well. He welcomed us in and shared

Lesole Elliot Dooms at age 79 standing in front of his former school, Colinda secondary school in Vryburg, the town his family relocated to after being forcibly removed from their village, Dithakwaneng.

stories about how the school performs poorly today because of poor government support for teaching and learning, and an even worse social environment in learners' homes and communities. He cited poverty, violence and unemployment as factors destabilising the home environments of young Coloured people, even in post-apartheid South Africa, and how these derail and demotivate many learners from taking their education seriously or doing well enough to use it as a step out of their circumstances.

We visited the gravesites of my father's mother, Onica Dooms, and his grandparents, Johannes and Elizabeth Dooms. We stood over their gravesites together for the first time, recognising them as our connections to broken pasts and our foundations for better futures. It was a moment of gratitude for lives lived in service of all of us, in times when barely any opportunities for better lives were possible.

We stopped by my father's home, which he inherited from his mother. This was not the home he was raised in, but it was where he brought his young bride, my mother, to stay when they visited my grandmother – first as newlyweds, then as young parents. The small house boasts a large and dusty yard that, for my sisters, is filled with childhood memories of play and grandmother's love. My paternal grandmother Onica died in 1982, two years before my birth, robbing me of any experiences with her or in that home.

Margaret Dooms at the celebration
of her 100th birthday.

My father also made sure that we made a stop at the shop he worked at as a teenager – the shop where the police had arrested him for not having the correct 'dompas', as well as the police station at which he'd been detained. The shop is still trading; Aunt Margaret owned it until her death in 2018 at the age of 101. At the time of our visit it was still owned by Aunt Victoria, Aunt Margaret's daughter, but run by a shopkeeper.

The enormity of seventy-odd years of history was brought to life by this old building still in use. Still owned by our family. Still carrying the stories of a different time with such significance for our understanding of who we are. I could not help but wonder how many Coloured families have the benefit of this much history on which to anchor themselves. We went inside. Watched as my father marvelled at how similar and familiar this little shop building remains. The narrow doorway led to a small counter, with many grocery items stacked behind it and no room for independent shopping. In this very room, he experienced an arrest that would change his life and forever change his name from Lesole to Elliot.

Our journey led us to the home of my father's last living aunt, Aunt Mpedi, who at 93 can still be found sitting in her lounge, chatting, with all her faculties present. She often reminisces about her sisters, who have now all passed on, one who lived to almost a hundred and the two who lived to see beyond that. It was in this conversation, with Aunt Mpedi hunched over in her overalls and doek, whispering in her way, that I got my first glimpse into the importance of the village called Dithakwaneng.

The late Margaret Dooms (centre) with her sisters, the late Kelehetswe Rose Dooms and Mpedi Emily Dooms (95), at the funeral of their eldest sister Elizabeth Dooms.

When my father mentioned to his aunt and cousins that Dithakwaneng was our next stop, everyone seemed pleased, if not a little envious, that we were going and wished they could come along. There was a fondness in everyone's voices when they spoke of Dithakwaneng that I do not re-member people using to describe Vryburg. This was strange, because the first time I had ever heard the name had been a few weeks earlier when my father had first suggested the trip. Although the conversation was about whether the roads would be good enough to travel to the village, my sisters and I were determined to make sure we included this destination in our trip. What a wise decision that turned out to be.

We got into the car again with anticipation of what we would find in Dithakwaneng. Google Maps alerted us that it was only 20 kilometres away. My father, however, remembered that the land our family inhabited in the village was not near the part of the village where the chief lives, although that is where our GPS took us. Emboldened, perhaps, by being home, my father drove straight into the chief's homestead and struck up a conversation with a member of the chieftaincy, explaining who we were and what we were searching for. The man immediately recognised the name Dooms and directed us to the land we were looking for, although it was no longer formally part of Dithakwaneng.

Off we went on a route that led us down a gravel road, flanked by farms, the path to my father's childhood memories. It was the first time he'd travelled this road in seven decades, yet was sure it was the road to his Dithakwaneng. Slowly, the picture began to form in my mind of the gap that this part of the journey filled in my father's history. He often spoke about growing up as a child in a farming area. Explained how he could not go to school until he was eight or nine years old, because children first needed to be strong enough to endure the 10 kilometres run to school, barefoot. As we passed fields, bush and rivers, he told us that this was the place his great-grandmother Mammila had moved the family to when his German grandfather had left for Whiter pastures. This was where Mammila rebuilt her family. Where he spent his childhood in the 1940s and 1950s, before apartheid laws transformed the landscape and the country.

With great sadness, my father recounted how, while he was playing with his White friends at the river one day, their parents had come and dragged them away from their game. He never saw his White friends again. He didn't understand in that moment what he or his siblings could possibly have done to cause this. Retrospectively, he understood that it was the first forced removal he would witness.

As we drove along the gravel road that began to feel endless, it seemed impossible to spot the land he was raised on. In the years since his family's

Lesole Elliot Dooms returning to Dithakwaneng for the first time in over sixty years after the apartheid government forcibly removed his family from their land.

displacement, the land had come to belong to mostly White farmers. But my father remained steadfast. We had not come this far not to find the large rocks and tall trees of his childhood that signalled home.

As we drove, my father peering over the steering wheel for familiar signs and my sisters and I crammed into the back seat, watching a foreign landscape go by that we were meant to be connected to, my father remembered a clue. They had Afrikaner neighbours who owned a farm called Naples. If we found Naples, he thought, we would have found home. Just minutes after he'd mentioned the name, in the distance a White-fenced farmhouse appeared. We stopped; my father stood at the gate until the owner, a White Afrikaner man, came to the gate to confirm that we had indeed found Naples. His family had not owned the farm 70 years ago, but he knew the man who had lived there before, a man now in his eighties. That man was one of the friends snatched away from my father at the riverbank many years ago. We all gasped.

It was unthinkable that a place my father remembered from when he was a child stood in front of us, intact, a landmark that gave us the assurance that we had indeed found my father's childhood home. He had finally brought to it the family he'd created in Johannesburg in the face of displacement and the stripping away of many parts of his identity. We were standing on his land. Our land. The land my father's aunts have been fighting to reclaim for many years. The land that raised the Dooms family to be a large, connected family of love and legends. We were not there to reclaim the land that day, but it certainly felt that we had reclaimed just a small part of our history and identity. My father could fully reclaim his childhood. Reclaim his joys. Reclaim his story. Reclaim his name.

When he was 16, the structural violence of the population registration process stole my father's name. Years later, the Group Areas Act stole his land and removed him from his home. But in those moments, in his Dithakwaneng, in the smallest of victories, we were able to introduce Lesole the Motswana child to Elliot the Coloured man. For Coloured people, the reclamation of identity is indeed a necessary part of shaping a more just and reconciled South Africa. My father took back his name, and as we returned to the life he had created in Johannesburg, he took Lesole with him this time: he asked us to start calling him Lesole.

If we truly believe in redress, it must include tending to the need for belonging and legitimacy that Coloured and indigenous communities across South Africa so desperately need. It can no longer be acceptable that Coloured and indigenous people feel underrepresented, misrepresented, or marginalised in our society. Yes, there is a need for difficult conversations. For honest accounts of the mistrust, hurt, harm, rejection and racism that cast shadows over Black communities' ability to unite and fight for the equality and humanity that continues to elude so many. That, however, must be done of we are to progress. If we choose a future that continues to marginalise any groups, we are only choosing to recreate the past. As Coloured people set out to reclaim our place in society, we continue to hope that the people of South Africa will indeed look beyond the classification and see the beauty and value of the cultures that Coloured people bring to the story of South Africa.

For Coloured communities, the work of reclaiming is crucial. It will take many forms.

The reclaiming of language and food as cultural expressions and shared experiences that bind us.

The reclaiming of music in ways that remind us about what connects us rather than what divides us. As a place of meaning-making for community, joy, hope and security. Music as a way of telling our stories and manifesting our aspirations. The kinds of music that connect us to other communities of struggle across the world, that make us feel more seen and less alone.

There is a need to reclaim our intersecting identities: our femininities and masculinities. To reflect deeply on why we have needed people to show up in particular ways as women and men. How those identities and expectations have limited our expressions of self in the world, empowering some and disempowering many who either fit the negative tropes or rebelled against the expectations too often.

Coloured communities must reclaim our political lives. Acknowledging that the political power of colonial and apartheid systems shaped us against our will, we must determine to take back our power to self-identify. Our power to shake off the power of old classifications, reappropriating if not reimagining them.

Our reclamation will never be complete without our ability to reclaim our people, to reclaim ourselves. Reclaiming cultural artefacts like language, music, food and politics has far less meaning if we do not reclaim ourselves. We need to reclaim our forefathers, and especially our foremothers. The people whose histories of love, pain, struggle, uncertainty, regret and courage pull threads from slave ships and nomadic treks through to apartheid registration offices and stolen land. Threads that are unwittingly tied to our hearts and minds as the ghosts of colonialism and the ruins of apartheid are the canvas on which we try to build our present-day lives and imagine our children's futures.

It is the names of Black mothers, the lost surnames of our fathers, the forgotten villages of our grandmothers and the fractured families that emerged from the violence of classification that we must fight most deliberately to reclaim. Not to embolden our already legitimate and real victimisation, but to own, understand, acknowledge and value the beautiful tapestries of humans who make up the colourful fabric of our communities now and into the future.

Reclamation is the beginning of a journey to a new future of Coloured identity. Taking back our power to be and belong opens the possibility of considering ourselves as the ones who can make the most of the future. Daring to invent the future is as necessary as boldly facing the past. Without an intentional intervention of the future, the best predictor of the future is the past. A call to reinvent the future is one not to be satisfied with creating a future that repeats past mistakes or inflicts past pain, but invents a future of impossibilities. Impossible progress. Impossible joy. Impossible stability. Impossible security. The impossible made possible only because Coloured communities determine that we are the makers of a future that truly is our ancestors' wildest dreams, and surpasses our wildest dreams too.

May every Coloured community, every Coloured mother, father, friend, child and neighbour find the courage and will to reclaim what we need for today and reinvent what we deserve for tomorrow.

NOTES

1. SOCIAL ORPHANS: NOT BLACK ENOUGH, NOT WHITE ENOUGH

1. Posel, D. 2001. What's in a Name? Racial Classifications under Apartheid and Their Afterlife. *Transformation* 47: 50–74.
2. Western, cited in Platzky, L. 1985. *The Surplus People: Forced Removals in South Africa*. Johannesburg: Ravan Press, p. 100.
3. Mabin, A. 1992. Comprehensive Segregation: The Origins of the Group Areas Act and its Planning Apparatuses. *Journal of Southern African Studies* 18(2): 405–429
4. Angelou, M. 1986. *All God's Children Need Travelling Shoes*. New York: Vintage Books.

2. LUCKY COLOUREDS AND FORGOTTEN ANCESTORS

1. Morrison, T. 1970, renewed 1998. *The Bluest Eye*. New York: Vintage International.
2. Adhikari, M. 2006. Hope, Fear, Shame, Frustration: Continuity and Change in the Expression of Coloured Identity in White Supremacist South Africa, 1910–1994. *Journal of Southern African Studies* 32(3): 467–487. DOI: 10.1080/03057070600829542.
3. Ibid.
4. Adhikari, M. (Ed.). 2009. *Burdened by Race: Coloured Identities in Southern Africa*. Cape Town: UCT Press, p. xi.
5. Christopher, AJ. 2002. 'To Define the Indefinable': Population Classification and the Census in South Africa. *Area* 34(4): 401–408. http://www.jstor.org/stable/20004271
6. Posel, D. 2001. What's in a Name? Racial Classifications under Apartheid and Their Afterlife. *Transformation* 47: 50–74.
7. Union of South Africa, House of Assembly Debates, 13 March 1950, in Posel, What's in a Name?, p. 55.
8. SAB NTS 1764 vol 2, 53/276, SNA to Secretary, Murraysburg Boere en Wolwerks Vereeniging, May 3, 1951, re 'Invordering van Agterstallige Naturellebelasting', in Posel, What's in a Name?, p. 55.
9. Union of South Africa, in Posel, What's in a Name?, p. 56.
10. Ibid.
11. South African History Archive. n.d. An Appalling 'Science'. https://sthp.saha.org.za/memorial/articles/an_appalling_science.htm
12. TAB TPD 886/1956, The Case of John Leach Lambert; Evidence from Johannes Marti Mante: 12, in Posel, What's in a Name?, p. 62.

13. TAB TPD 886/1956, The Case of Henry Abel Makue; Evidence from Makue: 12, in Posel, What's in a Name?, p. 62.
14. TAB TPD 886/1956, The Case of John Leach Lambert, in Posel, What's in a Name?, p. 62.
15. Ibid.
16. TAB TPD 886/1956, The Case of Henry Abel Makue; Evidence from Martin James Damons: 1, in Posel, What's in a Name?, p. 62.
17. Camissa People. 2016. The Story of the First Two 'Coloured' Governors at the Cape – Simon & Willem. 17 May 2016. https://camissapeople.wordpress.com/2016/05/17/the-story-of-the-first-two-Coloured-governors-at-the-cape-simon-willem/
18. A Coloured Tapestry. https://www.facebook.com/Colouredtapestry
19. Ibid.
20. The Making of a Runaway. https://www.youtube.com/watch?v=6H54yny_5cU
21. South African History Online. n.d. Pondoland. https://www.sahistory.org.za/place/pondoland
22. Ledwaba, L. 2018. amaHlubi's Battle Against Colonial Legacy Heads to High Court. *Mail & Guardian*, 19 October 2018. https://mg.co.za/article/2018-10-19-00-amahlubis-battle-against-colonial-legacy-heads-to-high-court/
23. Hadebe, SB. 1992. The History of the amaHlubi Tribe in the iziBongo of its Kings. Master of Arts thesis, University of Natal-Durban. https://researchspace.ukzn.ac.za/xmlui/bitstream/handle/10413/1015/Hadebe_Selby_Bongani_1992.pdf?sequence=1&isAllowed=y
24. Mohale, MR. 2014. Khelobedu Cultural Evolution Through Oral Tradition. Master of Arts thesis, University of South Africa. http://uir.unisa.ac.za/bitstream/handle/10500/14467/STUDENT%20NO%20%2044542356.pdf?sequence=1
25. Baloyi, P. 2021. Royal Council Claims They Had no Access to Princess Masalanabo Modjadji for Training on Monarch Duties. *SABC News*, 19 May 2021. https://www.sabcnews.com/sabcnews/royal-council-claims-they-had-no-access-to-princess-masalanabo-modjadji-for-training-on-monarch-duties/
26. *Matiwane v President of the Republic of South Africa and Others* (2047/2018) [2019] ZAECMHC 23; [2019] 3 All SA 209 (ECM) (16 May 2019). http://www.saflii.org/za/cases/ZAECMHC/2019/23.html
27. Davie, E. n.d. People Are Living There – A Story of Resilience. Hermanus History Society. https://www.hermanus-history-society.co.za/2019/09/11/people-are-living-there-a-story-of-resilience/
28. https://www.imdb.com/title/tt4428854/

3. NO, TREVOR NOAH ISN'T COLOURED

1. Noah, T. 2016. *Born a Crime: Stories from a South African Childhood*. New York, NY: Spiegel & Grau Publishers.
2. Irby, DJ. 2014. Revealing Racial Purity Ideology: Fear of Black–White Intimacy as a Framework for Understanding School Discipline in Post-Brown Schools. *Educational Administration Quarterly* 50(5): 783–795.
3. Distiller, N & Samuelson, M. 2005. 'Denying the Coloured Mother': Gender and Race in South Africa. *L'Homme* 16(2): 28–46.

4. Ibid.
5. Barnard, A. 1992. *Hunters and Herders of Southern Africa*. University of Edinburgh: Cambridge University Press, pp. 176–198.
6. Rory, C. 2003. The Black Woman – With White Parents. *The Guardian*, 17 March 2003. https://www.theguardian.com/theguardian/2003/mar/17/features11.g2
7. The British Broadcast Corporation. 2003. 'Black Afrikaner' Story to Become Film. *BBC News*, 29 May 2003.
8. South African History Online (SAHO). 1950. Population Registration Act. https://www.sahistory.org.za/sites/default/files/archive-files2/leg19500707.028.020.030.pdf
9. Stone, J. 2004. *When She Was White: The True Story of a Family Divided by Race*. New York, NY: Miramax Books/Hyperion.
10. Translated from Afrikaans to English, this means 'Caged girl'.

4. MUSICAL ROOTS

1. Mckinnon, A. 2010. The Sociology of Religion, in Turner, S. (Ed.). *The New Blackwell Companion to Sociology of Religion*. Oxford: Wiley-Blackwell, pp. 33–51.
2. Folan, K. 2015. Themes and Characteristics of Afro-American Slave Songs. https://www.researchgate.net/publication/274893394_Themes_and_Characteristics_of_Afro-American_Slave_Songs
3. Matthews, A. 2016. Looking Back Is Moving Forward: The Legacy of Negro Spirituals in the Civil Rights Movement. *International Journal of English Language, Literature, and Humanities* IV: 37–43.
4. Du Bois, WEB & Edwards, BH. 2007. *The Souls of Black Folk*. Oxford: Oxford University Press.
5. Stanley, B. 2011. Edinburgh and World History. *Studies in World Christianity* 17(1): 72–91.
6. Mason, JE. 2007. 'Mannenberg': Notes on the Making of an Icon and Anthem. *African Studies Quarterly* 9(4): 25–46.
7. Raph, T. 1986. *The American Song Treasury*. Minneola, NY: Dover Publications.
8. South African History Online. n.d. The Cape Minstrels: Origins and Evolution of Tweede Nuwe Jaar (Second New Year) in the Cape. https://www.sahistory.org.za/article/cape-minstrels-origins-and-evolution-tweede-nuwe-jaar-second-new-year-cape
9. Martin, D-C. 1999. *Coon Carnival: New Year in Cape Town: Past to Present*. Cape Town and Johannesburg: David Philip Publishers.
10. Haupt, A. 2001. Black Thing: Hip-Hop Nationalism, 'Race' and Gender in Prophets of da City and Brasse vannie Kaap, in Erasmus, Z. (Ed.). *Coloured by History, Shaped by Place: New Perspectives on Coloured Identities*. Cape Town: Kwela Books and South African History Online.

5. *HUISKOS*: IDENTITY ON A PLATE

1. Benayoun, M. n.d. Bobotie. 196 Flavours. https://www.196flavors.com/south-africa-bobotie/
2. Posel, D. 2001. What's in a Name? Racial Classifications under Apartheid and Their Afterlife. *Transformation* 47: 63.

3. Claasens, HW. 2003. Die Geskiedenis van Boerekos 1652–1806. Doctoral thesis, University of Pretoria. https://repository.up.ac.za/handle/2263/25523
4. Ibid., p. 354.
5. Ibid., p. 355.
6. Ibid., p. 356.
7. Musgrave, P. 2020. The Beautiful, Dumb Dream of McDonald's Peace Theory. *Foreign Policy*, November 26, 2020. https://foreignpolicy.com/2020/11/26/mcdonalds-peace-nagornokarabakh-friedman/
8. Korsten, L. 2018. What Led to World's Worst Listeriosis Outbreak in South Africa. *The Conversation: Africa*, March 12, 2018. https://theconversation.com/what-led-to-worlds-worst-listeriosis-outbreak-in-south-africa-92947
9. Heil, A. n.d. 'I Braai for a Living,' Says Jan Braai. *CapeTownMagazine.com*, https://www.capetownmagazine.com/jan-braai and South African History Online. n.d. Heritage Day, Braai Day or Shaka Day: Whose Heritage Is it Anyway? https://www.sahistory.org.za/article/heritage-day-braai-day-or-shaka-day-whose-heritage-it-anyway
10. Engelbrecht, S. 2005. *African Salad: A Portrait of South Africans at Home.* Leominster: Day One Publishing.
11. Ibid.

6. *AWÊ! MA SE KIND*: FINDING OUR MOTHER TONGUES.

1. South African History Online. n.d. Bessie Amelia Head. https://www.sahistory.org.za/people/bessie-amelia-head
2. The British Empire. n.d. Bantam. https://www.britishempire.co.uk/maproom/bantam.htm
3. South African History Online. n.d. Autshumao (Herry the Strandloper). https://www.sahistory.org.za/people/autshumao-herry-strandloper
4. Robertson, D. n.d. Khaik Ana Ma Koukoa of the Goringhaicona. The First Fifty Years Project. http://e-family.co.za/ffy/g17/p17309.htmKriel, M. 2013. Loose Continuity: The Post-Apartheid Afrikaans Language Movement in Historical Perspective. Doctoral thesis, London School of Economics and Political Science. http://etheses.lse.ac.uk/863/
5. Giliomee, H. 2004. The Rise and Possible Demise of Afrikaans as a Public Language. *Nationalism and Ethnic Politics* 10(1): 25–58.
6. Ibid.
7. Ibid., pp. 10–11.
8. Giliomee, H. 2018. *Die Afrikaners*. Cape Town: Tafelberg, p. 113.
9. Van der Ross, R. 2015. *In Our Own Skins: A Political History of the Coloured People.* Cape Town: Jonathan Ball Publishers, p. 111.
10. Ibid., pp. 127–129.
11. Esau, C. 2017. Die Impak wat 16 Junie 1976 op my Lewe Gehad Het, in Carsten, W & Le Cordeur, M. (Eds.). *Ons Kom van Vêr*. Cape Town: Naledi, pp. 171–181.
12. Titus, D. 2017. Afrikaans Boek van Bruin Kant: Taal en Identiteit op die Afrikaans Werf, in Carsten & Le Cordeur, *Ons Kom van Vêr*, pp. 196–197.
13. Boezak, W. 2017. Die Khoi-San as Afrikaanse Gemeenskap, Gister, Vandaag en Môre, in Carsten & Le Cordeur, *Ons Kom van Vêr*, p. 114.

14. Allison, S & Seiboko, R. 2020. Saving Southern Africa's Oldest Languages. *Mail & Guardian*, 20 July 2020. https://mg.co.za/africa/2020-07-20-saving-southern-africas-oldest-languages/
15. Trilingual Dictionary of Kaaps (TDK). http://dwkaaps.co.za/ and Haupt, A. 2021. The First-ever Dictionary of South Africa's Kaaps Language Has Launched – Why it Matters. *The Conversation: Africa*, August 29, 2021. https://theconversation.com/the-first-ever-dictionary-of-south-africas-kaaps-language-has-launched-why-it-matters-165485
16. Hamilton College. n.d. What Is Ebonics? https://academics.hamilton.edu/government/dparis/govt375/spring98/multiculturalism/ebonics/whatis.html and Rickford, JR. 1996. Ebonics Notes and Discussion. Stanford University. https://web.stanford.edu/~rickford/ebonics/EbonicsExamples.html

8. OF MEN, *MANNE* AND 'MOFFIES'

1. Adhikari, M, cited in Perkins, CS. 2015. Coloured Men, *Moffies*, and Meanings of Masculinity in South Africa, 1910–1960. Doctoral thesis, University of Virginia. https://libra2.lib.virginia.edu/downloads/v979v357h?filename=Perkins_Cody_2015.pdf
2. Smuts, JC. Africa and Some World Problems: Including The Rhodes Memorial Lectures Delivered in Michaelmas Term, 1929. Oxford: The Clarendon Press, 1930: 93, in Perkins, CS. 2015. Coloured Men, *Moffies*, and Meanings of Masculinity in South Africa, 1910–1960. Doctoral thesis, University of Virginia. https://libra2.lib.virginia.edu/downloads/v979v357h?filename=Perkins_Cody_2015.pdf
3. Perkins, CS. 2015. Coloured Men, *Moffies*, and Meanings of Masculinity in South Africa, 1910–1960. Doctoral thesis, University of Virginia. https://libra2.lib.virginia.edu/downloads/v979v357h?filename=Perkins_Cody_2015.pdf
4. Erasmus, Z. 2001. Introduction: Re-imagining Coloured Identities in Post-Apartheid, in Erasmus, Z. (Ed.). 2001. *Coloured by History, Shaped by Place: New Perspectives on Coloured Identities*. Cape Town: Kwela Books and cited in Perkins, Coloured Men, *Moffies*, and Meanings of Masculinity in South Africa, 1910–1960, p. 9.
5. *The Sun*, 10 December 1943, in Perkins, Coloured Men, *Moffies*, and Meanings of Masculinity in South Africa, 1910–1960, p. 128.
6. *Cape Standard*, 1 February 1944, in Perkins, Coloured Men, *Moffies*, and Meanings of Masculinity in South Africa, 1910–1960, p. 128.
7. Perkins, Coloured Men, *Moffies*, and Meanings of Masculinity in South Africa, 1910–1960, p. 182.
8. Ashwin Willemse Walks off SuperSport Set. https://www.youtube.com/watch?v=I5FepA12BVA
9. Qukula, Q. 2018. Willemse Wants to Restore his Dignity at SAHRC Hearing on Walkout. *CapeTalk*, 10 July 2018. https://www.capetalk.co.za/articles/310987/watch-ashwin-willemse-wants-to-restore-his-dignity-at-sahrc-hearing-on-walkout
10. Ratele, K. 2013. *Liberating Masculinities*. Cape Town: HSRC Press, p. 12.
11. Glaster, C. 1998. Swines, Hazels and the Dirty Dozen: Masculinity, Territoriality and the Youth Gangs of Soweto, 1960–1976. *Journal of Southern African Studies* 24(4): 719–736.
12. Wegner, L. 2016. Meaning and Purpose in the Occupations of Gang-involved Young Men in Cape Town. *South African Journal of Occupational Therapy* 46(1): 53–58.

13. Anderson, B. 2009. 'I'm not so into Gangs Anymore. I've Started Going to Church Now': Coloured Boys Resisting Gangster Masculinity. *Agenda* 23(80): 55–67.

14. Gottzén, L, Bjørnholt, M & Boonzaier, F. (Eds.). 2021. *Men, Masculinities and Intimate Partner Violence*. London and New York: Routledge.

15. Anderson, 'I'm not so into gangs anymore. I've started going to church now'.

16. Gear, S & Ngubeni, K. 2003. Your Brother, My Wife: Sex and Gender Behind Bars. *South African Crime Quarterly* 4, June.

17. Ratele, *Liberating Masculinities*, p. 23.

18. Perkins, Coloured Men, *Moffies*, and Meanings of Masculinity in South Africa, 1910–1960, p. 159.

19. South African History Online. n.d. Gayle: The Language of Apartheid South Africa's Gay Underground. https://www.sahisto ry.org.za/article/gayle-language-apartheid-south-africas-gay-underground

20. Khan, JF. 2020. *Khamr: The Makings of a Waterslams*. Johannesburg: Jacana Media.

21. Ibid., p. 162.

9. ON THE MARGINS: COLOURED POLITICAL IDENTITY IN SOUTH AFRICA

1. Delius, P & Trapido, S. 1982. Inboekselings and Oorlams: The Creation and Transformation of a Servile Class. *Journal of Southern African Studies* 8(2): 230.

2. Ibid.

3. Ibid., p. 241.

4. Wheelwright, CA. 1925. Native Administration in Zululand. *Journal of the Royal African Society* 24(94): 92–99.

5. Ballard, CM. 1980. John Dunn and Cetshwayo: The Material Foundations of Political Power in the Zulu Kingdom, 1857–1878. *The Journal of African History* 21(1): 75–91.

6. Venter, AJ. 1974. *Coloured: A Profile of Two Million South Africans*. Cape Town: Human & Rousseau, p. 280.

7. Ibid., p. 282.

8. Ibid., jacket.

9. Ibid., p. 282.

10. Ibid., p. 214.

11. Adhikari, M. 2009. From Narratives of Miscegenation to Post-modernist Reimaging, in Adhikari, M. (Ed.). *Burdened by Race: Coloured Identities in Southern Africa*. Cape Town: UCT Press.

12. Adhikari, M. (Ed.). 2009. Burdened by Race: Coloured Identities in Southern Africa. Cape Town: UCT Press.

13. Lee, C. 2009. 'A Generous Dream, but Difficult to Realize': The Making of the Anglo-African Community of Nyasaland, 1929–1940, in Adhikari, Burdened by Race: Coloured Identities in Southern Africa.

14. Giliomee, H. 2014. The Rise and Possible Demise of Afrikaans as a Public Lan¬guage. PRAESA Occasional Papers No. 14, University of Cape Town.

15. South African History Online. n.d. African People's Organisation (APO). https://www.sahistory.org.za/article/african-peoples-organisation-apo

16. Van der Ross, R. 2015. *In Our Own Skins: A Political History of the Coloured People*. Cape Town: Jonathan Ball Publishers, pp. 69–110.

17. Ibid., pp. 115–118.

18. South African History Online. n.d. South African Coloured People Organisation (SACPO). https://www.sahistory.org.za/article/south-african-coloured-people-organisation-sacpo

19. Gatvol, The Movement. https://www.facebook.com/profile.php?id=100064372644462

20. Interview with Peter Rafferty, 13 February 2022.

21. Pijoos, I. 2020. 'Nathaniel Julius Was Caught in Crossfire Between Cops and Gang' – Premier Makhura. *Sowetan Live*, 28 August 2020. https://www.sowetan-live.co.za/news/south-africa/2020-08-28-nathaniel-julius-was-caught-in-crossfire-between-cops-and-gang-premier-makhura/

22. Interview with Peter Rafferty, 13 February 2022.

23. Monaghan, R. 2004. 'One Merchant, One Bullet': The Rise and Fall of PAGAD. *Low Intensity Conflict & Law Enforcement* 12(1): 1–19.

24. Githahu, M. 2023. Pagad Leader Launches Attack on LGBTQIA+ Community amid Pride Month Celebrations. *IOL*, February 16, 2023. https://www.iol.co.za/capeargus/news/pagad-leader-launches-attack-on-lgbtqia-community-amid-pride-month-celebrations-9a1a8b35-ac0d-48e1-8875-b864144e09bb

25. Patriotic Alliance. 2013, amended 2014. The Constitution of the Patriotic Alliance. http://nebula.wsimg.com/fb14cd633db384529147cf3cdb6bec36?AccessKeyId=3F779A56590DC431C422&disposition=0&alloworigin=1

26. AmaShabalala, M. 2020. 'I Do not Play with Power': How Gayton McKenzie 'Captured' Key Joburg Dept. *Sunday Times*, 25 October 2020. https://www.times-live.co.za/sunday-times/news/2020-10-25-i-do-not-play-with-power-how-gayton-mckenzie-captured-key-joburg-dept/

27. Independent Electoral Commission. n.d. Municipal Election Results. https://results.elections.org.za/dashboards/lge/#

28. Seeletsa, M. 2023. Kenny Kunene to Evict Residents from Buildings During his Two-day Stint as Joburg Mayor. *The Citizen*, 15 May 2023. https://www.citizen.co.za/news/kenny-kunene-to-evict-residents-as-joburg-mayor/

29. Felix, J. 2021. Success Behind Cape Coloured Congress Based on People 'not Accepting Fate, Standing up' – Adams. *News24*, 28 December 2021. https://www.news24.com/news24/southafrica/news/success-behind-cape-coloured-congress-based-on-people-not-accepting-fate-standing-up-adams-20211228

30. Interview with Peter Rafferty, 13 February 2022.

31. South African History Archive. n.d. Origins of the United Democratic Front. https://www.saha.org.za/udf/origins.htm

32. Van Wyk, C. 2004. *Shirley, Goodness and Mercy*. Johannesburg: Picador Africa, p. 236.

33. Erasmus, Z, quoted in Strauss, H. 2009. '[C]onfused About Being Coloured': Creolisation and Coloured Identity in Chris van Wyk's *Shirley, Goodness and Mercy*, in Adhikari, *Burdened by Race*, p. 38.

34. Besten, M. 2009. 'We Are the Original Inhabitants of this Land': Khoe-San Identity in Post-apartheid South Africa, in Adhikari, Burdened by Race, p. 146.

35. South African History Online (SAHO). 1950. Population Registration Act. https://www.sahistory.org.za/sites/default/files/archive-files2/leg19500707.028.020.030.pdf

36. Ibid.

37. Besten, M. 2009. 'We Are the Original Inhabitants of this Land': Khoe-San Identity in post-apartheid South Africa, in Adhikari, *Burdened by Race*, p. 146.

38. South African Government. 2019. Traditional and Khoi-San Leadership Act 3 of 2019. https://www.gov.za/documents/traditional-and-khoi-san-leadership-act-3-2019-28-nov-2019-0000

39. Traditional and Khoi San Leadership Bill [B23-15]: Public Hearings Day One, 2 February 2016. Parliamentary Monitoring Group. https://pmg.org.za/committee-meeting/21968/

40. Parliamentary Monitoring Group. 2016. Traditional and Khoi San Leadership Bill [B23-15]: Public Hearings Day One, 2 February 2016. https://pmg.org.za/committee-meeting/21968/

41. Parliamentary Monitoring Group. 2016. Traditional and Khoi-San Leadership Bill Final Draft: Western Cape Public Hearings, 30 November 2016. https://pmg.org.za/committee-meeting/23801/

42. Department of Cooperative Governance. Minister Nkosazana Dlamini Zuma Appoints Commission on Khoi-San Matters. South African Government, 25 October 2021. https://www.gov.za/speeches/minister-nkosazana-dlamini-zuma-appoints-commission-khoi-san-matters-25-oct-2021-0000

43. Constitutional Court of South Africa. 2023. *Mogale and Others v Speaker of the National Assembly and Others* [2023] ZACC 14, heard on 23 February 2023, decided on 30 May 2023.

10. RECLAIMING KROTOA

1. Mellet, PT. 2020. *The Lie of 1652: A Decolonised History of Land.* Cape Town: Tafelberg.

2. Barnard, A. 2008. Ethnographic Analogy and the Reconstruction of Early Khoekhoe Society. *Southern African Humanities* 20(1): 61–75.

3. Landau, P. 2010. *Popular Politics in the History of South Africa*, 1400–1948. New York, NY: Cambridge University Press.

4. Al Jazeera. 2017. Outrage over Helen Zille's Colonialism Tweets. *Aljazeera*, 16 March 2017. https://www.aljazeera.com/amp/news/2017/3/16/outrage-over-helen-zilles-colonialism-tweets

5. Distiller, N & Samuelson, M. 2005. 'Denying the Coloured Mother': Gender and Race in South Africa. *L'Homme* 16(2): 28–46.

ACKNOWLEDGEMENTS

To Lynsey, my partner in this project – thank you for saying yes without skipping a beat. Thank you for trusting me and this process; even pushing through our insecurities, fears and my eventual floods of tears writing this book. I'm honoured to share the space of my first book with an internationally acclaimed writer who I know will bless the world with many more books for years to come.

To Nkanyezi Tshabalala and Sibongile Machika, our partners in publishing – we could not have started or completed this journey without you. Nkanyezi, this book would literally not exist without your vision and passion for telling uniquely African stories. I salute you and hope your role in African publishing grows rapidly. Sibongile, you stepped in to take us to the finish line. Thank you for taking time to build relationships and comradery with us. You have guarded our vision fiercely and for this I am deeply appreciative. Your patience, support and care gave a fledgling and unsure writer a chance to test her skills in a safe and warm environment. Thank you, many times over.

To my friends, my tribe, my humans who fill my WhatsApps, home and heart with unending support and love – thank you. All of you, even those unnamed. A few special shoutouts must go to Pearl Pillay, for believing in us, from pancakes to signing and completion. To the Youth Lab WhatsApp group, you are all part of this journey with cheers and encouragement that gave Lynsey and me confidence daily. To Toby Fayoyin, my partner in writing the stories of African people, thank you for reading every word, making them better and making me a better writer. Your commitment to words is infectious and your own books will show just how talented you are.

I have the most amazing family in the world. Being a Dooms, a child of Elliot and Irene, has always been a joy, but your allowing me to tell the story of our family has been an honour that you as my parents and sisters, Ruth and Phoebe, have given me, which I do not take lightly. I hope I have done our story justice. To Kaylin, Seth-lynn, Luke and Gabby – I hope this book reminds you that your dreams are forever valid. Also, Gabs, thanks for being the book's editor before the editor.

Finally, to the many people whose stories I have had a privilege to tell in this book, thank you for trusting me to hold space for you. May your stories heal and build this nation for years to come.

Tessa Dooms

In writing this book, I was struck and saddened by how much loss, rejection and orphanhood are a part of the Coloured story. My Coloured story has never been simple, but I have never been at sea or wandered the wilderness because my roots are deep and thick, thanks to my family. Our clan has kept us all grounded, shielded us from the worst of South Africa and prepared for us for the best. My grandparents Martha and Sidney built their home on a foundation of love and generosity and their 12 children each built on that, spreading it on a long table each Christmas and wrapping us all in it. Sometimes we squirm and sometimes we hug too tight, but we are always home. To each of you, from the youngest to the eldest, I am eternally indebted.

I am deeply grateful to the people who shared their stories with me, turning historical facts and social theories into lived experiences in which everyone could see themselves. To Leaveil Ward for your vulnerability, Peter Rafferty for your candour, Rasheed Pandy for your unbridled love of food, Heloise May, Anelle May and Philecia Figaji for the wash and blow and the open hearts, and Ruth Thomas for your story of love despite the loss, and Cheryl Carolus for the unflinching and empathetic look back at our and your past.

And to Tessa Dooms, for your early-morning faith and late-night patience and your deep belief in something bigger than both of us, bigger than this book. What a joy it is to watch you soar.

Lynsey Ebony Chutel

ABOUT THE AUTHORS

MALWANDLA RIKHOTSO

Lynsey Ebony Chutel is a Johannesburg-based journalist and writer. She is a reporter with *The New York Times*, has worked for South African and international news outlets, and has done stints in scriptwriting for an international Emmy Awards-nominated news satire show. Her short fiction has been shortlisted for the Afritondo Short Story Prize.

She grew up between Eldorado Park, Soweto and northern KwaZulu-Natal. She holds a Master of Arts degree in journalism from Columbia University and international relations from the University of the Witwa-tersrand. She was a recipient of the 2017 and 2018 African Great Lakes Reporting Initiative Fellowship by the International Women's Media Foundation. She was named as one of *Mail & Guardian*'s 200 Young South

189

Africans in 2015. Her reporting and storytelling have focused on gender, identity, culture and politics in a changing South Africa, and across the African continent. She makes her own pasta and grows her own herbs but has yet to keep an orchid alive.

Tessa Dooms is a director at the Rivonia Circle. She is a sociologist, development practitioner and political analyst. Having started her career in academia, Tessa has worked in diverse sectors including government, NGOs and the private sector, where she did work that aligns the objectives of various institutions and programmes with developmental objectives for the advancement of Africa. She has 15 years' experience as a development worker, trainer and researcher with expertise on governance, youth development and innovation, and has worked in over 10 African countries. In 2015 she was appointed to the National Planning Commission to advise the president on the implementation of South Africa's National Development Plan 2030. Tessa is a trustee of the Kagiso Trust. She holds a Master of Arts degree from the University of the Witwatersrand.

Printed in the USA
CPSIA information can be obtained
at www.ICGtesting.com
CBHW070017270624
10750CB00008B/397